LEGAL INTERVIEWING AND COUNSELING

IN A NUTSHELL

Fourth Edition

By

THOMAS L. SHAFFER

Robert E. & Marion D. Short
Professor of Law Emeritus
Notre Dame Law School

and

JAMES R. ELKINS

Professor of Law
West Virginia University

THOMSON

WEST

Mat #40217097

COPYRIGHT © 1976, 1987 WEST PUBLISHING CO.
COPYRIGHT © 1997 WEST GROUP
© 2005 West, a Thomson business
   610 Opperman Drive
   P.O. Box 64526
   St. Paul, MN 55164–0526
   1–800–328–9352
Printed in the United States of America

ISBN 0–314–15173–7

TEXT IS PRINTED ON 10% POST
CONSUMER RECYCLED PAPER

In the memory of Louis M. Brown, the founder and grandfather of so much what we have tried to work out in these pages.

—Tom Shaffer

To John Batt, my friend and colleague, who made psychology and psychoanalysis a part of my legal education, and whose innovations in legal pedagogy left me with the idea that I too might someday teach law. . .

—James R. Elkins

*

ACKNOWLEDGMENTS

Several sections in this book have been condensed and rewritten from our earlier work. Material which was used in the first edition, with permission, appeared originally at:

—45 Notre Dame Lawyer 197 (1970);

—57 American Bar Association Journal 123 (1970);

—18 UCLA Law Review 844 (1971);

—Sixth Annual Institute on Estate Planning, University of Miami (1972);

—17 American Journal of Jurisprudence 125 (1972);

—Seventh Annual Institute on Estate Planning, University of Miami (1973);

—Estate Tax Techniques (Lasser, ed.; Bender, 1973);

—113 Trusts and Estates 568 (1974).

Material used for the first time in the second edition, used with permission:

—48 Southern California Law Review 721 (1975);

—61 American Bar Association Journal 854 (1975);

—53 Notre Dame Lawyer 229 (1977);

—64 Virginia Law Review 735 (1978);

—30 American Journal of Jurisprudence 155 (1985).

ACKNOWLEDGMENTS

We have borrowed thoughts and other authors' ideas in a number of places from informal papers, talks, and notebook material published by the N.T.L. Institute for Applied Behavioral Science. Most of this material is acknowledged as it appears in the text. However, some of the N.T.L. material has been so thoroughly internalized (as the psychologists say) that we have not attempted to acknowledge it directly. We are grateful for that material; for the inspiration of those who worked with Shaffer in N.T.L.; and for David Bradford, at the Stanford Graduate School of Business, who made it possible for Elkins to participate in and lead an NTL-style small group.

We are grateful for permission to use copyrighted material, as follows:

From Professors Gerald P. Lopez and Alison Grey Anderson, permission to use unpublished material that appears, in this book, in Chapter Two.

From Pantheon Books, permission to use excerpts from David Hilfiker's "Healing the Wounds," copyrighted by Pantheon Books, a division of Random House, Inc.

From Houghton Mifflin Company permission to use excerpts from the short story, "Equitable Awards," from the volume entitled "Narcissa and Other Fables," by Louis Auchincloss; copyright 1983 by Houghton Mifflin Company.

ACKNOWLEDGMENTS

At places in the text, we quote from journals of law students and from tape recordings made of counseling sessions (some by students, some by practitioners). These sources are necessarily confidential and, in some cases, are rewritten slightly to preserve confidentiality.

John Schaperkotter, of the Class of 1977, University of Virginia School of Law, assisted on the first edition, and Nancy J. Shaffer assisted with the first and second editions. Brenda Waugh, at West Virginia, read the manuscript of the second edition and provided many helpful suggestions, and Andrew P. Shaffer assisted with research on the second edition. Our thanks to them.

                                    T.L.S.
                                    J.R.E.

April, 1976
February, 1987
September, 1997
November, 2004

*

OUTLINE

Page

Page

LEGAL INTERVIEWING AND COUNSELING

IN A NUTSHELL

Fourth Edition

*

CHAPTER ONE

INTRODUCTION

People deal with lawyers out of necessity. And when people deal with lawyers, they often complain that lawyers are not people-oriented, that lawyers are out of touch with those they serve. Many lawyers and law students find that there is something in the study and the practice of law that leads us to know more about legal strategies and techniques, and less about the people law serves. We lawyers tend to become identified more with law and less with people, the public interest, social welfare, and the common good.

This characterization of lawyers suggests something about who we are as lawyers, who we are as a profession, and what happens to us when we study and practice law. It is a characterization that presents a truth about lawyering, but it is not the entire truth of the matter. Many lawyers are sensitive, people-oriented professionals who relate to their clients as persons rather than problems. There are law-school courses on interviewing and counseling, negotiation, and mediation; there are clinical courses that involve one-on-one human-relations skills training; and there is in legal education a growing contingent of teachers who support and practice people-oriented humanistic lawyering. And

1

we suspect that there are tough-minded lawyers who, from years of practice and exposure to clients, courts, and the law, become more rather than less sensitive to their clients. So it would not be accurate to paint lawyers (and law students) as uncaring, insensitive, and unreceptive to the idea that the practice of law is the practice of human relations.

To talk about legal counseling is to talk about lawyers as they appear to those they serve, and that image is crucial. We argue that counseling is the heart and soul of lawyering. The practice of law is *not,* for most lawyers, a mechanical, repetitive, routine activity. One becomes a student of law, and makes a life of the practice of law to escape the confinements and restrictions found in much contemporary work. One attraction of professional life is that it will offer meaningful and fulfilling work. If that ideal is to be more than rhetoric followed by disappointment, disillusionment, and burnout, it must describe a working truth about lawyering, a truth that makes it worthwhile to search for the intrinsic value in lawyering, an intrinsic value encoded in the image of the lawyer as a counselor.

We are aware that some lawyers and law teachers and law students have a different image of lawyers and a different sense of what lawyers do with clients. Some law teachers believe that knowledge of the law and the ability to apply substantive rules of law constitute the core activities of lawyering. We find no conflict in the knowledge, skills, and attitudes of the lawyer as counselor and the acquisition of knowledge of legal rules, and the technical expertise of an able lawyer. The counseling orientation to lawyering complements legal knowledge and legal skills. Being a counselor while being a lawyer may, of course, create conflicts; most adventures in life are children of conflict, and, in some instances, the adventure of being a lawyer and counselor makes life difficult. Being a lawyer requires a life of knowledge, craftsmanship, skill, and virtue, but ultimately it is a life lived with those we serve.

The legal profession in America is not and never has been a homogeneous entity. We have never had a single model or image to portray the good lawyer, or, for that matter, the bad lawyer. This does not mean that anything goes in the practice of law; it means that lawyers may not always agree on what constitutes good lawyering and good counseling. Our point is that lawyering in America is not a uniform enterprise. Still, lawyers learn a body of knowledge and practice a craft as a community of practitioners. Law students learn a language and a way of thinking that set them apart. This doesn't make you a clone of the "typical" lawyer, but it can set you apart from non-lawyers.

We believe that there are persistent notions, attitudes, beliefs, and values that can be identified and associated with American lawyers. The lawyering ethos and ethic give rise to a legal *persona,* a way of acting and holding yourself out to the world that identifies you with the craft and craftiness of lawyering. Clients and the public form perceptions of lawyers based on their interaction with lawyers who give credence to the professional mask and to the stereotypes of lawyers paraded before us in the media and popular culture. As members of the legal profession, we can adopt and relish the lawyer *persona* or resist it. At least we can become aware of its existence and how the images others have of lawyers infect the image we have of ourselves and the work we do.

The presence of a legal *persona* does not mean that there is not diversity and difference in styles found in the legal profession. The truth is that lawyers are citizens, neighbors, spouses, parents, even novelists and poets. It is when we work with clients and help them respond to their problems that we become lawyers and succumb to or resist a *legal persona*.[1] As we become conscious of the mask, we learn how professionalism and lawyering set us apart—a distancing that is in part our own doing (even as it reflects an ideal associated with law and with being a professional). In being apart—adopting

---

1. We need to pause over this word *persona* as we use it throughout this book. C.G. Jung borrowed the word from classical theater: A *persona* is a mask worn by an actor. It is, in psychology, "what one passes for and what one appears to be, in contrast to one's real individual nature." It "corresponds to one's personal environment, and to the community," in this case, both the professional community, and the broader community that enfranchises and makes demands on the professional community. "The persona is the cloak and the shell, the armour and the uniform, behind and within which the individual conceals himself—from himself, often enough, as well as from the world. It is the self-control which hides what is uncontrolled and uncontrollable, the acceptable facade behind which the dark and the strange, eccentric, secret and uncanny side of our nature remains invisible." Erich Neumann, *Depth Psychology and a New Ethic* 37–38 (1973) (*See* Chapter Three).

the mask—we gain power, power to serve those who need our help and power to make our own way with autonomy and dignity, gaining along the way prestige, status, and financial well-being. A side effect of this *persona* is that we become out of step with, and hold ourselves apart from, those we serve.

A study of counseling is one way of addressing the professional *persona* and the odd way our profession both prepares us for and impoverishes our relations with those who seek our services. A study of counseling makes explicit what every course in law school involves—human relations. Law schools are now mandated to offer instruction in what is called "professional responsibility" and "legal ethics," a subject far more closely related to counseling than most legal ethics teachers would admit; a study of lawyer ethics requires an understanding of the moral dimensions of the attorney-client relationship. We consider a lawyer's ethic and ethics to be crucial to counseling; counseling is a moral art.

The ethical issues in counseling, and the concerns of the public and the profession about the human dimension of lawyering, raise social and political issues for lawyers. Some critics suggest that a counseling orientation based on a psychological model gives an asocial, apolitical cast to lawyering. William Simon, for example, argues that legal educators who emphasize human-relations skills tend to ignore the social and political dimensions of client problems. A counseling orientation grounded exclusively in psychology can be limiting, but we think it false and misleading to suggest that psychology, the study of the interior world of feeling and emotions, of the "felt experience" of what is going on around us and to us, inevitably leads to hostility or inattentiveness to the social, political, and cultural world in which a law practice takes place.

A counseling orientation and a sense of the psychological dynamics of lawyering, crucial as these are, do not and cannot address every concern raised by critics of law and legal education. There is a tendency, which should be resisted, to see in counseling (as in ethics, economics, or political theory) an answer to all that ails the legal profession and the study of law.

A REFLECTIVE EXERCISE: IMAGINING OURSELVES AS LAWYERS

Close your eyes and imagine yourself as a lawyer. Try to picture the office where you work, the kind of clothes you wear, the kind of activities that you are doing. Try to record all of the images that come to mind. One way to do this is with a partner: Lean back and daydream and tell what you see. What you're after are images: What you look like; what other people in your lawyer's life look like; the furniture and decoration in the place you work; the noises, the smells, the sights. You should come out with a catalogue of images.

To what extent do your images reflect stereotypes of lawyers—that is, what other people think of lawyers? (That is, what you think other people think.) To what extent do these images reflect your own notions about lawyers? How do these images and the phantasies they encode fit the story you tell about becoming a lawyer?

THE LAWYER AS COUNSELOR

Counseling exists in all professional disciplines—in the traditional professions of law, medicine, and the pastorate; in education (both in the teacher-student relationship and in specialized educational and vocational counseling); and in a wide array of business, industrial, and service occupations. Insurance underwriters, bartenders, appliance sales-people, employment security officers, and clerks in the courthouse all spend time counseling, as do social workers, nurses, physicians, and ministers.

Surveys suggest that lawyers spend much of their time in activities lawyers themselves describe as "counseling." One study found that lawyers spend more time "interviewing" clients than in any other professional activity. Lawyers spend less time in court and in the library than one would assume; many lawyers spend no time in either place, and the average time spent in court and libraries has been estimated at less than ten percent of a work week. An average lawyer spends more than half of her time influencing, facilitating, and implementing choices that are made not by courts but by individuals or small organic communities like families, boards of directors, or groups of neighbors. That professional activity—influencing, facilitating, and implementing a client's choices in the law office—is a good working definition for "legal interviewing and counseling."

For the most part this professional counseling activity will not require other professional activity (drafting, advocacy, research), or, if it does, the other professional activity will take less time and energy than did the counseling. Another way to put this is to say that the "problem" (or, as we prefer, the situation) in legal counseling is often more non-legal than legal.

Counseling decisions are as awesome, as authoritative, as binding, and usually as final as decisions of courts or legislatures. While counseling decisions are influenced by what is loosely called "legal thinking," they are not confined to it. Counseling proceeds from whatever makes it possible to relate to another person, to listen to his or her story, to respond to the needs of that person. Law office decisions proceed as much from subjective and emotional factors as from rules of law. This is also, often, the case with decisions by judges or legislators—but the subjective in counseling decisions is more obvious, because it is not hidden in procedure or rational explanation, and attributed to the necessity of rules. Counseling decisions often clearly proceed from feelings—so much so that any accurate assessment of law office decisions must begin with the proposition that *feelings* are to law office decisions (by clients and by lawyers) what *facts* are to common-law appellate decisions.

Counseling decisions are as important to the human lives they affect as are decisions of courts or legislatures. The settlement of a serious personal-injury claim by a client will mean more to him and to his family than the work of a session of Congress. A decision taken tomorrow morning, in a law office, by the president of a business enterprise who makes his decision in concert with his lawyer, and no one else, may mean more in the next year to thousands of employees, investors, and families, than all of the law a student will learn in a semester of law school.

Competence in counseling begins with two immediate questions, both directed to the lawyer: "What am I doing?" and "Where am I going?" These questions are directed to two crucial *dramatis personae*: I (lawyer) and Thou (client). The I–Thou reference is frightening and complicated and turns on self-awareness and the ability to become aware of others. We argue that competence in counseling begins with self-awareness as a primary skill. But there can be no authentic self-awareness absent knowledge about people. The best resource for learning about people is you; the next best resource is another person, a person you care about, the person Martin Buber called Thou. These resources for learning are intertwined. That is one of the landmark discoveries of Freud's psychoanalytic psychology: I can learn about myself with the help of another.

Those who say that counseling is the business of psychologists, not lawyers, are being defensive and short-sighted. They deserve E.M. Forster's bit of invective: "Man is an odd, sad creature as yet, intent on pilfering the earth, and heedless of the growths within himself. He cannot be bored about psychology. He leaves it to the specialist, which is as if he should leave his dinner to be eaten by a steam-engine. He cannot be bothered to digest his own soul."

* * *

The training that goes into learning to be a counselor often focuses on feelings: how we feel about the client we are trying to serve, how we feel about the choices the client is making, how we feel about the use of law to help the client implement these choices, how we feel abut the opposing lawyer, and how we feel about the law more generally and the life we have made for ourselves as lawyers. Counseling a client is influenced by what we bring to the relationship as well as what happens in face-to-face interactions. The past becomes the "trigger" of certain (sometimes predictable) feelings. (See Chapter Three and the discussion of countertransference.) The past has as much to do with feelings as the present. The past makes some feelings common, some occasional, and some unlikely. And it is also true that our feelings, what we are actually experiencing at the moment, or the feelings we have in being with another person, make us the kind of persons we are becoming. Empathy, the ability to put yourself in the shoes of another, to understand how he feels, and openness to and awareness of your own feelings are fundamental and basic *skills* in counseling. But immediate feelings are not everything.

IMAGINING THE LAWYER AS COUNSELOR

The lawyer is a counselor when she listens to and talks with a client. We follow the view that all talking and listening is a kind of counseling, and that all conversations between client and lawyer involve counseling. All lawyers are therefore counselors. They may not be good counselors, they may not call what they do counseling, they may not appreciate this aspect of their work; they are still counselors. Counseling is inherent in the talking and listening that lawyers do when they are with clients. Counseling is so fundamental to lawyering that all lawyers do it, which means that counseling is something that every lawyer knows something about. And it is something that law students already know about. When students talk and listen to each other, even in conversations about law, about their teachers, about summer jobs, about their lives and interests beyond law school, they are providing counsel to each other. It requires no psychological training, special degree, or license to be a counselor. Counseling is an ordinary activity that we all engage in, an activity inherent in the conversations that go on in law offices and law schools.

Counseling as a subject studied in law school provides an occasion to learn how to hold on to the ordinary, generic notion of trying to understand another person and in some way being helpful to them. It seeks to add some theory, sharpen skills, and explore the sensibilities needed when a lawyer decides to treat clients as persons rather than as problems. The risk and the deficiency—the lost opportunity—in treating our clients as problems is that the client's concern is recast, by the lawyer, into narrow and manageable categories—manageable in the sense that the client's concern is channeled into the legal system for solution: Interviewing becomes getting the facts; counseling becomes telling the client what the law is.

The interviewing and counseling that goes on in a narrowly defined, professional relationship consists of: (1) gathering the appropriate facts for the limited and obvious purpose of determining the nature of a problem; (2) securing the client's aid in gathering additional facts and obtaining necessary documents; (3) explaining the nature of the problem in legal terms; (4) exploring alternative resolutions of the problem; and (5) determining how to proceed. By this description the lawyer's role is straightforward, if not simple: Get the facts, define the situation as a problem, present alternatives, solve the problem (as defined). The counseling in this instrumental view of lawyering consists of surveying the facts, telling the client what the legal problem is and how the law regards it, and then presenting alternatives and consequences and the lawyer's evaluation of an appropriate course of action. In this view, counseling is breathtakingly simple.

Following this instrumental view of a lawyer's work, there is little need for collaboration with the client and little need for special training as a counselor. The activities that are ordinary and inherent in lawyering, in this view, are (1) eliciting facts, (2) reciting law, (3) minimized interaction with clients (and other people), and (4) presentations to decision-making tribunals. The lawyer doesn't need special training as a counselor to accomplish these tasks. (This is a view of lawyering that makes the psychology of counseling seem unnecessary, a business best left to psychologists.) Law school training in "issue spotting" (interviewing) and reciting the law (being a "counselor at law") are the only skills necessary for this kind of lawyering.

In this instrumental approach to the lawyer-client relationship the client comes to be regarded as a necessary nuisance. A client comes in to the law office talking; maybe he is all talk. The problem for the lawyer is to cut through the talk to see if there is a problem that can be defined as a legal problem. Or perhaps the lawyer has trouble getting the facts: A client schedules an appointment to talk about a problem. He enters the office and has difficulty establishing just what the problem is. He answers questions but volunteers only what the lawyer can pry out of him. (We pray for courtroom witnesses who will conduct themselves in this fashion, but this is not a witness.) Simply put, the client has trouble talking about his problem. Both clients are nuisances, but in both cases things get better once the lawyer gets the facts. Then she can get to work. The special skills a lawyer needs are skills for abating a nuisance.

The lawyer with counseling skills has a radically different perspective when talking and listening to clients. One client's talking too much and another's reticence are not obstacles to be overcome. The way we (lawyers and clients, students and teachers) talk and listen tells us—if we notice—how we see the world and how we try to cope with the world we see. The judgment that some clients talk too much and other clients don't talk enough (to suit the work we try to do as lawyers) illustrates a point about the lawyer-client relationship. When the relationship is healthy, it is not a matter of the client talking and the lawyer listening. Maybe the client does not share the lawyer's ideas of how conversation should go. Maybe the client is hurt, angry, vengeful; the legal consultation can be a vehicle for reconciling the hurt or finding appropriate targets for anger and vengeance. One way to see all this is to view the situation from a different perspective: Suppose the client uses the lawyer, or attempts to use the lawyer, for ends other than what the lawyer sees as the legal resolution of the problem. The point is this: The client wants to be a person as much as the lawyer does. The client wants to be somebody (too). A lawyer either promotes or obstructs his client's need to be somebody, to be the kind of person who doesn't have the kind of problem he now faces.

Some examples: A financially secure husband in a divorce case may seek custody of his children to punish his wife; or he may feel guilty, want to concede or confess, pay money, avoid litigation. Another client is terrified at the thought of being in a trial, or being interrogated in a discovery deposition; he misrepresents the facts, trying (sometimes successfully) to deceive his lawyer. A third client cannot decide whether to settle or proceed to trial; her feelings are in conflict as she tries to protect some individuals, knowing that pursuit of the case will reveal information that everyone concerned would prefer to keep secret. It is in situations such as these that the distinction between either lawyer or client talking while the other listens breaks down.

One way the distinction breaks down is that the lawyer silences the client while the lawyer takes charge. The response of the lawyer may be: "In this relationship, there are times for you to talk for yourself, and times for me to decide how it is best to speak for you. Yes, it is true that you are to decide what you want to do, what is in your own interest. But as we try to secure what you want (and need), to promote your interest, you must remember that I am the final arbiter of what I will say, and how it will be said. There is some limited part of our talking that is left to me, that is mine, an area of responsibility that I have to you, but which I must execute on my own."

Another case is presented by the client who hires the lawyer not only to speak for him, but to make his decisions. A client may be ambivalent, confused, or otherwise unable to make a decision on her own. Our clients depend on us: "Mr. Shaffer, what would you do in this situation?" ("Doctor, would you have the operation if you were me?") Some lawyers make decisions for clients because their clients ask them to. Others make decisions for clients because they *assume* that is what the client wants. Still others make decisions for clients because it makes life easier than trying to find out what the client wants. Other lawyers simply do not trust clients enough to let clients make decisions for themselves.

In each of these situations, the client who tries to dictate to the lawyer and the lawyer who makes decisions for the client, there appears to be an imbalance in talking and listening; underneath the imbalance we may find an issue of trust. Clients sometimes learn that they cannot trust their lawyers. Lawyers sometimes learn that their clients are not to be trusted. In the worst of cases, both client and lawyer engage in active deception, each mistrusting the other.

Trust is as much a matter of who we are as of what we are doing. By that we mean that the issue of trust, a client's trust of the lawyer, and the lawyer's trust of the client, is present from the very beginning. Some of us (lawyers and clients) have trouble trusting anyone. The problem of trust is one that we—lawyers and clients—bring with us to the counseling relationship, and it's a problem that gets addressed, in one way or another in the counseling we do. If we have difficulty with trust, it is going to present itself as a snag in our relationships, including relationships lawyers establish with their clients. The issue of trust calls for more than ordinary talking and listening. And it is when we experience the need to learn more about ordinary law office conversations, the need to transcend ordinary talking and listening, that we develop counseling skills, a way of listening and talking that is responsive—as instrumental legal thinking is not—to the needs of both clients and lawyers.

CHAPTER TWO

SOLVING PROBLEMS AND TELLING STORIES

The work day of most lawyers is so busy that we have difficulty slowing down to think about what we do. And during the course of a busy day there are interruptions of many sorts. Our clients interrupt us with telephone calls to provide new information, or to find out what has happened in their cases; a spouse or friend calls to talk; a lawyer in the office interrupts to talk about a case that she is working on. These interruptions in the well-organized, planned day of the professional are important; they are the fragments of telling and listening which carry us through a day; some of these fragments become part of more extended, complex conversations, some will be pleasurable, others will be experienced as an annoyance or a disruption of what we've planned for the day (or our life).

These conversations differ, from the slight and insignificant to those in which we exchange needed information (give and get directions on how to do something, or how to proceed) to those in which we actively listen to what a client is saying and attempt to say something to the client that is responsive to her concerns. The work that lawyers do with clients depends upon conversation, the talking and listening that forms the basis of what we call counseling. From a counseling perspective, conversations matter. Alasdair MacIntyre, a philosopher, suggests that "a conversation is a dramatic work, even if a very short one, in which the participants are not only the actors, but also the joint authors, working out in agreement or disagreement the mode of their production. For it is not just that conversations belong to genres in just the way that plays and novels do; but they have beginnings, middles and endings just as do literary works. They embody reversals and recognitions; they move towards and away from climaxes. There may within a longer conversation be digressions and subplots, indeed digressions within digressions and subplots within subplots." MacIntyre suggests that we focus on conversations as narratives, as stories in progress.

* * *

It is one of those hectic days, the phone ringing, a settlement conference that lasted two days, and a trial to prepare for at the end of the week. Your secretary reminds you that you have an appointment at 3 o'clock with Ron Barrett, a young man that you have not previously met. When you meet with Barrett you ask him what you can do to be of help. He tells, in outline form, the following story: He owns a small print shop that keeps prices low by hiring high school kids enrolled in a training program at a local high school. The program is innovative and educational, and it helps the kids financially. The customers know the kids and patronize his shop because they support what he is doing. The problem, as Ron Barrett describes it, is that one of the kids, who had helped in the store, working the cash register and taking customers' orders, is now threatening him. Ron fired the student because he thought he was taking money from the cash register. The student has now threatened to file a complaint with the state wages-and-hours authority, claiming that he was not paid overtime wages, as the law requires, unless the print shop owner pays him two months' severance pay. There was, of course, no mention of overtime or of severance pay in the student's contract of employment.

The story that Ron Barrett tells you interrupts your day, but you realize that without such interruptions you wouldn't have new clients, and without new clients you would be stuck with all your "old" cases and clients and that might be an even worse fate. So there is something pleasurable in taking on a new client, in starting at the beginning, in listening to what the client has to say and trying to figure out what the legal problem is and how it can be resolved.

Lawyers work for clients. We (and they) sometimes think of what lawyers do as problem solving. Ron Barrett has a problem and the lawyer knows how to solve it or knows who can, or knows that it isn't the kind of problem that lawyers try to solve. This view of what lawyers do is descriptive, accurate, and incomplete. Lawyers do work with certain kinds of problems and not others, seeking particular kinds of resolutions, in particular kinds of places;

but the description and the images of the lawyer
that accompany it don't go as far as a lawyer's life
goes. The traditional image of the lawyer in court,
or the lawyer drawing up a legal document, or even
the lawyer listening to an individual client like Ron
Barrett, is not the whole story. There is more going
on in this meeting with Ron Barrett, for example,
than the description of a legal problem (which is *one*
of the things going on), and the counselor in you
intuitively knows that Ron Barrett is not *just* a
legal problem, not *just* a new client, not *just* the
owner of a small business.

There are tough-minded lawyers, law teachers,
and law students who argue with us on this point,
maintaining that the image of the lawyer as a
problem-solver is adequate. Our response is that
this image of the lawyer and other images embedded in seemingly straightforward descriptions of
lawyers tell us something about the way lawyers
work, but not enough. There is *adventure* in the
practice of law, adventure beyond and beneath solving problems.

The lawyer sitting at a desk, a pile of papers and
books before her, looking for an answer in the law
books, is an image of the lawyer as problem-solver.
It is an image rooted in experience. Consider your
first association with problem-solving, perhaps doing math problems as a kid in school. The problems
were what followed the explanations and examples
in the math book. You came home from school at
night and tried to solve the problems. Or you asked
for help from your parents; more often, solving

problems was something done in your room alone. In solving math problems, you were doing a relatively well-defined task and doing it by procedures you had been taught. As your father might have put it: "You just have to read the book and learn to do them yourself." It is from just such early experiences that we develop a sense that problem-solving is the use of clearly defined rules and procedures to find an answer. We sometimes want law to work like mathematics.

Louis Auchincloss is a lawyer and a teller of stories about modern, big-firm lawyers in America. His novel "The Great World and Timothy Colt" tells a story about a problem solver, a lawyer who came to legal education and then to law practice as one who had learned to work alone, and to solve problems alone: "All his youth he worked, at night, during summers, in laundries and restaurants, in banks and garages; he put himself through Columbia with only a minimum of unexpected aid from a Colt cousin." Tim lived with his mother (his father was dead) and, of course, had to take into account this other person in his life: "It was as if she were an actual part of him, the looser, lighter side of his own nature, the one that he had to make up for before the great golden eye of a demanding God. . . . Only in the spare neatness of his own small room, under the green lamp with his law books, was there rest from the pressure of his imagined overseer, as in childhood at the same desk he had sought the solace of the solved equation, the translated stanza."

Tim becomes a senior associate in his law firm, a deal-maker and a competent engineer at the complexities of corporate mergers. Auchincloss tells the story of Tim and a demanding corporate magnate who resents the fact that the firm has assigned a young lawyer to do his work. The great advantage of Timothy Colt's temperament, of his seeing his legal work as he saw his law books and, before that, his math books, in his room, alone, is that the obnoxious client need not be known—his story, as we might say—need not be known. "Timmy's defense was ... inflexible courtesy and unvarying patience, and if these sometimes formed the grey panes and lattices behind which an equally inflexible dislike could be just detected, he did not care. The client was entitled to the job done and the job done well."

This is one way to look at problem solving by lawyers. It is technical in the sense that you have to know the formal rules of a system so that you can apply those rules and get what the system tells you is the answer. In solving math problems we were looking for an answer and knew it when we got it. In problem solving there was (and is) the right answer (and there are clearly wrong answers). What emerges from all this is the idea that the problem-solver is doing something precise and by following rules and procedures we are able to find an answer and verify it as correct. It was and is all very cut and dried when you know what you're doing. Ron Barrett's "legal problem" may thus be a simple one, but only when narrowly described—it is a simple problem from the perspective of the lawyer who likes his problems to be like math problems.

This notion of the lawyer as problem-solver brings to mind the image of a highly trained technician who can examine a situation, diagnose the problem, and take whatever corrective means are necessary to get things going again. In this view, a lawyer's work is technical because it involves a high level of specificity, *i.e.,* some legal rules rather than others apply and you have to know what you are doing to apply applicable rules to reach a proper conclusion; the application of rules to specific facts takes practice, as every law student learns. (In the hands of some lawyers and judges, the use of rules becomes the work of an artist.) When the rules are known and the facts are presented, an answer should be available. Finally, the work is technical because it lends itself to an established procedure for solution. The problem is resolved by the use of a methodology that produces answers.

In legal education, this image of the lawyer as a technician is given credibility and at the same time systematically undermined. Becoming a lawyer is not as simple as learning rules and applying them, and virtually every law student either learns this or suffers for failing to learn it. What, one might ask, is going on, when a man like Ron Barrett goes to a lawyer with the story he is telling? The images of Ron Barrett as a legal problem and his lawyer as technician are law school images, one kind of truth about the work that lawyers do. These images are both valid and dangerous; the danger is that they compete with other images, including good, useful images that each of us brought to law school, the kind of images that many professionals secretly harbor during hectic days in the office, and many suppress.

In this book we are suggesting a way to think about lawyering that honors the problem solving element of lawyering and provides an alternative set of images, drawn from within and outside the legal profession, that have to do with being a companion to Ron Barrett as well as someone who can solve whatever legal problem he might present to us as a client.

In Chapter One we suggested that counseling is an attentive, focused, engaged way of talking and listening, the kind of talking and listening we sometimes find in everyday conversations, the kind of exchange we might have with Ron Barrett if he was our friend. But counseling is more than just talking (free advice is readily available) and listening (also free but in short supply). The talking and listening that we associate with counseling takes place when the counselor knows the limits of advice (talking at the client about law) and has learned the art of listening (hearing what is said and hearing beyond what is said). Another way to look at counseling is that it is a highly skilled, artful way of talking and listening. Counseling is an intense and purposeful conversation which draws on knowledge and skills.

A conversation with clients is both like and different from other conversations. If there were no difference, law school would consist of a single year instead of three and lawyers would make far less money than many of them earn today. Conversations in the law office are different from ordinary conversations because law itself influences what you will say to Ron Barrett and how his story will unfold and how his story will be retold to others and how his problem will eventually be resolved.

James Boyd White, writing about conversations between lawyers and their clients, points out that "[l]aw establishes roles and relations and voices, positions from which and audiences to which one may speak, and it gives us as speakers the materials and methods of a discourse. It is a way of creating a rhetorical community over time." *Law* itself is a kind of conversation, one in which the way we speak, the audience, and the nature of the responses of those who participate are distinctive, but not limited to the legal system. This is a focus, like MacIntyre's, on having a conversation rather than fixing things.

The conversation between the lawyer and Ron Barrett, and the lawyer and the discharged employee (or his attorney) may be sufficient to deal with the problem and to satisfy Barrett that he is getting what he wants from the lawyer. But conversation may not be enough, and a lawyer is educated (and trained) to get the kind of facts and structure the relationship in such a way that Barrett can use the law, to the fullest extent possible, to get what he wants. But even when informal conversations (and how is a conversation in a law office ever to be viewed as really informal, at least by the client?) fail to resolve the issue, and there is a resort to litigation, conversation does not stop. White tells us that a litigated legal case "proceeds by a conversation in which each speaker is invited to present an ideal version of himself, speaking to an ideal audience." A litigated legal case, like the case of a client whose concerns are resolved by informal conversation (sometimes a little talk and a letter are enough), begins as a story and over time is presented to a decision-maker in the form of a narrative, one that places special demands on judges. If the law is a conversational process that proceeds by way of narrative, then the judge, White observes, "will have to speak in an extraordinarily rich and complex way, not in a voice that is merely bureaucratic and official. To be true to the actual difficulties of a real legal case, an opinion must be full of the kind of life that comes from a set of acknowledged tensions: between the two versions of the story before the court; between the stories so told and the language of legal conclusion; between the demand that like cases be treated alike and the recognition that cases never are 'alike'; between the fidelities owed to the past and the future; between an awareness that the case is a particular dispute between individual persons and a sense that it is typical as well; and so on.... In the complexity and formality of his speech, its metaphoric character and its openness to uncertainty, in its tension between the general and the particular, the judge must indeed be something of a poet."

White speaks of lawsuits, but he could speak as well of the more common kind of legal decision made by and with a counselor at law, in a law office, what a lawyer might do with Ron Barrett. In White's view of the law as narrative, the client plays an integral role. We contend that the client is a resource, the best resource that you as his lawyer have. Ron Barrett's problem is with the law, but it is also a problem with himself, and a situation that brings law into the story. For Barrett, White would say, "the case is, at its heart, an occasion and a method in which he can tell his story and have it heard." Ultimately, Barrett may, as White puts it, have "the right to a jury, to insure that he will have an audience that will understand his story and speak his language. The presence of a jury requires that the entire story, on both sides, be told in ordinary language and made intelligible to the ordinary person. This is a promise to the citizen that the law will ultimately speak to him, and for him, in the language that he speaks, not in a technical or special jargon."

Barrett has a legal problem, a problem that you as his lawyer may help resolve. But Ron Barrett also has a story to tell. It is a story about success (the print shop is doing well); the American dream (the client wants to get the legal matter cleared up so that he can take his wife on their first trip to Europe); short-cuts (everybody in this business makes under-the-table arrangements with employees); betrayal (putting trust in employees and having that trust violated); and fear (what will happen to me now). Ron Barrett comes to the lawyer as a person who may, it is true, even see himself as a legal problem. He can be a print-shop owner with a legal problem; he can be reduced to his problem and encased in a file folder; he can become just another part of a hectic day. Barrett's problem—this person *as* a problem—is, when you are a lawyer, legal. Your role is to *solve* legal *problems*. But the client has a story to tell, and in the enactment of that story (or stories) now seeks to involve you as his lawyer. It is now your story, for you listen and decide (or go along by not deciding) where you fit in to what you are learning about Barrett and his problem. You will hear a story, perhaps not all of it, that Barrett wants you to hear. Maybe you will tell his story for him. Maybe what you will tell is some story that you and he will create together.

BEYOND LISTENING: STORYTELLING AS ADVOCACY

Gerald Lopez and Alison Grey Anderson, have described the lawyer as storyteller, and in doing so, create an image of the lawyer that stands along with, if not against, the image of the lawyer as technician and problem-solver. "A lawyer is a storyteller. To be sure, she is an instrumental storyteller—she wants something from her audience. But every storyteller wants something from her audience—attention certainly, but also a reaction—

laughter, tears, shock, joy. Lawyers want attention, too, but usually in order to obtain remedies (some desired outcome) from their audience for their clients. They must therefore learn to tell a story that will persuade the audience (whether judge, jury, opposing party, government official, or other person in control of the desired remedy) to grant whatever it is the client desires or needs. The story may be a simple one—'X hurt my client, X was careless, X must pay the damage'—or a much more complicated one—'The language in this agreement may appear to mean X, but once I tell you about the context of the agreement, the expectations of the parties, the customs of the industry, the nature of the technology involved, and the consequences of a literal interpretation, you will see that the language can only mean Y'—but it must make sense as a story. Put differently, the story told by the lawyer must develop, both in human terms and in legal terms, a narrative that is plausible and that suggests to the audience some obvious, indeed necessary, conclusion—what the client wants.

"The lawyer's job, then, is to 'make sense' of the client's problem, first to her own satisfaction, and then in a way which will persuade the relevant audience to grant the desired remedy. Note that this is as true of contracts that have to work, or of wills that affect people, as it is of lawsuits. How does she do that? Most likely by asking herself a series of questions: For example, Do I really understand what happened (or is happening, or is about to happen) in my client's world? Do I understand why whatever is happening is a 'problem' for my client? Do I understand what my client wants in terms of solutions?''

Lopez and Anderson go on to suggest that when law students read appellate judicial opinions they should do so from the perspective of the potential storyteller, a perspective we find equally applicable to the way a lawyer might try to listen to a client. The questions suggested are: "What is the human story here? What is at stake? Why did the client seek legal help? How did this problem come to be seen as one to be dealt with by the legal culture? What decisions by the lawyer and client in this case were made that led to litigation ... ? What other choices did the lawyer and client have? Are there other legal stories that might have been told about this human story? Are there audiences other than a judge or jury that the client or lawyer might have approached ... ? Why are the legal stories that can be told about this case so limited? Why are they shaped the way they are? What do the legal stories that apply to this problem tell us about the society which produced these stories? Can we write new stories?'' Lopez and Anderson suggest that this is only a small sample of the questions that can be asked about the human and legal stories reflected in a single appellate opinion, and, we might add, appellate opinions are only a small subset of the stories heard and told by lawyers.

Lopez and Anderson see in the lawyer as storyteller a need to explore:

— What it means to represent others, to tell other people's stories, that is, to be a professional storyteller.

— What it means to try to understand the human story told by another person, and to work with that person to investigate, shape, and create "the facts" of a particular case.

— How we translate what we do with the client into a legal repertoire, into a language that can be acted upon by a judge or other decision-maker.

— The relationship between storytelling and argument, between different forms of persuasion, between stories and their meanings and the meanings suitable to particular legal settings.

— How stories work with different audiences, e.g., juries, judges, arbitrators, legislators, government officials, opposing counsel, journalists, and just plain folks.

— Where our legal stories come from, that is, their psychological, philosophical, historical, social, and political roots.

— The art and politics of legal storytelling, that is, using, not using, and changing an existing repertoire of legal stories.

Law, from the perspective of storytelling, and from the reality of our clients as storytellers is, in James Boyd White's opinion, "best regarded not so much as a set of rules and doctrines or as a bureaucratic system or as an instrument for social control

but as a culture, for the most part a culture of
argument. It is a way of making a world with a life
and a value of its own. The conversation that it
creates is at once its method and its point, and its
object is to give to the world it creates the kind of
intelligibility that results from the simultaneous
recognition of contrasting positions. . . .

"The fact that the conversation of the law is
largely argumentative has important consequences
of its own. Legal argument exposes in clarified and
self-conscious form—in slow motion, as it were—the
processes of agreement and disagreement—of persuasion—by which this part of our culture, and our
culture more generally, are defined and trans-
formed. For in legal argument the state of the
discourse itself—how we should think and talk—is a
constant subject of conscious attention and debate.
This means that the contours of the culture are
pushed to their limits and marked with extraordinary distinctness. As the argument proceeds, each
speaker tests the limits of his language, subjecting
its every term and procedure to all the strain that it
can take—that we can take—in order to make
things come out his way. And since he must always
operate within strict limits imposed by time and the
interests of his audience, he is constantly forced to
discriminate among the arguments he might make,
putting forward what seems best, holding back
what is weak or unimportant, and so on. As the
materials of the legal culture are tested in this
manner, are put to work—they are defined and
reorganized in especially clear and reliable ways.

This makes it possible to think clearly about their transformation."

Legal stories are "imaginative forms," forms derived from local knowledge, from what happens and is said, felt, thought, and experienced when law is invoked, when disputes are settled, when lawyers and clients talk about problems and how to address them. The anthropologist Clifford Geertz argues that law is a form of "local knowledge, local not just as to place, time, class and variety of issue, but as to accent—vernacular characterizations of what happens connected to vernacular imaginings of what can happen." Geertz understands "legal sensibility" as a complex of characterizations and imaginings, "stories about events cast in imagery about principles."

Lopez and Anderson, writing for law students, trying to bring the image of the lawyer as storyteller to the classroom, find that, "Contrary to popular belief, the practice of law is not a lot of rules, but a set of stories and storytelling practices. Law is not simply a collection of definitions and rules to be memorized and applied, but a culture consisting of storytellers, audiences, a set of standard stories and arguments, and a variety of conventions about story writing, storytelling, argument-making and the structure and content of legal stories.... In order to transform human stories effectively and persuasively into legal stories, you must not only learn about and internalize the conventions and values of the legal culture, you must also be able to relate that culture to the varied ways in which human beings perceive, interpret and represent the world. In order to be an effective legal storyteller, you must be able to see all the possible meanings in legal stories and use those meanings to persuade different audiences to see the world as you want it seen."

Lopez and Anderson present some other observations on how we use and embody stories that are richly suggestive for the lawyer as counselor. "We depend on a stock of stories to help us organize our knowledge about people, events, objects, and their characteristic relationships." Another way to say this is that stories locate us in the world. Stories show how we find a place in the world of others and at times how we live a life trying to escape from them. Whatever place I find, whatever role I accept or reject, whatever stance I take, it is ultimately in relation to some story, a story told within the context of a community and a culture.

Stories reflect a fundamental human need for narrative, for the kind of telling that gets beyond routine, standard descriptions of our work and our relations with others. Work that otherwise dries us out is given meaning and purpose in the plots of our stories. We find out who we are as lawyers and persons (as persons who are lawyers) by the story we tell, by the conversations we have with clients and other lawyers, in court and on the street corner. Our stories about being lawyers, shaped by the way we imagine ourselves and our clients, are central to the way we understand and reflect on the way our lives unfold and interact.

Living a story is one thing, becoming the teller of stories is another. As we live and tell stories, we live a life bound by the stories of others. We don't see the objects of our service as persons until we hear the story being told, until we realize the story that we live out in our work and in our interactions with our clients.

Lopez and Anderson suggest that "given our limited information-processing capabilities, we need stories to allow us to figure out what's going on and what we should do about it. By simplifying the world, however, stories may distort our perceptions and responses.... Studying our use of stories can thus help us both to improve our ability to use stories to change the world and to become aware of ways in which our stock stories constrain our views of ourselves and the world.

"Our stock stories embody our values and assumptions about the way life is and the way it ought to be. Because telling a particular story implies acceptance of a set of political, human, and social values, telling a story is always a [moral] political act. One of the important things to learn about stories is which ones you *don't* want to tell, and when, and why. A story may present the story-teller or other characters in ways that they'd rather not be presented. A story may also incorporate values that you don't want to accept, even for the moment, even if telling that story would be an effective way to achieve a short-term objective.

"If you're telling someone else's story, it's even harder to sort out good stories from bad stories. We don't often recognize how hard it is to understand someone else's life, the story someone else is living or wants to live, and we often don't appreciate how little we know about the kinds of stories that a friend or client is willing to have told about her. It's never enough just to pick any story that will compel the audience to grant the desired remedy. Responsible storytelling requires sensitivity to the needs and values of the subject of the story, and to the values embodied in the story itself.

"We learn to use stories to understand the world and to solve problems by living in a culture. We learn stories and storytelling by hearing people around us describe 'what is going on' or 'what we have always done.' Each person's practical, working knowledge includes a set of stock stories and storytelling techniques appropriate to her everyday needs, whether or not she is aware of it. People naturally absorb lawyering skills from their cultural environment, but may not recognize them as skills which may be useful out of the context in which they were learned. . . . "

A REFLECTIVE EXERCISE:
PERSONAL CLIMATE

We intend nothing mystical or puzzling with the idea that relationships are embedded in stories. One aspect of this embedded quality of significance to

the counselor is the "personal climate" that surrounds a relationship. The way we feel when we are
with particular people, in certain places, creates a
climate, an environment. The attorney-client relationship, the primary focus here, does not exist as a
single pattern or defined set of feelings and cannot
be fully described on the basis of an idealized or
conventional view of the lawyer role.

An analogy to "personal climate" in law-office
relationships is the "personal climate" in the law-
school classroom. Pick out one of your law school
courses. How does the view of the law that you and
the teacher take into the classroom affect the "personal climate" there? Is the teacher's view of the
law different from your own? How does the difference affect your learning? What kind of assumptions have you and your teacher made about the law
that create a "feeling" or climate that you can
identify and describe?

Does the teacher seem to have a general philosophy (a story or theory of human nature) that provides a framework or structure for his or her teaching? If you do not immediately perceive such a story
or philosophy, does that mean the teacher does not
have one?

It is sometimes argued that even those who contend most vehemently that they have no philosophy
do nevertheless have one. Do you agree with the
assertion? And if that is the case, is it possible for a
teacher to teach without reference, in some way, to
such a philosophy? Or for a lawyer to practice law

without one? What kind of teaching would that be? What kind of lawyering?

Now reverse the situation. Ask each of these questions concerning general philosophy and story in relation to yourself and your learning in class.

Finally, how are you regarded by the teacher? As a colleague? A friend? A companion? A pest? An enemy? How is the teacher's view of you communicated? That is, how does it become part of the "personal climate" of the classroom? And how do you respond? What are your feelings about the dynamic that has been created, and in which you participate (with others)? How do you view yourself as a student? What metaphor would you use to describe your view of yourself: player? sponge? roadblock? pest?

At what point in these musings about your teachers do you find yourself telling a story–a story about yourself, about law teachers, about your education, about law school?

* * *

The object of all these questions is to suggest a way to study counseling. The situations we are already in, the relationships we already have, are a laboratory for learning. What we have to do is to pay attention to them. Learning to be a counselor involves making use of these situations for the explicit purpose of learning more about ourselves and how we relate to others. Human-relations skills are those we use every day, skills we can learn more about, skills that can be improved as we become more conscious of how we experience something as ordinary as the relationship you have with each teacher, in each course in the law school.

The lawyer you will be, and the manner in which you relate to your clients, will not be so radically different from who you are now, the way you relate to others now, and the way you are learning to relate to others from the relationships you see around you. When you leave law school you will undoubtedly try to get away from being a student and adopt a stance more appropriate to being a lawyer and a person of influence. Does that mean that you will reject the perceptions and philosophies you now enact, or act toward your clients as your teacher now acts toward you?

By reflecting on these questions about your teacher, her relation to the law, to the classroom, and to you, you have been exploring how "professionals" relate to others. And when you see yourself as a student in relation to a teacher, you have come close to putting yourself in the position of a client vis-a-vis a lawyer. What sorts of working relationships will you have with your clients, if they feel toward you as you now feel toward your teacher(s)? What stories will you, in your relations with clients, tell with your life as a lawyer?

A CONCLUDING NOTE

Jacqueline Winspear, in her debut novel, *Maisie Dobbs* (Soho Press, 2003), takes her protagonist, Maisie Dobbs, on a climb up Britain's social ladder. Along the way she receives some clear-headed, astute advice from Maurice Blanche, her wise old guru: "Never follow a story with a question, Maisie, not immediately. And remember to acknowledge the storyteller, for in some way even the messenger is affected by the story he brings." We translate Maurice Blanche's advice for the lawyer to mean: Your client is always a storyteller. Never let your questions of the client about his problem, lead you to forget the person he is and the story he has brought with him to your office. You will do best when you remember: "acknowledge the storyteller."

CHAPTER THREE

THE LAWYER PERSONA AND FEELINGS IT DISGUISES

LEARNING THE MASK

Law professors identify two goals for their students: to think and to talk like a lawyer. These goals are established for you at a crucial time—as you begin to try to learn the law and to find a place for yourself in the profession. Their significance on the lawyer as counselor is profound. But what does it mean to "talk" and "think" like a lawyer?

TALKING LIKE A LAWYER

Lawyers often speak a foreign language; clients hear it as "legalese." In a polemical attack on the language of lawyers, almost 50 years ago, Fred Rodell argued that the law deals with ordinary facts and occurrences but that lawyers use "a jargon which completely baffles and befoozles the ordinary literate [person]." Rodell berated lawyers for the use of "professional pig Latin" and for their failure to relate legal concepts to clients in simple English. "It is this fact more than any other—the fact that lawyers can't or won't tell what they are about in ordinary English—that is responsible for the hope-

42

lessness felt by the non-lawyer in trying to cope with or understand the so-called science of law. For the lawyers' trade is a trade built entirely on words. And so long as the lawyers carefully keep to themselves the key to what those words mean, the only way the average [person] can find out what is going on is to become a lawyer, or at least to study law, himself. All of which makes it very nice—and very secure—for the lawyers." E.B. White, the greatest of American wordsmiths, said, "I honestly worry about lawyers. They never write plain English themselves, and when you give them a bit of plain English to read, they say, 'Don't worry, it doesn't mean anything.' " When we talk to clients we must remember, as James Boyd White points out, that lawyers "still speak an inherited and traditional language with marked peculiarities of vocabulary and construction." The language of law can become a barrier between lawyers who know the language and clients who do not.

The United States Tax Court once held that a lawyer who tried to learn the English language was not acquiring a skill that is necessary to his profession. We suspected as much, but were depressed to see it become official. Steven J. McAuliffe in that case lost his claim for a deduction of $1,822 for taking English courses at Georgetown University. He argued that the study of poetry, Victorian literature, and writing were important to his being a lawyer. Not so, said the Tax Court. "We are unwilling to declare that the study of English literature . . . bears the sort of proximate relationship to the improvement of an appellate attorney's legal skills to justify the deduction," Judge Howard A. Dawson, Jr., said. An unfortunate decision. If Judge Dawson had taken the courses Mr. McAuliffe took perhaps he wouldn't have said things like "bears the sort of proximate relationship" when he meant "is close enough."

It is not that lawyers speak in a single voice or use a unique language, for there is no special language reserved for law. From the perspective of lawyers, legal language is ordinary English (some of it very old), or foreign phrases that an educated gentleman of the 19th century was supposed to understand, to which we lawyers give special and sometimes technical meaning. It is difficult for a lawyer to talk without using these special meanings, and when we work with other lawyers there is little reason to avoid legal expressions and phrases or the special meanings we sometimes attach to lay terms. Gaining mastery of the way law uses (and abuses) language is an integral part of learning to be a lawyer. But words that mean something to lawyers can become obstacles to communication with clients. The words we use and the way we use them with (and against) our clients are of special concern to the lawyer as counselor. A counselor monitors what he or she is doing with and to the client with words. We look for the effect, and the *affect* of our words.

There is another perspective to be considered—that of clients. Clients have their ways of saying things, too; as we note in Chapter Five, in reference particularly to Alfred Kinsey's interviews, using words the client uses is often indispensable to understanding what the client wants to say. (Not just hearing those words, Kinsey says—but using them.) Failure in the art of understanding words (and, Kinsey said, understanding means using) may mean failure to understand the client.

THINKING LIKE A LAWYER

Social scientists—psychologists, sociologists, anthropologists—concur that every person has a patterned way of seeing things. Bandler and Grinder write, "Each of us creates a representation of the world in which we live—that is, we create a map or model which we use to generate our behavior. Our representation of the world determines to a large degree what our experience of the world will be, how we will perceive the world, what choices we will see available to us as we live in the world."

A world view consists of the underlying postulates and assumptions that an individual (and her social group and culture) uses to understand and explain the world. The legal profession has its own world view, one that functions much like a computer software program; it programs our interaction with others, our way of being in the world as lawyers, and even our way of being persons outside the law. Some computer users know enough about programming to "patch" the software to get the program and the computer to do what they want it to do. In a similar way, some lawyers make the practice of law into an art, one they devise, a craft to serve clients' and their own needs; they remake an existing role of the lawyer into forms and activities that fit who they want to be as lawyers. Others take what the legal profession gives as standard fare; they take it on as a job, as if the law were a drill press on an assembly line, and clients were pieces of metal.

A lawyer thinks about client problems, about clients, and about herself through a veil of role and rules. She tells her that she is a neutral, rational, objective problem-solver. Jerald Auerbach argues that it is the lawyer's dislike of vague generalities, the preference for case-by-case treatment of social issues, the structuring of human relations as sets of legal claims and counter-claims, that constitutes the lawyer's way of thinking—what the social scientist might call a *weltanschaung*. Stuart Scheingold writes, "When we accuse someone of being legalistic, we suggest an excessive zeal for purely formal details which becloud rather than clarify the real issue. The legalist is someone who is lost among the trees and cannot or will not consider the overall shape of the forest. So it is a sense of willful closure together with an obsession for procedure and minutiae that we associate with the law game."

Lawyers, it will surprise no one, become confirmed legalists in law school. Judith Shklar defines legalism as the ethical "attitude that holds moral conduct to be a matter of rule following and moral relationships to consist of duties and rights determined by rules." Legalism in her view is "a way of

thinking about social life, a mode of consciousness.''
Of course, ''legalism'' may be an epithet, a word
used to describe rigid, formal, or narrow reasoning.
But Shklar's point cuts deeper; it has more to it
than the identification of an insult. Legalism is, she
said, characteristic of a certain way of thinking; a
way of thinking characteristic of a way of being.
Jungian psychology has a term for a way of being
derived from the mask used by actors in Greek
theater: *persona.* What Shklar was talking about,
and what, when we get down to it, we are talking
about here, is the lawyer *persona,* the way a lawyer
is being when she acts like a lawyer.

The lawyer *persona* is not just a tool or device put
to use in a law office, but a world view. Our work is
carried out by wearing the mask. Our wishes and
fears are filtered through the mask. The mask
frames the way we talk to our clients, and what we
hear our clients say. We see our clients through the
persona that forms the basis of an identity and
shields us from what we are unwilling to hear—
feelings that are painful, anything we do not understand, all that we want to deny.

The *persona* becomes significant in determining
the kind of information we call facts and excluding
from awareness and consideration the kind of information we view as irrelevant. The verbal stuff of
law practice—what lawyers call facts, or legal problems, or law—is made subjective by the legal *persona.* First, the facts that we derive from our legal
world view are based upon the selection of what we
hear, and how we are able to organize, verbally,

what we hear, for use in responding to what we have decided in advance is a problem. Lawyers typically obtain their facts from clients (complemented in some instances by outside investigations). The attorney reviews, selects, organizes, and synthesizes facts. By selecting and excluding that which is unneeded and unacceptable, a coherent, organized, and orderly view of the world is maintained. We lawyers communicate with one another not only or even principally with words and facts but also by way of a world view; we define reality with our professional masks.

A *persona* is functional. That is why a person begins to use it in the first place. The problem is that the *persona* becomes a habit; we forget we have it, forget that it can be a barrier put between us and other people. And of course when that happens, the *persona* is not functional at all; we only tell ourselves that it is. Function is not the issue anyway; character is the issue. (How we mislead ourselves into believing we are serving the client when we are serving ourselves is the issue.) It is important to understand that the lawyer *persona,* even when it is functional, and especially when it is not, operates to exclude and to screen, to limit what we see and think. It leads to self-deception and injustice when we try to convince ourselves that we are not, in fact, limited by what we have become, by what we have learned or will learn about how, say, to practice law. "Law professors and lawyers," Scheingold points out, "do not believe that they are either encumbered or enlightened by a special view of the world.

They simply feel that their legal training has taught them to think logically. In a complex world, they have the intellectual tools to strip a problem, any problem, down to its essentials."

Legalism, a way of being taken on in the form of a lawyer *persona*, is promoted and maintained by the legal profession; its roots are deep in the pedagogy, curriculum, and everyday activities of the law school. Law schools claim to teach a way of thinking that creates (or narrows reality to) a universe of rights and obligations, causes of action, forms and procedures. An association of people calls itself a profession and then acts for the community (or the state) in creating a sense of obligation, in each of its members, that refers to and gives definition to the *persona*. The professional role of the lawyer is represented in but is not fully realized by assuming a professional mask. The *persona* represents both an idealized way of presenting yourself to a client and a cover or disguise for the underlying self, a disguise used in conspiracy with those in the community who find it safer to deal with a mask than with a person. As a result, the *persona* shapes character. It imposes a morality; we come to talk of the lawyer *persona* as having a life of its own. We then, as lawyers, become a community (of sorts), in which we claim the masks we wear as an emblem of status.

FEELINGS AND THE PERSONA

One of the primary ways we establish a professional identity is to adopt, often unconsciously, a psychological "style" that we use in our relations with clients. We tend to adopt a style dictated by conventional role expectations and common usage of the professional mask. The interaction with the client may be adequate and effective in soliciting facts, but it will also be a style developed out of the lawyer's own conflicts, anxieties, and fantasies, a style that serves all that is unconscious as well as that of which he is conscious. The problem with a style left unexamined is that it becomes rigid and inflexible. Each client is exactly that—a client. And a client is "seen" and "heard" through the mask. The mask is in large part unconscious: Remember that the lawyer learns the mask (style) and over time begins to accept it as natural and intuitive, rather than constructed. The mask is easy, because it is already there; efficient because we don't have to think about it; and effective enough to lure us into ignoring it. It has its purpose, sometimes serves us well, and we pay the price (as does the client): Every client is a case; finally, like every other client. No client is a person. No client is an adventure.

Since no one is capable of responding to the entire range of human feelings and emotions, we tend to select some, filter out others (ignoring, suppressing, denying, compartmentalizing, partitioning and walling-off feelings that are problematic or threatening). When this selective filtering process takes place, which it does whether we are conscious of it or not, a style develops, a mask constructed, a *persona* presented to the client. And it is to the effort to become more aware of the feelings behind the mask that we now turn our attention.

There are some general points that can be made about these feelings:

— Most human behavior expresses a striving for satisfaction or the avoidance of threats. We move toward comfort and stay away from what we fear or dislike.

— Many of us ignore feelings as long as it is possible to do so. The person or lawyer who pretends to himself that he is a rational calculating machine, moved only by the business at hand and concerned only about solving a client's legal problem, suffers from a grave illusion. He may have ceased to recognize his feelings, but few of us, other than the psychopaths, ever learn how to erase their emotions. He cannot be whole until he addresses his repressions and experiences his own feelings. It is not surprising that a lawyer who for years pretends to others that he feels what he doesn't really feel should lose his ability to discriminate among his own emotions.

— Lawyers say, "We have work to do. We need not be emotional about this!" Feelings are forced aside and allowed to operate surreptitiously.

— Problems arise, not because emotions are present, but because they are denied. People get into trouble, not because they have emotions, but because of attempts to repress, deny, or disguise their emotions.

— The test of a good decision (tough choice), one which is carried out wholeheartedly, is not whether it has been unemotionally made, but rather whether all of the emotions involved have been expressed, recognized, and taken into account. Innumerable business and law-office decisions are bad because they have been devised on the assumption that feelings can be laid aside or ignored.

What is the lawyer to do with her feelings, in particular those about her client? One alternative: Repress them through habitual, unconscious mechanisms, which means not being aware of them at all. Wall them off from the on-going relationship with the client and then find a "release" outside professional relationships: running, sailing, weaving, family life, gardening, church work. Another possibility: feelings, always present, are channeled secretly back into the relationship and used as tools of manipulation. A third alternative (and one we advocate): bring feelings openly into the relationship with the client.

A common way we relate to our feelings for a client is to put the feelings aside or ignore them, by trying to focus on the "problem" the client presents. We do this because we adopt a narrow definition of lawyering, and we often do this unconsciously. The lawyer is able to create and take up a lawyer role that minimizes the need to take account of her feelings. In this role-oriented, instrumental approach to lawyering, feelings are consistently devalued or ignored. We emphasize objectivity and independent judgment. Professionalism itself comes to be defined in terms of the ability to keep the client at arm's length. The good lawyer, in this view, *controls* the client, and does so for the specific purpose of pursuing the client's interests. In medicine, this is translated as "the doctor knows best." It is an interactional style supported by the lawyering ethos, by individual psychological needs, by the fantasies we entertain about the lives we live as lawyers, and by the rules of professional ethics.

The interactional psychological and professional style we describe here cuts the client off from her story (see Chapter Two). When we focus on the legal problem to the exclusion of the client, or on the client as a problem, attention and energy are directed outward, toward an imagined safe zone of objectivity represented by knowledge and skill, and away from the relationship. But the client's problem cannot be separated from the client, and the lawyer cannot keep the energy and focus of the relationship solely on the problem. Relationships premised upon a problem fail even as they succeed. The relation of the lawyer, client, and problem are in reality too complex and overwhelm the problem-oriented focus of the lawyer. If the problem were a ball, and both lawyer and client could keep their gaze directed on the ball, the psychodynamics of the attorney-client relationship would be a relatively simple matter. But the client's problem is not separate from the client. Ron Barrett does not experience his legal problem as outside him or outside the relationship he has with his employee, and will not experience it that way even at the behest of the most authoritarian lawyer.

THE AUTHORITARIAN STYLE, THE PROBLEM OF POWER, AND THE NEED TO BE HEROIC

There are lawyers who actively assert dominance over their clients, letting it be known, from the beginning, that clients can take it (submit), or leave it. Some clients want a "take it or leave it" lawyer, a lawyer that will assume control, and will get them what they want. A client may be willing to acquiesce, and pay the price of submission, in the hope that she will actually get what she wants. And it takes little imagination to speculate on the dynamics and the pathologies of the authoritarian lawyer who dominates his client and does so routinely and as a matter of course cuts himself off from his client and the world of his client. This lawyer retreats into an Olympian world of his own making. When we live in a world of self-designed Olympian heights, we begin to act like the Greek god Zeus, taking on an assumed power and lofty unreachableness that calls for competition, power-plays, and the pushing and shoving that goes with a "top-dog" mentality. The authoritarian lawyer can, and sometimes does, become a legendary figure, renowned for his success, revered for his exploits, a folk hero in both professional and public circles. The authoritarian lawyer is often a mesmerizing figure, a subject of controversy and gossip, setting about (whether consciously or unconsciously) to make himself a legend.

We admire our pop-culture lawyer heroes (whether they are heroes in the fuller sense of what it means to be an authentic cultural hero is another matter). They represent, symbolically, our own struggle, and our will to compete, to overcome mediocrity, to fight for something that we believe in, and the hope that we will prevail whatever the odds. The popular lawyer hero is a symbol and a projective screen for our fantasies of prevailing, of overcoming, of securing just rewards for the injuries and damages to ourselves and our clients. The lawyer hero is a winner who overcomes great obstacles. The hero is a version of myself. I, too, feel (or desire to feel) heroic, engaged in meaningful struggles, having acquired the power to overcome all that stands against me. To actualize this heroic image I require that my clients place themselves entirely in my hands.

A point of clarification. We are not suggesting that it takes an authoritarian lawyer to become a cultural hero, or that popular lawyers, some of whom achieve local and national acclaim (and some of whom are real heroes), are all authoritarian. (A wonderful counter-example is the southern lawyer-hero, Atticus Finch, in Harper Lee's novel *To Kill a Mockingbird*.) There are different kinds of heroes, as there are different kinds of lawyers. We can distinguish between popular figures admired by the public, made heroes by the press and television, and lawyers who are less well known but in quiet ways are genuinely heroic. And, we might note as well, there is the hero we associate with the heroic quest, the mythic journey that each of us takes when he enters the world fully as a public citizen and seeks to do something significant, as we do when we take on the causes of others, advocating and professing for other people.

The authoritarian lawyer style is both a caricature and a reality. It is one way lawyers protect themselves from their own feelings and the feelings of others, a form of protection associated with objectivity in professional relationships. It is one way lawyers measure their success, a success that makes some lawyers popular heroes. In the reality of the law office—which is our concern—the authoritarian lawyer points to the problem of power: who will control a relationship, who will feel powerful and who will experience feelings of helplessness when clients work with lawyers. We assume it inevitable in the course of a professional relationship (and perhaps, any relationship) that the "helper" will feel strong or subtle pressure to take command of the situation and to wield power over the client. Power, the desire for control, is never absent from human relationships. In the relationship of lawyer and client, the lawyer is pushed from many directions, internal (psychological) and external (social, political, and cultural), to take charge and be in control. In Freudian and Jungian psychology, this need is analyzed from the perspective of countertransference, a name for those strong feelings that are directed toward the client, that are linked up with other relationships (often past), needs, and feelings that are not specifically related to those of the client who is the real person before us and with us in the room.

Evidence of the need to be powerful (a need that is itself a countertransference reaction) includes unsolicited advice, false reassurance, grandiose claims and arguments, browbeating, insisting on rigid compliance with the lawyer's plan on how to proceed, frequent references to aspects of the law that are beyond the client's understanding, trivializing the work of other lawyers. Every lawyer recognizes the impulse to get and maintain control over clients and their "cases." The need for control (and the power that goes with control) is something we take into relationships with us (a need that runs from functional to neurotic) and is often enough exacerbated by the client's needs and the nature of the work that we are called on to do for and with the client.

More problematic still is the need for control that emanates from the feeling that the client is making a similar bid for power, so that lawyer and client compete for control. Clients, no less than lawyers, have a need for control and a wish for power. A client can take control, assume a power position, and dominate a lawyer—a situation that is not in the best interests of either client or lawyer. The power issue is not solved by giving up control or forcing the client to make decisions that he does not feel capable of making.

Murray Stein, a Jungian analyst and one of the psychologists whose work we have drawn on for this description of the need for power in professional relationships, makes this useful observation: Sometimes the need for power comes from "a professional attitude," what we have called the lawyer's *persona*. The *persona* brings power with it, and so we control our clients in order to live up to, and live out, the demands of the mask. The power dynamic of the professional attitude that comes from this *persona* leaves the client in the position of accepting the situation or looking for a different lawyer. As Stein puts it: The client "either accepts it and adapts, or rejects it and leaves." That Olympian clarity is a possibility, but more frequently the power dynamic is set into motion *during* the relationship, as the case proceeds, or, as Stein puts it, "as the complexes of each partner become engaged with those of the other. Here the power pattern derives from the psychodynamics that operate between two specific individuals, while other areas of each person's life remain relatively free of this pattern." Stein gives an example of the patient who brings out the sadist in the psychotherapist. This kind of person is not unknown in law offices. "They are unconsciously looking for someone to take charge and to assert power over them, to tell them what to do, to give them tough advice, to punish them for their inadequacy.... " In such a case, it doesn't take an overwhelming need to control, a neurotic power drive, for a lawyer to find himself controlling the client. That is, after all, what the client wants. It is in fact what the client has tricked you into doing. The effect of the power dynamic, viewed from either client or lawyer perspective, is that it creates psychological distance between two persons. It produces isolation.

A REFLECTIVE EXERCISE: COMPETITION AND OTHER THREATS TO A WORKING RELATIONSHIP

We have identified two initial threats that pose a danger to a good working relationship between attorney and client: competition and professional domination (often called "paternalism"). Competition and paternalism are not things that just happen in professional relationships; nor are they inevitable. Competition and paternalism are learned. You learned competition and paternalism before you came to law school; law school helps confirm what you've learned and gives it a new status and justification. One way to understand competition and paternalism as threats to a working relationship with clients is to unravel the complex history of your own learning about competition and paternalism.

As a law student you are now in a competitive world, for law schools are places of intense competition. Is it possible that you found your way to law school because you are a competitive person? Do you see the competition that is going on around you, now? Do you see where and how you fit into this competitive world? Competition may be a reality but what kind of reality is it for you? How has it affected your experience of law school?

Competition is commonplace in our culture, so much so that we tend to think of those around us, and even ourselves, as winners and losers. Competition may, of course, be the spur to "doing a good job" and, for many, the motivation to reach higher levels of personal achievement. There is, at least on first appearance, nothing inherently wrong with competition. Much of what we see and hear as we grow up in America says that competition is good for us—and this in a culture that otherwise exalts cooperation, community, and loving our neighbor. Competitiveness, in American culture, is considered a virtue. But the experience of many law students is that the competitiveness promoted in law school is destructive. The concern of many students (and teachers) is that competitiveness tends to usurp other virtues and can blind one to the intrinsic worth of the activity which has been translated into a competition with winners and losers.

Return, now, to the questions posed above and see if you can describe how you and your feelings about the competitive academic world have been worked out. Or have your feelings and concerns about competition been articulated and addressed at all?

COUNTERTRANSFERENCE

It is uncommon, in professional relations outside the therapeutic setting, for the professional ("helper") to learn how to take account of his feelings; feelings are simply left to take care of themselves or we find ways to help us forget the feelings we have. Feelings are just there, to be left alone, undisturbed, or perhaps, more problematic, actively suppressed. They receive little attention (in legal education or continuing legal education programs) or conscious thought, and there is generally no effort to understand how they might influence interactions with clients (or with other lawyers, or judges), or how one might identify and make use of these feelings. We take our feelings for granted, and in doing so give little thought to the kind of questions that might make us more aware of these feelings: How am I as a lawyer and a person (a Christian, a wife, a Mason, a father, a daughter) to act toward and with my clients? Do I approach all my clients with the same kind of attitude, a professional attitude that has become a legal *persona*? Or do I allow myself to put aside the mask and respond to each client as the person he or she is or wishes to be? Do I respond to the story the client tells with its unique particulars or to the story as a genre whose plot I have memorized so well that there is no longer a need to listen? (See Chapter Two.)

When we talk about the feelings of a lawyer for and about a client (and feelings *against* the client), we have entered the realm of transference and countertransference, terms probably not familiar to most lawyers. Feelings associated with a counter-transference can be witnessed in unexpected behavior, strong feelings (affection and hostility are common), a quick reply, a rebuke, browbeating, abruptness, verbal threats, power moves, seductive behavior. Here are a few clues, from Saxe and Kuvin, clues that signal countertransference in lawyer-client relationships. They may lead to awareness of lawyer needs that are not being met, or to a recognition that the feeling level of the relationship needs attention. When these signals are ignored, the client rather than the lawyer is made to bear the burden of them:

— Feelings of discomfort during or after meetings with the client ("most likely indicate inability on the part of the attorney to understand and honestly deal with certain kinds of material which touch on the attorney's own problems").

— Carelessness and discourtesy toward the client, such as being late for appointments, permitting avoidable interruption, or making appointment arrangements that are inconvenient for the client. ("Despite the rationalizations ... this is usually an ... indication of his hostility toward his client or his fear that the coming appointment will further produce material that will cause anxiety in the attorney.")

— Strong affectionate feelings for the client, which feelings are usually recognized when the client is of the opposite sex and repressed when he or she is not.

— Inclinations to boast, to colleagues or client, on the importance of the matter the client brings in ("indicative of the attorney's damaged self-concept and his lowered self-esteem . . . a reparative maneuver").

— Avoidance of the client and neglect of his case (the principal source of complaint about lawyers to bar-association grievance committees) ("may indicate serious neurotic conflicts").

— Gossip with others about the client ("[c]ausations may include . . . need to associate with peer group . . . psycho-sexual pathology . . . self-defeating or self-destructive mechanism").

— A tendency to "hammer away at minutiae beyond the scope of even the most intelligent lament." Saxe and Kuvin see this as a manifestation of aggression, and note that it often occurs with a client who is perceived as dissatisfied with the lawyer. "If the attorney is blind to his vulnerability in this area, and contracts with a client who is neurotically 'pain-dependent,' the conduct of the case is usually chaotic, and the end result is usually a disaster for the client. . . . "

— Boredom or drowsiness—"the most important of all responses." Saxe and Kuvin believe this to be "almost inevitably an indicator of extreme anxiety produced in the attorney." The agenda then, of course, would be to locate the source of the anxiety.

Howard F. Stein in his work on countertransference in physician-patient relationships observes that "we discover and recognize its power only by stumbling on it, by feeling disturbed by it, or by having someone else identify it." There is an element of surprise (sometimes confusion, anger, or shame) that comes from this stumbling onto our own feelings. "When we 'accidentally' let slip our feelings—through words, tone of voice, gestures, impulsive actions—we often feel surprised if not overwhelmed by such lapses in self-control." Whenever a feeling is denied or ignored and then finds its way back into the conversation or is acted out in behavior, it is overdetermined, which means it is differentiated from on-going reactions by having an unexpected power, a way of making itself known that is unexpected and that takes us by surprise. "It strikes us," Stein says, "unprepared."

The countertransference is threatening because it conflicts with the role expectations we have consciously shaped into an operative professional mask. In the world of feeling, a lawyer has no more expertise or knowledge than her client. The compartmentalization of role and self collapse in professional life when we recognize and work with countertransference feelings. Role and *persona* are ways to institutionalize, that is, regularize and routinize, the professional's response in confusing and threatening situations. But feelings are embedded in even the most routinized response. By gaining insight into countertransference, we see the subjectivity (an essential aspect of human caring) operating inside the mask of professionalism.

There is, one suspects, a healthier and more truthful way to work through the three-cornered reality of client, lawyer, and problem. Instead of allowing power to create distance, the lawyer and client become partners, in meetings and between meetings. The lawyer and client work together. The work (the work of being together and the work that is the legal problem) bring them together. It is like Robert Frost's farmer (in the poem "Tuft of Flowers") who begins the day feeling alone but comes in his work to see that, "We work together when we work apart."

A REFLECTIVE EXERCISE: ACTIVE LISTENING

The client is a lecturer in sociology at a local university. He has had recurrent, frequent, and recent clashes with the head of his department and has reason to believe that his contract will not be renewed. He explains this, and adds that he wonders whether there is anything a lawyer can do to help. You know this much from your secretary, who talked with him when he made the appointment to talk to you.

What follows is a series of statements by the client during the course of an interview. We interrupt the interview to pose alternative responses by the lawyer. Select the response that you would make to what the client has said.

C–1: "I don't know what's the matter with that place. You walk across the campus and don't even see anyone you know. You can walk into offices and they give you the cold shoulder. Faculty members are not treated with any respect at all."

I would:

    1.   indicate my understanding of the client's bitterness.

    2.   convey the idea that attitudes typically taken toward young teachers at large universities might understandably cause him to feel bitter and rejected.

    3.   get the client to continue talking so that I can get a better idea of what he has to deal with.

    4.   lead the client to consider that his present worry about unemployment may be in part the result of his own attitudes.

    5.   indicate to the client that this doesn't sound like the kind of problem that a lawyer can deal with effectively.

C–2: "It wasn't this way where I taught before. It was tough there, but you had your job and you did it. I had a fifteen-hour teaching load some semesters. I could have let the classes slide, but I never did. I always prepared thoroughly."

I would:

1. lead the client to explain in more detail what the memory of his old college means to him.

2. gently point out that the present situation is different and that memories of the old college are irrelevant.

3. try to convey the feeling (my feeling) that I mean to sympathize with how difficult the new situation has been for him.

4. let him know I recognize his feelings, that in his old college his hard work was appreciated.

5. help him to recognize that his feelings of bitterness are probably due to the fact that the university he now teaches at is much larger and that therefore there is bound to be less of a sense that others depend on him.

C–3: "You see, there are teachers all around me who do so little, and do it so poorly, that it makes you sore. There are a lot of teachers who let the teaching assistants do all the work. It makes me boil, just like it used to when I was a kid and my big brother would sneak away on Saturdays and leave me all the work."

I would:

1. get the client to realize that criticism of others is not a solution to his problem.

2. try to convey an appreciation (my appreciation) of how he sees the situation as one in which he has been taken advantage of and not appreciated.

    3. tell him: "You have difficulty working with people who complain about others."

    4. explore further how this situation reminds him of his childhood, with the idea that he might need psychological counseling.

    5. reveal my own feelings about his feelings of being taken advantage of.

C–4: "You know, it's a funny thing, but when I go in to talk to them about this contract thing I feel shaky all over. It's the silliest damned thing. Why should I do that?"

I would:

    1. help the client to minimize his concern over this problem of feeling shaky all over.

    2. try to help the client connect his feelings of rejection with his anxiety about going in to the head of his department to talk about the contract (so that he will understand his feelings better).

    3. express as directly as I can that I can see how his reactions must puzzle him and cause him concern.

    4. ask him if he has given thought to some things he might do to deal with his anxiety.

    5. ask him to talk more about his relationship with the department chairman and his colleagues in the department, to determine if they might be terminating his contract for a good reason.

C–5: "I think it would be a screwy thing to do, really, but I think sometimes that I will write to the old college where I was teaching and see if they will take me back. It would be a lot easier than fighting over this mess here. It would be good to see some of the old crowd back there. But it would be a silly thing to do."

I would:

1.   point out to the client that it sounds like he is ambivalent about pursuing legal action.

2.   ask for more information about what he wants to do in this case, including his feelings about possible legal action.

3.   tell him that he has some escapist attitudes and that these attitudes will simply interfere with my ability to help him in his legal case.

4.   help him see his present situation is really not as bad as he now thinks it is.

5.   suggest to the client that I am probably not going to be willing to represent him.

C–6: "I can go live with my mother, if I have to. She doesn't have much; I've been sending her money for years. I never know just what to do about that. It seems to me that I had a right to what I earned. I didn't live very high; I send home two or three hundred dollars a month. What do you think? Does that seem fair to you?"

I would:

1.   help the client see that his relationship with his mother has nothing to do with his legal case and my representation of him.

2. help the client see that his present ambivalence about what to do about his contract is related to his ambivalence about his mother.

3. encourage him to talk more about his situation with his mother.

4. try to reduce his anxiety and uncertainty by telling him that I am sure he has always done the right thing with his mother.

5. tell him that what matters is that he feels he did the right thing, regardless of whether I or anyone else feels it was right or wrong.

C–7: "When I'm feeling discouraged, I wonder if there will be anything for me to do next year. Maybe I've lived my life. Maybe I should just drop out, or maybe what I've got to live for is second rate in comparison with what I have had."

I would:

1. convey to the client the idea that, if he continues to look at his future this way, it will be more likely to become true, and that it would be better to put his mind to the problem at hand.

2. try to elicit more information about what he will do if he loses his job.

3. point out that one alternative seems to be going back to his old position.

4. indicate that I understand—or that I am trying to understand—that he feels disillusioned.

5. point out that his discouragement is a natural result of his present stressful situation, and therefore that he should try not to worry about it.

C–8: "I am beginning to wonder if my abilities are even marketable. I am wondering if I am going to have to live on the damages you collect for me. I don't want to go back to my old college, and I can't bear the thought of starting all over at some new place again."

I will:

1.   sympathize with the client that the situation looks hopeless.

2.   try to help him see that regardless of his immediate situation, he has important talents and abilities that will help him find a position.

3.   suggest that he rethink his decision about not going back to his old college.

4.   discuss with him the difficulties of getting damages in this kind of situation.

5.   help him see that his present assessment of the situation is not accurate, that he has real abilities, and that with a lawyer in the case the university might be willing to extend his contract.

* * *

This exercise is adapted from an early treatise on non-directive counseling, by psychologist E.H. Porter, Jr. It bears the title *An Introduction to Therapeutic Counseling*. It is a valuable source on reflective counseling (and interviewing); it includes exercises such as this one, and systems for scoring responses. It may be helpful to evaluate your answers in by reference to Dr. Porter's suggested scoring categories:

— *evaluative* ("the counselor has made a judgment of relative goodness, appropriateness, effectiveness, rightness")

— *interpretive* ("the counselor's intent is to impart meaning to the client, to show him ... what the client might or ought to think")

— *supportive* ("reassure ... reduce the client's intensity of feeling, to pacify ... the client need not feel as he does")

— *understanding* ("to ask the client whether the counselor understands correctly what the client is 'saying,' how the client 'feels' about it ... how the client 'sees' it")

Dr. Porter sought to show how some choices of words are more reflective and indicative of active listening than others. He invited attention to various aspects of the words the counselor chooses:

— *content* ("in large part ... simple repetition")

— *shallow or partial* ("limited.... involving only a portion of what the client expressed or ... 'undercutting' or 'watering-down' the feeling ... expressed")

— *reflection* ("rephrasing in fresh words the gist of the client's expression without changing the meaning or feeling")

— *interpretive* ("goes beyond the meaning ... adds meaning not expressed by the client")

As the interview continues, assume that you want the client to feel that you understand him. Your responses now are for the purpose of trying to reflect to the client that you understand how the client feels, or, at least, that you are trying to understand. Choose a response or draft one using your own words.

C–9: "So, I guess that what I want you to do is to make sure I keep my job. I suppose, though, that I probably will bungle it. Things couldn't get much worse."

    1.   You want work and yet you feel that if I can get them to give you another contract, something will go wrong anyway.

    2.   You feel that your lack of self-confidence makes you incapable of holding the job even if you keep it for now.

    3.   This inability to hold a job has been troubling you and you're turning to me for help.

    4.   You feel it's almost futile to try to get the job back.

C–10: "Oh, well, I guess it's all sort of hopeless. The days go on. Everyone's planning for next fall's classes except me. My landlord says the papers are full of stories about the shortage of people in my field who have jobs in industry. A manpower shortage. Maybe that's what's wrong with me—a shortage of manpower."

    1.   You feel that you're not quite up to the fight, is that it?

    2.   You feel that, if you're not hired again for next year, it will be because of your own shortage, is that it?

3. You feel, do you, that this hopelessness may be something inside you?

4. In other words, you feel pretty inadequate.

C–11: "You know, last year I really thought I was going places. My classes really clicked for a while. Then I had a bad break. Oh, well, you're probably not interested."

1. You feel, do you, that to explain it to me would only bore me?

2. Things looked pretty hopeful for a while but then the bottom just dropped out, is that it?

3. You'd really like to tell me about this but you feel uncertain about going ahead, is that it?

4. I take it you feel pretty disappointed.

C–12: "Well, what happened was that I stood up for a fellow professor in a faculty meeting—a man who was terminated last year. And I spoke up. And what I said was met with stony silence. Like it was in bad taste. So I am getting the skids now. There may be other reasons for my getting the boot, but that reason sticks in my mind."

1. In other words, while you see other factors involved, you are pretty sure that, if you are terminated, it will be because of your exercise of free speech in a faculty meeting.

2. In other words, you feel that there is a connection between your defenses of a colleague and your possible termination.

3. You feel you are being treated unfairly and you just can't get that out of your mind.

4. That's the reason that sticks in your mind, but you feel there may be other reasons.

C–13: "Do you ever have anything grab onto you so you couldn't shake it loose? (Angrily) Well, I have. I've got a habit that if I don't cut it out, I'm going to ruin myself and my career—everything!"

1. In other words, this thing is just driving you over the precipice, unless you can bring it under control.

2. It's a habit you can't shake. It may be ruinous.

3. This thing bothers you quite a bit, doesn't it?

4. In other words, you feel you just don't have enough will power to meet this thing.

C–14: "You see, it all started when I was a kid. We had a club in high school; we used to go out and drink beer. We did that every week. Well, beer got to be quite a habit with me. My folks were German; they didn't think anything of it. Well, that was okay, but after I got into graduate school I drank more and more, and I've been drinking awfully heavily in the past few years. My colleagues at the other college told me to lay off. If I could quit drinking, I'd be okay."

1. You begin to slip in your work when you start drinking too much.

2. This drinking is something you want to conquer.

3. You feel that you used to drink to drown your disappointment in yourself.

4. It may have started out innocently enough, but now it's become something that's a real problem to you.

CHAPTER FOUR

ESTABLISHING A WORKING RELATIONSHIP

PERSONAL CLIMATE

The key to tough decisions in law offices and to client choices that work, is the climate lawyers create for the relationship with clients. (See Reflective Exercise, in Chapter Two). The heart of counseling effectiveness, wherever it falls on the spectrum from legal problem-solving to advice to therapy, is the client's ability to trust the counselor. A climate of trust involves acceptance, understanding, and empathy. The issues of trust, dependence, personal growth, and client choice turn on the climate the counselor creates. Many legal counselors are poor at building a healthy, constructive, non-manipulative office climate for the people who come to them with worries, troubles, and confusion. Yet, we know that many lawyers are remarkably skillful at it.

It is obvious that two people who propose to work together have to come to a working agreement, a sense about how they will proceed, how they will talk and listen to each other, and how the stories they tell each other will be reconciled. Life is filled with working agreements, from the resolution of who is to go through the door first to comity among the three branches of the federal government. The working agreement between a lawyer and client will develop, in most cases, all too quickly, based on some mix of the following:

— Each party's view of the law. Lawyers tend to regard law as something necessary and functional; clients may regard it as oppressive, intrusive, or tyrannical, puzzling or mysterious.

— Each party's view of lawyers. Research indicates that many citizens have a low regard for lawyers. People who have dealt with lawyers retain this low regard for the profession but tend to have a higher regard for the lawyer who represented them. The client who expects his lawyer to file a lawsuit, immediately, has a different feeling about what lawyers do than the client who appears to seek personal guidance.

— Each party's view of the client's situation. Virginia Anne Church put it well: "The fact that a client first seeks you, an attorney, rather than a minister, marriage counselor, psychologist, therapist, or doctor, may have little to do with the nature of his underlying problem (or even with the best means of effectively resolving it). Most likely he will choose a lawyer because of his stereotypes of the other helping professions in relation to his self image, or his view of the lawyer as an authoritative, rational, and respectable power source." In his work with divorced spouses, Robert Weiss, a sociologist, found that individuals with marital difficulties seek lawyers for a variety of reasons: "Some retain a lawyer because they want a specific legal service: a separation agreement to be negotiated, legal pressure to be brought on a non-supporting husband or on a wife who refuses visitation, or simply a divorce. But others retain a lawyer for all sorts of non-legal reasons. They may want to demonstrate to themselves and their spouse that they are seriously dissatisfied with their marriage: 'I saw a lawyer today' can be of decided dramatic value when dropped into an evening's dispute. Or they may be unhappy and confused, and perhaps fearful of the future, and want the reassurance of having talked with someone knowledgeable. Many among the separated see a lawyer initially just for information regarding their legal situation, without any immediate desire to proceed beyond this. Some retain a lawyer almost against their will, because their spouse has insisted that they do so, or because their spouse has retained one and they believe that in self-protection they must follow suit."

— Some lawyers see themselves as available for warfare (they even speak of themselves or colleagues as "hired guns") and are not very interested in anything else. Some see themselves as society's keepers of the peace and will go to extraordinary lengths to avoid warfare. Some see themselves as sources of wisdom, and still others as vindicators of justice.

There is common agreement that an open, reflective, supportive atmosphere in the office, is likely to produce better rapport than a climate in which one or both parties in the relationship have secret agendas. An open, reflective atmosphere requires: (1) active listening, (2) empathic regard for the client's feelings, (3) acceptance (what Carl Rogers called "unconditional positive regard"). A reflective, supportive relationship can prevent an early and troubling emotional dependence on the lawyer. It can also help avoid a dependence based on misplaced perceptions of a lawyer's expertise. Our professional ideals, the dynamics of interpersonal relationships, and a decent respect for human persons require that clients remain active in the development of their own legal relationships. This client activity varies depending upon what the lawyer sets out to do for the client: drafting a complaint, devising appropriate language for a letter written on the client's behalf, preparing provisions of a will, conducting a trial. It is astounding, though, how many clients say, "Why do I want to read the draft of my will? What do I have a lawyer for?" Such remarks are evidence of a working relationship in which the lawyer's technical expertise is being made to carry more weight than it should in an open, reflective, professional relationship.

The best working arrangement is one founded on an understanding of the client that he is being encouraged to talk freely, to become a working partner in the relationship. The dialogue between lawyer and client, early in their association, has much to do with how the working agreement is formed. Consider for a moment the words of an initial dialogue. Communication research suggests that the more leading the professional's words are, the more likely the resulting contract will be a contract based on undue reliance. Appel and Van Atta report a continuum which ranges from a category of Acceptance Remark (illustrated by a simple, "Uh huh" or "I see") to Rejection Responses ("I'm sure you don't mean that" or "I'm afraid you're wrong about that"), a category of maximum lead. To encourage client talk, they recommend fewer leading techniques. When leading is necessary they suggest "general leads": "Could you talk a bit more about.... " Conversely, a counselor who wants to assume responsibility will employ techniques that involve a high degree of lead, such as interpretation remarks: "It appears to me that your situation boils down to" or urging remarks, such as "It seems to me that what you need is.... "

Here is part of an initial interview of the owner of a photography studio who consults a lawyer because she thinks she is being (unfairly? wrongly? illegally? corruptly?) excluded from a school's business. She has been describing how competing studios that are given yearbook contracts provide free services, or outright cash, to the schools involved:

1   C: But I know the time that I bid, I had given the best bid. I know. But the studio that ended up getting it did both. They gave both money and services.

2   L: I see.

3   C: But the actual work that the studio did, or the prices that we were going to charge the seniors—it really was not important.

4   L: The studio—the charges to them—was—were—presumably, high.

5   C: Oh, yes. Well, you have to—what else are we going to do? You know, somewhere the money—

6   L: Umm.

7   C: It's going to come out of somewhere. You take a yearbook—I don't know whether you were on a yearbook committee when you were in school—I don't know—

8   L: No. But I had my picture taken.

9   C: That you had done. But the yearbook committee—when you consider that they have a printer. The printer doesn't donate his work. They don't go to the printer and say, "Okay, sir, you print up the book for us, and then you can come in and sell them. And if you sell a few, you can get some money, you can cover your printing expenses." No. The printer charges. You know it's going to cost so much to get those books printed up.

10   L: Right.

11   C: But the only one in this whole area of professional people, that has to give free things, is the photographer. And this seems wrong to me.

The lawyer's responses here do not interrupt flow. The client's story is not diverted or interrupted by what the lawyer says. The responses are, as counselors' say, acceptance remarks. However, the client needs more than the absence of interruption (although the restraint necessary to provide even that would be difficult for many lawyers). She also needs some encouragement, and that is most naturally provided by responses that demonstrate that the lawyer feels some empathy for her. The difference between acceptance and empathy is that empathy brings the lawyer's feelings into the interview. What, for example, would have been a good response to the last-quoted client remark?

(1) I can understand that you feel strongly about that.

(2) You really feel that that is wrong.

(3) Yes, and this probably reflects the fact that business has been a struggle for you.

(4) Oh? Why is that?

The second response—from the standpoint both of rapport and working arrangement—is, in our opinion, preferable. It expresses both acceptance of the feeling and empathy for it. But, to be effective, it must be sincere, and some lawyers would probably not have received and shared the feeling well enough to express themselves empathically; they would not have experienced empathy, and it would be false for them to attempt to express it. In that case, the first answer, which shows understanding, seems best. The third answer would fit the category of interpretative remarks; it may come across as presumptuous. The fourth answer is probing and, even if it might be effective later in the interview, may throw the client off course.

This lawyer in fact responded: "And the reason you have come to see me is—?" That seems to us a poor response. It does not demonstrate acceptance of the client's strong feeling. Silence on the issue of acceptance, as here, is rejection (of the feeling and, inevitably, of the client too). The response was also abrupt and premature. The remainder of the interview demonstrates that the client had more to say, including facts crucial to her claim, and it demonstrates that the lawyer did not do enough to establish a sound working arrangement. If the lawyer were experiencing time pressures, it would have been more honest and much less damaging to say so and to arrange for a second interview. Response "10" is an earlier indication of this—what? impatience?—and is also an ineffective response; client statement "9" presented an occasion for acceptance of feeling. The lawyer mistook agreement for acceptance of feeling, which is not the same at all. If the client says (as she, in a way, was saying), "I'm damned mad," an accepting response would be something like "Yes, you really are mad," said with feeling; the response, "Right," fails to reflect the feeling and also implies that client feelings are presented for agreement or disagreement by the lawyer.

Evidence that a working agreement was not being adequately developed in the most effective manner occurs in two statements that followed:

11   C: ... And this seems wrong to me.

12   L: And the reason you've come to me is—?

13   C: I don't know. (Laughter.) That's what you're supposed to decide. I don't know. There's [such] a lot of problems that I don't know that you can do anything for me.

Here, by way of contrast, is a short dialogue between Carl Rogers and a young woman who came to see him about problems in her family:

14   C: I mean I hate the idea of everybody telling me what to do. Even my husband, he'll tell me what to do. Even though I'm young and I'm married, I mean I'm a human being and I like to run my life myself.

15   R: M-hm.

16   C: I mean I don't want to feel like I'm still in a baby buggy or something like that.

17   R: You feel that your mother and your husband and everybody tries to run your life.

18   C: Yes, that's why I feel that I was old enough to bear a baby and that's surely a lot of pain but yet they won't let me make up my mind for myself.

19   R: M-hm. M-hm. (Pause; the client might have continued, but did not; Rogers apparently decided he had to say something.) Here

I was old enough to have a child and yet nobody thinks I can make my decisions or run my own life. Is that what you're saying?

20   C: Yes.

21   R: M-hm. M-hm.

22   C: I mean, like, uh, now this is when my husband and I went to California with my little boy. I mean we were happier out there. He didn't have to run home to his mother all the time, and his mother is another one that, that we just don't get along. She hated me right from the day she saw me. But when we went to California, we had a good time out there.

23   R: I guess you're saying that kind of shows that when we're just by ourselves, we really get along better.

24   C: Yes, we get along better. . . .

Notice several things about these exchanges: (1) They probably took less than a minute, but, in them, Rogers learned about the significant effects on the marital relationship of the client's mother-in-law. (2) Rogers uses very slight non-verbal sounds of encouragement to keep the client talking. When the client stops talking, he uses reflective statements that carry much of the client's feeling, and therefore encourage her to go on. (3) Rogers checks with the client to see if his understanding is correct ("Is that what you're saying?" "I guess

you're saying that.... '') (See also the Reflective
Exercise at the end of Chapter Three).

CLIENT EXPECTATIONS

There are two aspects of the client's world that
the attorney often overlooks and that have an important bearing on the attorney-client relationship,
matters that can be addressed in the early stages of
the interview process. First are the client's *conscious* expectations. If these are not explored, they
become a kind of hidden agenda. Second, the
client's *unconscious* motivations for seeking legal
assistance affect fact-gathering. The lawyer needs to
understand and address both conscious expectations
and unconscious motivation.

It is essential that the lawyer determine what the
client wants and expects. To what degree is the
client seeking information, support, aid in decision-
making, friendship, or skills that only a lawyer
might be expected to have? What kind of role is the
attorney being asked to play in securing what the
client wants? Are the client's expectations and role
demands (that is, what he wants the lawyer to *be*)
compatible with the attorney's image of his role and
sense of self? In all likelihood, the client comes to
the attorney with a broad range of expectations.
These expectations may be uninformed or more
often based on stereotyped images of lawyers derived from representations of lawyers in the media
(TV, films, novels, newspapers).

When client expectations are unrealistic or distorted, they may severely interfere with the attorney-client relationship. The simplest direct technique for handling client expectations is to simply ask the client at the first meeting but not at the beginning of it, "What do you want?" During the course of the relationship the attorney may become uncertain on the answer to this question, or may detect unrealistic expectations on the part of the client, and there will be a need to discuss this issue again. The lawyer can and should discuss with the client these distorted images, beliefs, and expectations. Everyone has expectations; it is only talking about them and bringing them to conscious awareness that we can openly deal with them. Everyone has unconscious needs that affect their relationship with professional people, and everyone uses such relationships to satisfy psychological needs. These motivations are least harmful, and can be put to use when we are aware of their existence.

There are times when the client's needs are so unclear that the problem (and the story) is presented in a rambling and incoherent form. A lawyer's time is money, and there may be concern about a client who "rambles." Certainly, demanding formal, courtroom, casebook coherence stops the flow of information. Nonetheless, too much rambling, as Gerard Egan warns, "destroys the concreteness, the focus, and the intensity of the helping experience." In other words, rambling puts the client's payoff at risk, because the theme of the client's story and the supporting facts get lost in the rambling and tangled account the client gives of them. It can become impossible to deal with all of the implications of what the client is saying. When this happens, the attorney can (and should) be more directive, focusing the client's attention on discrete elements of the problem. Lawyers learn in law school how to use the law to do this; our argument is that we focus also on the client's need for it rather than the lawyer's psychological need to control the conversation and the relationship.

CONTENT AND PROCESS

A relationship between a client and her lawyer can be examined in terms of content and process. Content is the information and advice about the law and the context in which the client's decision will be implemented. Process includes the feelings of lawyer and client about each other, about themselves when they work together, and all of the ways they act toward each other that do not pertain directly to the business they transact. Content is the reason a person seeks legal assistance, those aspects of a consultation which can be taken down on a yellow pad. Process can be captured only by a perceptive human being. Process includes gestures, sounds, voice inflection, and posture. Non-verbal ways of communicating often give better clues to process than words do. Process is always pervasive and often has more to do with content and the way things turn out than one would suspect. Process shapes the twists and turns in the professional relationship. It reflects the depth of attraction, the feeling, and the understanding between the client and the lawyer.

Most lawyers and law students understand the difference between content and process. But for some, understanding process can be elusive. Part of the reason is that we are usually more aware of the content of our interactions than we are of the process. The way we live, the way we are educated, and the way we come to think about the world and ourselves is focused on: (1) what we do, (2) how we do it, and (3) how we experience the doing, that is, how we feel about ourselves and the way our actions take on meaning. In philosophical (and theological) terms, we are more attuned to *doing* than to *being*. When we meet someone we do not know there is a strong temptation, one that is hard to resist, to ask: What do you *do?* Knowing what a person does lets us make assumptions about him and about who he is, based on the work he does, the position he holds. This interest in what a person does is an example of the way we focus on content.

A REFLECTIVE EXERCISE: CONTENT AND PROCESS

Part A

An example of the distinction between content and process comes from the way we relate to our dreams. When you recall a dream, or write it down, you are focusing on content, a description of the images that appeared and the actions that took place in the dream. Freud called this descriptive element of the dream its "manifest content." But the content of dreams doesn't tell us everything we want to know. The problem is that the dream's content doesn't announce its message. The dream doesn't tell us what we want to know, about it or ourselves, until we get beyond content. If the dream is to have any meaning, if it is to be understood, at least in relation to our own lives, then we have to explore what Freud called the *latent* aspect of the dream. The latent part is what we would call process.

In the terminology that we borrow, this deeper level of the dream works as process and is out of awareness. When we look at the process level of the dream, how it is working, what the images might mean to the dreamer, the feelings that the dream evokes, and the way that the dream returns throughout the day, then we are at the process level: The process is the dreamer's relation to the dream.

Choose a day in which you set for yourself, as part of your agenda, observations that will help you distinguish between content and process, manifest and latent aspects of your interactions. You might begin with the first conversation of the day. And then, when you are in the classroom, see if you can distinguish between the manifest and latent communications of your teachers.

Part B

In a reflective exercise on "personal climate" (Chapter One), we posed questions about the law school classroom and your relationship with one (or more) of your teachers. If you tried to respond to all the questions raised in that exercise you made use of what you know about the teacher, what you know about yourself, and what you are able to describe about the way the two of you affect one another; that is content. It is what you imagine to be the views and philosophy of the teacher and of yourself that affects the way you learn. Some, although perhaps not all, of your responses to those questions about personal climate come from your feelings about what happens (to you) when you are in the presence of this teacher. The feelings—yours and the teacher's and those of other students, and perhaps even other teachers—operate, for the most part, out of sight; they are not an explicit part of the classroom learning. They exist at the process level. Feelings tend to point toward the process level of an interaction and of a relationship.

Review your responses to the "personal climate" reflective exercise in Chapter One and see if you can distinguish how your evaluation of the "personal climate" of the classroom draws on content and how it draws on process, on what you know and on what you feel, on what you are being asked to learn and how you are asked to learn it.

Part C

Using the content (manifest) and process (latent) distinction, see if you can describe a conversation (either one in which you were a participant or one that you observed), an interaction (with a friend, a stranger, the Dean, your spouse), or a situation in the classroom by focusing on content and process.

Remember that process is a response to the question: What is going on here? Process reflects the "personal climate" of the conversation. Process is more a question of "how" than a question of "why." For example, if, as you describe this conversation, you ask, "Why did he say that?" you will not necessarily move from the content to the process level. The process level is more likely to be reached when you ask about feelings, rather than reasons: Do I know or have any indication of what she was feeling when she said that? How did I feel when I heard what she said?

We know that content and process are not rigid categories of human interaction, but we believe the distinction to be an important one. Seeing how the distinction works in your own life, in the way you learn law, even in the way you talk to your friends, can provide valuable information about how you interact with others. Good counselors train themselves in the art of taking feelings into account. Awareness of the distinction between content and process is a device for doing that.

Note: The distinction that we are making here is sometimes discussed in terms of objective and subjective aspects of communication. Content is, in this dichotomy, associated with what we think to be objective, while process is labeled subjective. We find the objective/subjective labels problematic, indeed, more problematic than helpful.

Law office process relates—at least initially—to a lawyer's *persona* and role. Lawyers try to be lawyers by acting like they assume lawyers should act. Lawyers groom themselves (in more than one sense) to be lawyers. "In considering the individual's participation in social action," Erving Goffman says, "we must understand that in a sense he does not participate as a total person but rather in terms of a special capacity or status; in short, in terms of a special self." Law-office conversations illustrate this. A husband and wife are talking to a lawyer about wills:

L: My secretary has told me that you would like to discuss a will, so I sent you a small form to fill out. A couple of basic questions. Did you—uh—fill it out? Bring it with you?

H: Uh. I didn't fill it out because I didn't think you needed that information.

L: Didn't need it. You didn't think I'd need it.

H: I mean, what relevance does it have?

L: Well—really—

H: I mean, how much do you need for a will? My wife tells me we need a will. But do we really need a will?

L: Well, let's find out. Why don't you tell me something about yourself and your wife, and—uh—your background.

H: Go ahead, Mary. You're the one who wanted to come down here.

W: I think everybody needs a will—and I think he probably needs to know as much information as is relevant to decide, if we really need a will.

H: Why?

L: Well, there's a certain amount of information that an attorney needs to know. . . .

At the process (or what psychologist Eric Berne called the ulterior) level, this transaction is a ritual in which chairmanship is being worked out. The husband challenges both the lawyer's control of the transaction and his wife's concerns in a conversation–an interview–where the husband's strong feelings of an undetermined nature and source are playing a leading role as the driving force in shaping the "personal climate" of the interview.

Deference. Process in lawyer-client relationships involves questions of deference as does process in all human relationships. We see deference being worked out in the elevator, the dining room, the board room, the law-office waiting room, and the classroom. It reveals itself in the way people greet one another, the invitations—express and implicit—

that they issue, the compliments they pay, and the minor services

they render. If these daily rituals are, in process terms, symmetrical, what they say to the world is that the actors regard themselves as equals. If they are asymmetrical, they say that one actor is expected to defer to the other. Law-office deference rituals are usually asymmetrical. A client is not likely to address his lawyer by the lawyer's given name unless the lawyer indicates that this conduct is acceptable (and maybe not even then); certain territory in the office (behind the desk; in front of the filing cabinet) is restricted to use by the lawyer; the telephone is available only for his use. The deferred-to member in a professional relationship usually has implicit permission to inquire into the private life of the deferring member, and the deferring member is expected to honor the inquiry.

Deference is illustrated in formal law-office rituals, such as will-execution conferences—where the lawyer acts as a master of ceremonies in a sort of liturgy (or as a judge) would act—and in informal ceremonies such as explicit directions to clients on which chair to sit in, and implicit directions on whether clients may smoke, or argue with what the lawyer says. All of this behavior awaits stage directions from the lawyer; it often does not appear in the content of the transaction, but it always has a significant influence on the content.

A REFLECTIVE EXERCISE:
DEFERENCE

Given the society we (you and the authors) live in, it is likely that you have spent time in physicians' offices, their waiting rooms, and their examination rooms. We ask in this Exercise that you recall an occasion when you were in a doctor's office, as a patient, and you talked with the doctor about some "problem."

How did the talking and listening take place in the doctor's office? Who initiated topics of conversation? Was the talking and listening a *conversation?* What other terms might describe what took place? (Lecture? Reprimand? Interrogation?) Did the physician do any counseling? Did the counseling include: Explanation? Instruction? Reassurance? Intimidation?

Think about your relationship with physicians, with your family doctor. Do you pay deference to the physician? How does the deference work? How is it encouraged? How does it help the physician get her work done? How does it get you, the patient, what you want from the physician? How do you know what it is that you actually want? Is the deference working for you (is it in your best interest) or for the physician (in management of the illness or the office? her peace of mind)? Or is it simply a matter of, "the doctor knows best" (take it or leave it)?

Does it matter to the establishment of deference that the physician is a man and the patient is a woman (or vice versa)? What can you say from your own experience (or from what you know or have read) about the way deference in relationships with physicians affects the health care of women?

Demeanor. A similar process occurs in matters of demeanor. Clients who work with their hands will normally put on "Sunday" clothes to come to a law office (but may not when they go to a physician's office). Clients demonstrate by the way they sit, the tone of voice they use, and the way they open and close doors whether and how they wish to show deference. Their behavior will indicate whether or not they wish to be thought of as comfortable in the lawyer's world, a reluctant visitor to that world, or confused and baffled by it and therefore dependent on the lawyer as a guide and protector in this world.

Openness. From the lawyer's side, signals indicating relative openness to the client will determine the course of an hour in the law office or even of the entire professional relationship. If the lawyer says, "What is your problem?" he reduces his client to a thing. If the lawyer says, "What can I do for you?" he limits his client to the client's preconceived idea of the range of the lawyer's usefulness. Here, by contrast, is the way Carl Rogers greeted one of his clients:

R: Now, what I would like would be for you to tell me anything you're willing to tell me about yourself and your situation, how you feel about yourself. Or I guess another way of putting it is that anything you are willing to tell me that would help me to know you better, I'd be very glad to hear.

C: Where do you want me to start?

R: Wherever you would like to.

A lawyer might feel unprepared to begin a relationship with a prospective client this way. But the psychotherapist's approach does illustrate, by way of contrast to "What is your problem?" or "What can I do for you?" an effort to be open to the client as a person as well as to the client as a problem.

Lawyers often attempt to fashion a communication of openness by beginning the conversation with small talk, or offering the client coffee. These are sometimes effective—that is, the client sometimes responds to them with relaxation and freedom. But attempts at friendly gestures and idle banter can also be done in ways that produce awkward moments, in ways that make the client feel more uncomfortable than is otherwise necessary. The more direct way to go about this effort at openness is to simply be open to the client, whatever is on the client's mind, and however she wants to present the problem. Here is a young lawyer who attempted to do that:

L: Come in.

C: Hi. Are you Mr. Harris?

L: Yes, I am. Have a seat.

C: Sit here?

L: Fine.

C: How are you today?

L: Fine. How are you?

C: Oh, good.

L: I would like to offer you coffee, but our new offices don't have a coffee machine yet.

C: No problem. I don't drink coffee anyway. So we're all set. Let me think a second.

L: Sure.

C: I came right from work and I have not had a chance to sit down and think about this.

L: Fine. I don't know anything about why you're here, but perhaps you can tell me a little about it, and a little about yourself.

A sadder example is the public defender, appointed to represent a juvenile offender, who first met the client in an interview room at the jail. These were her opening remarks:

L: Would you like to tell me about your past record? I have some notes here that you've been in trouble before. If you think there's anything that's relevant, and want to tell me what happened—

C: Yeah. I been in trouble. A lot of trouble.

L: What for?

This relationship was thus characterized, at the beginning, as the relationship between a criminal and a defender of criminals. The process, in these opening remarks, implies, "I have no interest in you aside from the fact that you are in trouble."

Of course, an inept opening question does not mean a more authentic working relationship can never be established. And a good beginning can fade quickly, as it tends to do, for example, when a lawyer receives "irrelevant" personal information from the client with indifference, or when he rejects the client's curiosity about the lawyer as a person. The relationship between lawyer and client—the way they are together—warms and cools, moves forward and regresses, opens and closes throughout the relationship. The principal objective in learning to attend to process is to be aware of these shifts and changes and of their implications for helping the client and serving her interests. The objective is to be as aware of the process in lawyer-client relationships as we are the words we use in drafting instruments, or the strategies we use in litigation.

INITIAL THREATS TO A WORKING RELATIONSHIP

We can expect a well-trained, experienced lawyer to be relatively comfortable in dealing with clients (some, of course, are more comfortable than others). It is comfortable to be one who helps others. It is comfortable to deal with other people who come seeking help, who are willing to pay for it, who admire our learning and composure, and who listen with respect to what we say about the nature and resolution of the problem presented to us (or as we define it) and who express a willingness to follow our advice. Helping is such a comfortable thing to

do, in fact, that it may end up blocking awareness of
the process that underlies the on-going interaction
in the relationship. The real test for whether one's
image as a helper is useful to the client or harmful
to him is whether the help leads to *growth* in the
client. The growth test would have us focus on who
is making the decisions, the lawyer or the client,
and whether the client will be better enabled to
make his own decisions once the relationship with
the lawyer ceases. If the client is encouraged to be
passive about the decisions being made, then
growth is unlikely as an outcome of the relationship.

In terms of content, the object of a lawyer-client
relationship is a mutually satisfactory resolution of
the concerns that the client brings to the lawyer. In
terms of process, the object is a healthy relationship
between the lawyer and the client. Process affects
content. As R.S. Hunt puts it, the "problem" orientation in the relationship is evaluated (by lawyer,
client, and others) in terms of whether the client
will follow the course of action that has been
worked out in the law office—whether he will, as it
is commonly put, "take the lawyer's advice." That
result depends on how the client feels about the
lawyer. Process also affects itself, that is, it affects
the relationship. The way two persons in the law
office feel toward one another today affects the way
they will act together to resolve problems that it is
the purpose of the professional relationship to resolve.

* * *

A significant and initial issue in law-office process is the identification of dangers to the working relationship. Two principal dangers are identified in this section—the danger of competition and the danger of domineering paternalism.

Competition and domineering paternalism are threats to the process of a working relationship. Both can become serious when they are ignored or neglected. Time and energy spent in attending to them—in preventing them—are time and energy spent in developing and protecting the working relationship itself. Neglect of them is likely, at worst, to end in a bad professional result—advice the client will not follow, or a decision by the client not to return for further legal assistance. At best, neglect of competition and domination is likely to lead to a crisis in the relationship that will cost more time, energy, and emotional stress to resolve than it would have cost to prevent their development in the first place. The point is illustrated by a favorite story of the late Dean Joseph O'Meara: A hiker came upon a man chopping wood. The hiker noticed that the chopper's ax was dull. He said to the chopper, "You should sharpen your ax." And the chopper said, "I can't. I have to chop all this wood."

What must be attended to are: (1) our tendency, and the tendency of our clients, to adopt strategies of competition, rather than strategies of collaboration, in the law office; and (2) our tendency to invite dependence from clients, and clients' tendency to emotional reliance on us. Both forces are subtle.

Each tends to destroy the working relationship. (See the first Reflective Exercise in Chapter Three).

Competition. Lawyers are trained in law school to be competitive; in fact we are selected, and we select ourselves, for rituals of competition. The educational atmosphere professors and students live in, and practicing lawyers are nostalgic about, is a jungle atmosphere—more of a jungle than the practice of law. Lawyers are people who need to win arguments. Many of us have only one way to deal with our own internal conflict, our doubt, our hurt and that way is to slug it out with somebody else.

The alternative is to learn non-competitive strategies. What we have to be able to say, verbally and nonverbally, to clients is: "There is no need to compete in this office. I am your companion on a journey which I know can be strange and anxious for you. I will prove that I am your companion by being willing to tell you how I feel. I am going to try to take down the barriers that I and my law teachers and my colleagues in the practice have built between me and the people I care about."

Competition is built into law offices. Law-office interviews can be games that lawyers prepare in advance to win. The typical prosperous law office suite is a case study in one-upmanship, from decor to copies of *Barrons* to rooms lined with the Law Reports. Some law offices are only a trifle more subtle than the chair Mr. Tutt kept for unwelcome visitors which had an inch cut off each of the front legs, or the federal judge who has chairs for visitors in his cavernous office positioned ten feet away from his desk. Lawyers present themselves to clients in coat and tie, sit behind massive desks in high-back chairs, and barricade themselves with superior demeanor, yellow pads fourteen inches long, and gadgets such as computers and speaker telephones. Our heady language creates an atmosphere. The process signaled in the atmosphere is a mighty nonverbal claxon directed at clients: SIT UP AND PAY ATTENTION. I'M IN CHARGE HERE.

Dependence. A working relationship is as seriously threatened from the other direction, from dependence of the client on the lawyer. In response to client expectations and psychological needs, the attorney is often cast in a directive, dominant role. Feelings of dependence on the client's part may arise from a variety of factors: the client's expectation that the lawyer will step in and straighten things out; the client's attempt to avoid responsibility for making a decision; the client's expectation that the lawyer is able to manipulate the legal system or people in the client's world so as to achieve what the client desires; the client's inflated view of the legal profession; the client's low self-esteem or sense of failure; and, finally, the attorney's psychological need to occupy a dominant role in the interaction.

The counseling relationship where the lawyer treats the client as a child, and the client treats the lawyer as a domineering parent, creates a setting that calls forth unproductive and misplaced feelings. Freudian and Jungian therapists know these feelings as transference. In a transference response the client relives an emotional relationship from the past, and cast his lawyer in an unrealistic role. The lawyer is being made to stand in for an important person in the client's life—typically, in the Freudian view of things, the client's father. The result is a distorted dependence on the lawyer—not only the normal dependence common in people who think that lawyers know a lot, but a focused, emotional dependence. Critical choices and biases are then likely to come from the lawyer—or, rather, from the way in which the client regards the lawyer—rather than from the client. It is a well accepted tenet of Freudian psychology (one accepted by various "schools" of counseling) that this distortion in relationships is a common occurrence, that it happens in law offices, and that decisions apparently made by clients are in fact made by lawyers, because clients are too dependent on lawyers. Transference feelings are a significant feature of most lawyer-client relationships. (We explore the phenomenon of transference and countertransference below.)

The lawyer's reaction to those client feelings that are the product of transference—of emotional distortion, in other words—either advances or retards the incipient dependence that occurs in most professional relationships. The lawyer's reaction, to the transference, is critical. We begin with the proposition that it is not possible not to react. Some lawyers may think they can say to clients, "Okay, whatever you want," but, as a matter of fact, they cannot. The lawyer has feelings, and his feelings are picked up by the client; they matter to the client, especially as the client moves toward emotional dependence. The client may not understand the lawyer's feelings accurately, but he will act as if he does. Lawyers tend, as everyone does, to feel moral disapproval, or rebellion, or panic, or a lack of control, or a need to protect the client. The point is that clients perceive and guess at these feelings and, often, conclude that they are more negative than they are. The lawyer's feelings, and the client's perception of them—or guesses at them—have everything to do with whether the dependence issue will be resolved in a productive way.

If the lawyer reacts as a domineering parent would react (or if the client believes that the lawyer is reacting that way)—with judgmental approval or disapproval, dependence is encouraged. Dependence will sometimes be expressed in submission (and a fantasy of rescue), sometimes in rebellion, but it will be dependence, however expressed. The result is a situation in which the client is being led to believe, or is leading himself to believe, that he is not prepared, not wise enough, to act for himself. He has to have an authority figure who will tell him what to do.

Dependence in those situations where the client abdicates to the lawyer decision-making responsibility can be "moves" or "stances" in what counselors sometimes describe as the game of "rescue." Strong negative feelings develop from low self-esteem and dependency on the lawyer which give rise to a perception of helplessness and the need for a rescuer. In the language of transactional analysis, "the victim's position" is "I'm not OK, you're OK (I am helpless and hopeless, try and help me)." The rescuer's position matches the victim's: "I'm OK, you're not OK (you are helpless and hopeless; nevertheless, I'll try to help you)."

Claude Steiner, a therapist who practiced transactional analysis, explained the pleasures and danger of this rescue game. "No one enjoys being one-down, but it is pleasurable to let go and have others take over. One can let others take over for short periods of time without playing the game, especially if one has agreements to reverse the situation later on. The feeling of being a powerless victim, however, is hellish and is only made worse by rescuing. No matter how we feel, it is good to hear that we are not completely powerless; and it is energizing to be asked and expected to take our power and do our part by someone who is willing to help."

How should the attorney approach the client who has the victim's attitude? Carl Rogers points out that the natural tendency in such a situation is to try to convince the client that feelings of powerlessness and low self-esteem are exaggerated, and that there is no logical reason for him to feel that way. This attempt, however, may not be successful. "The client feels worthless, no matter how many good qualities may be objectively pointed out to him. . . . The counselor is giving more genuine help if he assists the client to face these feelings openly, recognize them for what they are, and admit that he has them."

There is an alternative to the game of rescue and other forms of client dependence. The alternative is to sort out the feelings involved, to discover with the client where the boundaries are between his feelings and the feelings of his lawyer. This requires that the lawyer level with the client about his own feelings. It requires honesty, self-awareness, genuineness (what Rogers calls *congruence*), and a level of openness that may be uncomfortable for the lawyer. Our point here is that locating boundaries in the relationship is not a matter to be left to the client's guesses, and it may require practice.

Another part of sorting out feelings is to accept that both client and lawyer have feelings and that, while we may be called to judge actions and behaviors, feelings are best accepted as is. A lawyer might refuse to be a judge of another's feelings. He might want to say to the client, in effect: "I hear what you are saying; I understand your feelings, but I refuse to judge them, one way or another, because it is you who are important to me."

The key, in Carl Rogers's phrase, is to enter into the client's world. To see it as he sees it. This kind of empathy is a subtle and difficult skill. The empathic response to people is acceptance without judgment—what Rogers calls "unconditional positive regard"—and an affirmation of the client's dignity and ability to choose for himself.

In addition to facing the client's (and our own) need for dependence (and feelings of powerlessness), the attorney is in a position—by virtue of professional status, knowledge of the legal process, and previous experience with clients—to function in a strong supportive role towards the client. Support is not the same as parental approval. Support is a matter of saying, as advocates have always said, "I am on your side; my knowledge, and what I can do, are on your side. You are not alone." Attorneys should consider support as an integral and specific part of the lawyer's counseling function, especially for clients in crisis. A strong supportive stance is what advocacy is all about. It is not always called for, but, when it is, it helps reduce client anxiety and the discomfort of clients who have little experience dealing with lawyers and the legal system.

CONTINUING THREATS TO A WORKING RELATIONSHIP: PROJECTION AND TRANSFERENCE

One way to live with ourselves, and those aspects of self that we find unacceptable, is to see in others what we cannot see in ourselves. Unable to tolerate the possibility of our own weakness, vulnerability, fear, we see these things in others. I am far more likely to see and object to your rigidity than I am my own. Freudians (and psychologists from other schools of counseling) call this ego defense *projection*. The root meaning of projection is "casting out" or projecting from self to others. Psychology regards the maneuver as defensive, as an unconscious process by which the ego defends the conscious self.

A similar process, and another way that the ego protects the conscious self, is in the *displacement* of feelings. For example, hostility toward one partner in the firm that could be threatening if expressed can be displaced and expressed against another. The experience of frustration in the office is directed toward one's spouse at home who had no part in producing the frustration. Displacement is defensive, as are projections; by displacing feelings a person may avoid confronting in a realistic way the feelings which might materially affect relationships with significant people in her life.

By bringing together these two ways that the ego works to defend itself—projection and displacement—we can begin to understand the psychology of a professional relationship that gives rise to strong feelings of attachment and anger. These feelings are often a product not of the present interaction but an unconscious psychological need that lies outside the immediate relationship. This is what Freud called *transference* (the strong feelings of the client for the helper)(while *countertransference* is the strong feelings of the helper for the client).

Transference is not limited to psychotherapeutic relationships. It may occur in any relationship in which one person becomes dependent on another, or where one person in a relationship is viewed as an authority figure (one to be accepted or rejected). Andrew S. Watson suggests that transference is an essential "tool" in the relationship between lawyer and client. Transference is, he says, an "ubiquitous phenomenon"; lawyers who bother to understand the phenomenon "can profit immensely." He quotes the late Justice Abe Fortas and sociologist Talcott Parsons in support of the proposition that transference and countertransference are commonplace in law office, client-attorney relationships and often develop between young lawyers and senior partners. "The capacity to accept the possibility that one's feelings about another may be due to unconscious and unrealistic coloring rather than to the other's reality traits," he says, "is a major step toward understanding relations among lawyers and in lawyer-client encounters."

Jung spoke of this with a characteristic avuncular chuckle, but he had important words to say to lawyers about transference:

So, if a patient [client] projects the savior complex onto you, for instance, you have to give back to him nothing less than a savior. . . .

So he [the professional] begins to feel, "If there are saviors, well, perhaps it is just possible that I am one," and he will fall for it, at first hesitantly, and then it will become more and more plain to him that he really is a sort of extraordinary individual.

Transference is likely to exist in any professional relationship in which rapport has been attempted and dependence permitted (or required); one psychiatrist even attempted to gauge transference between students and their teachers in an engineering class.

Transference and countertransference are pervasive in everyday "helping" relationships. But lawyers, even though expected to serve in the role of professional helpers, are given little opportunity in the course of their legal education and training to work out principles of relatedness (attachment, dependence, authority, awe, disgust) in their interaction with those they help. The problem of "relatedness," however, is present everywhere. "Early experiences in interpersonal relatedness," Frieda Fromm–Reichmann said, "affect ... later relationships with [a] family doctor, dentist, minister, etc. Even the mere anticipation of consulting any kind of qualified helper ... may pave the way for the development of transference reactions." She added that "as a result, present-day persons and interpersonal situations will be misjudged, incorrectly evaluated, and ... distorted along the lines of the patients' unrevised, early, dissociated experiences." "The transference itself," Jung said, "is a perfectly natural phenomenon which does not by any means happen only in the consulting room—it can be seen everywhere and may lead to all sorts of nonsense.... "

Transference is treated in one fashion or another in all schools of psychotherapy and is fundamental in Freudian psychoanalysis and Jungian analytical psychology. Carl Rogers reports similar discoveries about transference in counseling. Rogers believes that transference in his "client-centered therapy" develops to some extent in almost all cases. In each situation, he sees four indications that transference is present: (1) "a desire for dependence upon the counselor, accompanied by deep affect [feeling]"; (2) "fear of the counselor, which is ... related to fear of parents"; (3) "attitudes of hostility ... beyond the attitudes ... realistically related to the experience"; and (4) "expressions of affection, and a desire for a love relationship."

Rogers believes that the milder—and more common—transference disappears as the client is led to rely on his own judgment rather than that of his counselor. He reports the case of a young woman who wanted to drop her sessions with her therapist because of a dream:

> I was up for trial, and you were the judge.... I didn't see how I could come back into the situation. I mean the circumstances, you already judged me, and therefore I didn't really see how I could possibly talk any more.... I suppose in my own way I was judging myself.

In the process of talking about the dream, Rogers believes, this woman came to see that she was projecting her assessment of herself. She was seeing in Rogers a disapproval which did not come from him, but from her. She was doing that because Rogers had come to occupy a parental position in her feelings. The source of disapproval was old experiences of parental disapproval being reexperienced. She came to understand, Rogers reports, that she was capable of recognizing the source of her feelings, and when this happened:

> the "transference attitudes" . . . simply disappear because experience has been reperceived in a way which makes them meaningless. It is analogous to the way in which one attitude drops out and another entirely different one takes its place when I turn to watch the large plane I have dimly glimpsed out of the corner of my eye, and find it to be a gnat flying by a few inches from my face.

C.G. Jung's treatment of transference is at the center of his view of psychology and psychotherapy. Jung regarded transference as a natural phenomenon, rather than a manipulative device to be used by the analyst. When it occurs, he said, it poses a delicate and sometimes insurmountable obstacle to the physician: "What seems to be so easily won by the transference always turns out in the end to be a loss; for a patient who gets rid of a system [of symptoms] by transferring it to the analyst always makes the analyst the guarantor of this miracle and so binds himself to him more closely than ever."

Jung seems to be fundamentally at odds with Freud, who viewed psychoanalytic treatment of the "transference neurosis" as the central task of the psychoanalyst and the focal point of healing in the psychoanalytic relationship. Mental disorders that interfere with the formation of the "transference neurosis" were, in Freud's view, unsuitable "to a greater or lesser extent" for psychoanalysis (a view modified in contemporary psychoanalytic theory). This idea leads the Freudian and his patient to work for transference, a venture Jung believed to be futile: "Transference is only another word for 'projection.' No one can voluntarily make projections, they just happen. They are illusions which merely make the treatment more difficult." When transference does occur it is delicate, time-consuming, and not easily or methodically erased. Jung's insight is valuable for the lawyer who is often puzzled over the way clients seem to become "hung up" on him. Jung would say the "hang-up" is the most natural thing in the world.

Psychotherapeutic relations rest, in Jung's view, on a rapport which is coextensive with transference, although his discussion suggests that transference overwhelms rapport. Transference, when it occurs, is a projection; and projections are dissociative—they are unintegrated bits of the personality wrongly seen as belonging outside the self. The cure for them is integration—individuation—and this involves first and foremost, honest rapport to minimize the transference: "The transference," says Jung, "is the patient's attempt to get into psychological rapport with the doctor. He needs this relationship if he is to overcome the dissociation. The feebler the rapport ... the more intensely will the transference be fostered.... "

The physician's personality is unavoidably involved in the transference. The very survival of the patient may depend, as Jung put it, on "the doctor's knowledge, like a flickering lamp ... the one dim light in the darkness." The physician then has an opportunity to lead his patient to the integration of personality—"[n]o longer a mere selection of suitable fictions, but a string of hard facts, which together make up the cross we all have to carry or the fate we ourselves are." This idea is central:

> So long as the patient can think that somebody else (his father or mother) is responsible for his difficulties, he can save some semblance of unity.... But once he realizes that he himself has a shadow, that his enemy is in his own heart, then the conflict begins and one becomes two. Since the "other" will eventually prove to be yet another duality, a compound of opposites, the ego soon becomes a shuttlecock tossed between a multitude of "velleities," with the result that there is an obfuscation of the light, i.e., consciousness is depotentiated and the patient is at a loss to know where his personality begins or ends.

But Jung is at some pains to make it clear that this "therapeutic," helping process is not a matter of manipulation but the result of dealing honestly with the client.

Both Freud and Jung took account of the sexual element of transference and countertransference. Freud linked it to the infantile Oedipus complex, the child's desire to replace his father in his mother's life. Transference to a female therapist by a male patient would therefore involve these sexual feelings. (Not all modern Freudians would agree.) Jung thought that the projection was fundamental-

ly of the contrasexual element within the patient
himself. A man tends to project the female within
him—the *anima*. (The female, in this scheme, is
more likely to project the *animus* or inner masculine.) In childhood he has made this projection on
his mother and sisters; he later projects it on other
women, but it often retains a certain incestuous
character. (He also projects homo-erotic feelings
from within himself on his father, his brothers, his
male physician.) This *anima* projection in its purest
form involves the incest taboo; but it affords also
the therapeutic opportunity for a "spiritual marriage" in which the projected and unprojected elements of the patient's personality are integrated
into a renewed, conscious self. This process, insofar
as it is therapeutic, is a process that needs some
substitute for the biological unity of the family—
"family" here in the sense of ancient, archetypal
"kinship." An important insight of Jung's is that
the sexual element in transference is archetypal—
that is, rooted in the "collective unconscious" we all
share. His idea was that integration (cure) takes
place in a human association that is libidinal but
not sexual. That idea is complex—almost mystical—
but it is obviously central to what Jung says about
transference in everyday life:

> Everyone is now a stranger among strangers.
> Kinship libido ... has long been deprived of its
> object. But, being an instinct, it is not to be
> satisfied by any mere substitute such as a creed,
> party, nation, or state. It wants the human con-
> nection. That is the core of the whole transfer-

ence phenomenon, and it is impossible to argue it away, because relationship to the self is at once relationship to our fellow man, and no one can be related to the latter until he is related to himself.

Jung used a medieval book on alchemy to explain transference. He built his explanation around woodcuts that illustrated the conjunction between symbolic, mythical male and female figures. His theory was that transference involves the projection of contrasexual contents (the *anima* of a man, the *animus* of a woman) in the unconscious of the transferring person. Although he did not confine transference to this sort of projection—it was possible, he said, to have a transference even onto inanimate objects—it is clear that the Jungian prototype of transference is contrasexual.

Freud's view of transference, in contrast to Jung's, was tied to his view of the Oedipus complex. Feelings transferred by the patient originated in competition between the patient and his father for the love of the patient's mother—a necessarily contrasexual relationship.

It is possible to exaggerate the importance of the sexual element in transference. Fromm–Reichmann appears to disagree with Freud's view on the Oedipus complex in transference; she regards the affective, or feeling element, in the transference as a "wish for closeness and tenderness with the beloved parent ... without recognizable sexual roots," and attributes the apparently contrasexual character of transference to the fact that people in our culture find it easier to talk about sex than about "friendly, tender, asexually loving aspects of . . . interpersonal relationships." However, the evidence for some contrasexual tendency in transference is at least strong enough to justify seeking a parallel between clinical experience with the phenomenon and the incidence of contrasexual transference in the law office.

* * *

Transference relationships may become exceptionally strong. Examples from Freud and Jung illustrate the point. Freud's case involved a Herr P. who had developed a strong positive transference to Freud. Freud had decided he could not help Herr P. and had told him so, but Herr P. wanted to continue therapy for some few weeks until his duties at a university began. Freud agreed, although he recognized that his only link to the patient was that Herr P. "felt comfortable in a well-tempered father-transference to me," and that this indefinite arrangement was "in disregard of the strict rules of medical practice." The relationship became so intense that the patient seemed to know facts—most notably the name of a foreign visitor to Freud's office—that were, objectively, hidden from him. Freud was tempted to believe that the relationship between him and Herr P. caused a transfer of thought.

Jung's examples are even more candid; one of them involved Freud, older than Jung, and with whom Jung had a strong father-son relationship, which Freud acknowledged and encouraged. Before Jung's eventual break with Freud, Jung had a dream that signaled to him their forthcoming break and that represented both aspects of the ambivalent transference relationship:

He still meant to me a superior personality, upon whom I had projected the father, and at the time of the dream this projection was still far from eliminated. Where such a projection occurs, we are no longer objective; we persist in a state of divided judgment. On the one hand we are dependent, and on the other we have resistances. When the dream took place I still thought highly of Freud, but at the same time I was critical of him. This divided attitude is a sign that I was still unconscious of the situation and had not come to any resolution of it. This is characteristic of all projections.

Jung cited another example in explanation of parapsychological phenomena. A patient, with whom Jung had formed a strong countertransference, was progressing toward cure when he discovered that his wife resented Jung. In the face of stress between wife and surrogate father the patient relapsed into depression. One night Jung was awakened as if someone were in his room. While awake he felt a dull pain at the back of his skull. The next day he learned that his patient had shot himself in the head, at the time of Jung's experience. "The collective unconscious is common to all," Jung said of this experience. "It is the foundation of what the ancients call the 'empathy of all things.' In this case the unconscious had knowledge of the patient's condition."

CHAPTER FIVE

GETTING THE FACTS (INTERVIEWING)

LAW–OFFICE FACTS AND LITIGATION FACTS

Lawyers in law offices need to find out the facts about their clients' situations, in order to help the clients, or to help the clients help themselves, just as lawyers in litigation need to learn the facts required by the logic of litigation, or appellate judges whose function in government it is to consider, shape, and proclaim legal doctrine need to learn the facts required by the logic of policy. Facts are a prelude to problem-solving. We're talking here abut the facts at the beginning of case briefs, facts on the first pages of briefs in litigation, and facts in the opening paragraphs in appellate opinions.

There are three critical differences between fact-finding in litigation or policy-making and fact-finding in the law office:

1. *Relevance.* Relevance in litigation is expressed, more or less, by rules of evidence. Rules of evidence (and pleading) are political limitations on the operation of the law in courts. (Courts are part of the government; law offices are not.) Feelings

and perceptions are usually excluded from proof in litigation—so that statements that begin "I feel" or "I think" are not proper in courts, and statements which begin "I saw," "I heard," are proper there. Relevance in law offices, if political considerations limit what is said there, are political considerations imposed not by the law but by lawyers.

2. *Malleability.* Louis M. Brown referred to facts in law offices as "hot facts." Judge-made law turns on "cold facts," that is, historical facts. (This is true only more or less; facts in judge-made law are also made as they are presented, as they are embodied in the stories conveyed in and by the decisions of a court.) Or, as Brown put it, law follows facts in judge-made law; facts follow law in office-made law. An example occurs early in the movie "Anatomy of a Murder," when the defense lawyer (James Stewart) sees his client for the first time (in jail) and tells the client he does not want to hear the "facts" until the client has an opportunity to consider the law of temporary insanity. The film presents an example of "hot facts." Office practice abounds with examples. Whether a contract or declaration of trust is oral or written, for example, makes a legal difference. That fact is within the client's control in the law office; it is beyond control and cold fact once litigation is brought on the contract or the trust.

3. *Organization.* Facts in litigation come when they are supposed to—at the beginning of a brief, oral argument, or judicial opinion, or with controlled precision during an evidentiary hearing. Facts in law offices, come when they are ready to

come. Forceful attempts to elicit them by directive questions, or limiting their production to a limited time-frame, are likely to frustrate the client and reduce the amount of information ultimately obtained from the client. If decisions and plans are formulated too quickly in the office, facts that appear later, during the processes of decision and planning, may render useless much of the work that has preceded their discovery.

FACT GATHERING

One of the tasks for a lawyer working with a client is to get enough facts to form an accurate picture of the client's situation, facts as the client sees them and facts that the lawyer helps the client to see. The manner in which the attorney gets the facts sets the "personal climate," the tone and structure of the relationship, and is a central feature of the working agreement (most often implicit) on how the relationship will proceed. The breadth and depth—the adequacy—of the information the attorney gathers depends on:

— the attorney's approach (or "bedside manner");

— the client's initial impression of the attorney and of the place where they work together;

— the initial feelings the two people have for each other (and this usually includes who they remind one another of);

— the manner in which the attorney goes after information;

— the attorney's perception of the facts as the client begins to provide them;

— the client's expectations and images concerning the law and lawyers;

— the attorney's understanding of the client's concerns as these are placed in their broader context (the client's story and the story of how the client sees the world); and

— theories and models used by the attorney to explain the client's behavior (and his own) (See Chapter Six).

Analysis of these factors presents us with the essence of fact-gathering by lawyers, an essence that goes beyond and underneath facts that are, in case-book terms, relevant or irrelevant. When lawyers seek "relevant" facts, they are influenced by the model of directive interrogation in trials and depositions. Relevance here means related to legal doctrine: Lawyers want facts that are relevant to legal problems and are not concerned with facts relevant to the client's feelings. The trial lawyer forcefully guides the client's (witness's) responses with direct questions designed to elicit the facts the lawyer thinks will produce a legal result.

This trial-lawyer approach to fact gathering as the primary task in interviewing is one aspect of a powerful, traditional professional model of the attorney-client relationship: The client talks and the attorney gathers the facts. When the lawyer talks it is to tell the client about the law and how the law regards the facts presented. It is this emphasis on fact relevance and the attorney's rational, logical, analytical approach to problem-solving that focuses on legal issues and legal determinations and eschews client expectations and feelings. The detachment (what traditional lawyers call professionalism) does not provide a relationship in which a client's *emotions* are recognized as facts. The traditional model of lawyering requires that both lawyer and client keep their eyes on facts that fit legal doctrine. Other facts are not important; they are not even facts.

The most serious drawback of this approach to "facts" is that it does not allow for the expression of client and attorney feelings, feelings present in every relationship, including those between clients and attorneys. A relationship in which feelings are valued—that is, any human relationship worthy of the name—is dependent upon each person's understanding that feelings *are* facts. To understand that feelings are facts is to understand that feelings are guides to behavior; even feelings that appear to be irrational—the most "irrelevant" facts of all—are a form of communication. For example, the client may confront the attorney with an accusation that the attorney has not pursued his case vigorously or has not worked to negotiate a favorable settlement (an accusation which, if true, presents an ethical problem as well as a counseling issue). A client may obstinately adhere to unreasonable demands or vehemently attack the attorney. The client may react angrily or seek to dismiss the attorney with little or no provocation. In each of these cases the client is saying something, something that usually relates to the legal work that is being done for the client.

REFLECTIVE EXERCISE: FEELINGS

In counseling theory, there are a minimum number of what would be called principles. But there are some, even if few in number. One we have adopted in this book is that "Feelings are facts." Feelings are something that counselors learn to pay attention to, learn about, and learn from. Learning from feelings means learning who the client is, who I am, and what it means to me to be a lawyer. The learning moves in both directions, and from the counselor to herself. (The movement in learning shifts throughout the relationship and when it does not shift you can assume something has gone wrong.)

The way to learn about feelings is to work with them, to see what you know about feelings and how they work. It is easy enough to define feelings and emotions (some psychologists and counselors draw a distinction between feelings and emotions; we see no purpose in doing that here), but the important thing is to check and see what you actually know about your own feelings. Most of us make assumptions about feelings—first, that we have feelings, and, that we know what they are, that we can name them and, if need be, describe them. We now want to explore those assumptions, to see what assumptions about feelings you have and how those assumptions work. The goal is to find out how your views on feelings will affect your work as a legal counselor.

Part A

How do you *see* yourself in regard to your feelings? What do you *know* about your feelings? How do you *see* them working (for you and against you)?

It will be a good idea to write down your answers to these questions (and the questions that arise about feelings).

Some of us feel overwhelmed by feelings and some of us do not. Some of us are guided by our feelings and some of us try to lessen the impact of feelings on our decisions. The kind of knowledge (certainty) we have in regard to our own feelings varies widely. Some people are more confused about their feelings than others. Some of us claim to know what our feelings are and others aren't so sure.

Part B

Read the following commentary on feelings gathered from various sources and when you have finished reading return to what you wrote in response to Part A. How does your stated relationship with your own feelings reflect what is being explained in these comments? How could you relate to your feelings in a way that would better reflect the psychological knowledge reflected in the commentaries?

— A feeling, or emotion, might be seen as a message that contains information that we send to ourselves about an experience. Feelings are part of an internal communication system. They provide feedback to us about ourselves and others. David Viscott points out that "our feelings are our sixth sense, the sense that interprets, arranges, directs and summarizes the other five. Feelings tell us whether what we experience is threatening, painful, regretful, sad or joyous." Viscott goes on to make an even more dramatic statement. "Not to be aware of one's feelings, not to understand them or know how to use or express them is worse than being blind, deaf or paralyzed. Not to feel is not to be alive. More than anything else feelings make us human. Feelings make us all kindred." David Viscott, *The Language of Feelings* 9 (Pocket Book edition, 1977).

— Feeling lies in the realm of affect, which is often viewed in contrast to the cognitive realm, the realm of thought and intellect. Feeling "is a message to the cognitive processes, to the thinking brain and to our intelligence. . . . " Willard Gaylin, *Feelings* 7 (1979).

"The most intelligent of men [and women] have no particular advantage over others in understanding what they feel. Indeed a high intelligence is often a severe handicap when it is used to rationalize feelings and offer logical, but none the less elusive, detours away from the truth. Everyone knows intelligent people who do not seem to have any understanding of their feelings, and as a result make poor and untrustworthy companions. They distort the world, although at times with a convincing elegance and even grace, but still remain far from understanding themselves." (Viscott, *The Language of Feelings*, at 21).

— It is from our feelings, contends Gaylin, that we find the means to "judge the importance of our activities. We want to feel pride and joy, but we also want to sense others' delight, love, appreciation, and respect. Emotions, then, are not just directives to ourselves, but directives from others to us, indications that we have been seen; that we have been understood; that we have been appreciated; that we have made contact" (Gaylin, *Feelings*, at 9).

— Feelings serve yet another function: "Feelings of anxiety, boredom, tension, and agitation alert us to the sense of something wrong, and, more importantly, by the subtle distinctions of their messages they indicate something of the nature of the impending danger and direct us to specific kinds of adaptive maneuvers to avoid, prevent, or change the incipient threat. Feelings of guilt allow us to model our behavior against certain ideals and register when we have moved away from those ideals, or have not yet achieved them" (Gaylin, *Feelings*, at 7).

— When we say that feelings are facts, we are saying something about the nature of reality, at least reality from a counseling perspective. Viscott argues that "reality can't be comprehended without taking into account feelings." He goes on to observe that "the reality we derive from our perceptions is largely a creation of our own needs and expectations.... Thinking is a much more indirect way of handling reality than feeling" (Gaylin, *Feelings*, at 13, 19–20).

— John Welwood, a psychotherapist knowledgeable about Eastern philosophy, particularly Zen Buddhism, has some interesting things to say about emotions. "Emotions are our most common experience of being moved by forces seemingly beyond our control. As such, they are among the most confusing and frightening phenomena of everyday life. People often treat them as a nuisance or a threat, yet failing to experience them straight-forwardly undermines sanity and well-being." Welwood then raises this question: "Can we ever befriend our emotions and accept them as part of us? Why is emotion so hard to come to terms with in our culture?" John Welwood, "Befriending Emotion," in *Awakening the Heart* 79–90, at 79 (J. Welwood ed., 1983).

In a rationalistic oriented profession like law do we experience an even more pronounced impulse to act in disregard to feelings?

— Welwood sees feeling and emotion as "what arises in response to letting the world in." (Welwood, at 81). Welwood's idea is contrary to the prevailing notion that emotions and feelings are private and idiosyncratic to the individual. If the emotion is the way we experience the world, that is, the way we let the world in, then our feelings are about being in the world. They are fundamental to any connection with other people.

— Welwood's view is also reflected in the work of James Hillman, a Jungian analyst who has worked out a substantial revision of Jung's ideas (a revising that is most often referred to as archetypal psychology). Hillman says, "It is through emotion that we get the exaggerated sense of soul, of honor, of hurt, of anxiety, of our own person. In emotion we get the awareness that we are not alone in ourselves, not in control over all of ourselves, that there is another person, if only an unconscious complex, who also has something—often a great deal—to say about our behavior.... We fall into emotions, moods, affects, and discover a new dimension which, much as we wish to rid ourselves of it, leads us downward into depths of ourselves." James Hillman, *Insearch: Psychology and Religion* 53–54 (1967).

— Welwood suggests this approach to thinking about emotions: "The first step in taming the lion of emotions, in transmuting their fierce energy into illumination, is to befriend it by letting it be, without judging it as good or bad. Running away from a fierce animal or trying to suppress its energy only provokes attack.... Although emotions may seem to have us in their grip, as soon as we turn to face them directly, we find nothing as solid or fixed as our judgments or stories about them.... " (Welwood, at 86).

"We usually try to keep them [emotions] from flowing through us because they threaten the control we try to maintain. Since ego by definition is the activity of holding on, 'I' cannot let go, 'I' want to ward off anything that threatens this hold. What is possible, however, is to let the emotions wash through me, and, in so doing, wash the controlling part of me away from them. If I can really open to the actual texture and quality of a feeling, instead of trying to control it or churn out story lines for it, 'I'—the activity of trying to hold myself together—can dissolve into 'it'—the larger feeling process itself." (Welwood, at 86).

THE KINSEY MODEL

Alfred C. Kinsey's *Sexual Behavior in the Human Male* (1948), an elaborate analysis of 12,000 interviews about the sex lives of American men, was at the time a shocking book. When the book appeared, the elder author of this book (Shaffer) was a serious Baptist boy in a small western town; he did not read Kinsey's book or know anyone who did. But there were newspaper stories about it. When he read the Kinsey book many years later, the second chapter revealed a remarkable treatise on interviewing.

There is much to be learned from the methods of Kinsey and his little-known co-authors Pomeroy and Martin, who arranged to have thousands of men and (for a second book) women talk to them for hours about the most intimate, taboo, shocking, shameful corners of their private lives. The Kinsey researchers conquered a formidable set of obstacles to communication (more formidable then, by the way, than they would be now) to gather their information. Their methods and their results bear on the human activity in which one person is attempting to elicit personal information from another.

Interviewee as Helper

The most fundamental fact about the Kinsey style, a fact relevant for lawyers, is that Kinsey asked people to help him. He did not pay them for their information; they talked to him readily and for free. It is radical but nonetheless valid to suggest to legal counselors that they ask their clients for help—that we treat the legal interview as a process in which we seek help rather than give it.

Some lawyers would reject the analogy, but we might ask these lawyers: What would it cost you? What would happen if you approached legal interviewing that way? Theoretically the idea is sound. The object of an interview is information. The most important means to information is cooperation from the person who possesses information. Alfred Kinsey knew how to garner information. Kinsey's interviewing and his ability to get people to help him were premised on the regard he expressed for those he asked to help him; not only did he respect these people, he was fond of them. As Kinsey put it:

Learning how to meet people of all ranks and levels, establishing rapport, sympathetically comprehending the significance of things as others view them, learning to accept their attitudes and activities without moral, social, or esthetic evaluation, being interested in people as they are and not as someone else would have them, learning to see the reasonable bases of what at first glance may appear to be most unreasonable behavior, developing a capacity to like all kinds of people and thus to win their esteem and cooperation— these are the elements to be mastered by one who would gather human statistics.

Notice that this call for a humanistic approach to gathering information did not come from a psychologist. Kinsey was a professor of zoology. Notice, also, that "legal issues" are to law-office interviewing as "statistics" are to social research. Lawyers learn to take human facts for granted and "get to the issue," just as research-oriented psychologists learn to ignore the people they're talking to and to concentrate instead on the data they seek to gather from their "subjects."

Affection

Kinsey believed he was successful, but he admits to a sense of wonder and a feeling that no interviewing theory can quite explain his success: "We are not sure that we completely comprehend why people have been willing to talk to us." Encountering another person was, Kinsey said, a drama. That is a touching observation from a man who was, his colleagues report, incredibly single-minded about his purposes. Kinsey attributed his success in these dramatic encounters to honesty. He made his purposes clear. Once he communicated his own need (a need, remember, for astounding information) and his own integrity, people wanted to help him. Many of his interviewees—especially the relatively simple and ignorant among them—required, he said, "only a gesture of honest friendship." He gives an example:

The little gray-haired woman at the cabin door, out on the Western plain, epitomized what we have heard now from hundreds of people: "Of all things—! In all my years I have never had such a question put to me! But—if my experience will help, I'll give it to you." This, in many forms, some of them simple, some of them sophisticated as scientists and scholars like them, some of them crude, incisive, and abrupt as the underworld makes them, is the expression of the altruistic bent (however philosophers and scientists may analyze it) which has been the chief motive leading people to cooperate in this study.

Pay-off

Kinsey found a pay-off for the interviewee as the subjects could obtain information about sex and how the interviewee's behavior compared with the behavior of others. There was, between interviewer and interviewee, a spirit of cooperation. There is a lesson here for how lawyers go about conducting interviews. The lawyer interviewer wants to learn and is willing to help; the client interviewee wants to explain and is seeking help. Pay-off is involved in their two-way experience of being helpful: The interviewee also cooperates for altruistic pay-off, the good feeling that comes from cooperation, and he cooperates because he has trust in the competence of the interviewer-advisor. The client may also find it of interest that in working with a lawyer she is able to learn, from an insider, something about the law.

Trust

Kinsey's techniques were quaintly conventional. He seems almost to have acted without calculation and elevated his behavior to the level of technique only when he sat down to write about it. In building rapport, for example, he said the key factors were acceptance and trust: "It is imperative . . . that the investigator be able to convince the subject . . . that he . . . offers no objection to any type of sexual behavior in which the subject could possibly have been involved, [and] that the confidences . . . will be kept without question." Kinsey was obviously adept at convincing people that he was not judging them, and at demonstrating somehow that he could be trusted. How did he do it?

Meaning

The technique he mentions most prominently is a negative one. He said he avoided "cold objectivity." He said he could not achieve rapport of any sort with his interviewee unless he managed first to convince the interviewee that he was "desperately anxious to comprehend what this experience meant

to him." It is important to notice that he did not
say what the experience *was,* but what the experience *meant.* Notice that that fact would be "irrelevant" in litigation and is rarely to be found in a
law-school casebook, but that Kinsey considered it
fundamental to getting the information he wanted.
Kinsey said this quest for meaning was necessary
because the information he sought involved—as
law-office information usually does—hurt, frustration, pain, unsatisfied longing, disappointment,
tragedy, and even catastrophe. Presumably—one
hopes—it also involved joy, victory, achievement,
and happiness. The point is that these human victo-
ries and defeats are important to the client; he will
not hand them over as readily as he puts coins in a
parking meter. "The subject feels that the investigator who asks merely routine questions has no
right to know about such things.... The interviewer who senses what these things can mean, who at
least momentarily shares something of the satisfaction, pain, or bewilderment which was the subject's,
who shares something of the subject's hope that
things will, somehow, work out right, is more effective, though he may not be altogether neutral."

Kinsey emphasized a point made throughout his
book—that it is impossible to hide one's reaction to
clients. "Reactions ... are ... readily comprehended by most people. A minute change of a facial
expression, a slight tensing of a muscle, the flick of
an eye, a trace of a change in one's voice, a slight
inflection or change in emphasis, slight changes in
one's rate of speaking, slight hesitancies ... one's

choice of words . . . or any of a dozen and one other involuntary reactions betray the interviewer's emotions and most subjects quickly understand them." The claim that we are objective because we have been trained to be so as lawyers is a phantasy, a pose.

The client comes to the lawyer to find something he needs, and that something is fundamental to the interpersonal communication that makes fact-finding possible. Kinsey's point is that clarity in the lawyer's reactions has everything to do with this preliminary agenda in the interview. "If his [interviewer's] reactions add up right, then the subject is willing to tell his story. The interview has become an opportunity for him to develop his own thinking, to express his own disappointments and hopes, to bring into the open things that he has previously been afraid to admit to himself, to work out solutions to his difficulties."

Presence

However much Kinsey explains it, the impression remains that, for him, no amount of *technique* was sufficient. His success was the art of being fully and manifestly present to the interviewee. Another clue, which he only hinted at in his chapter on interviewing, was mutuality. Kinsey was trusted by his subjects and he trusted them: "The interviewer should be as interested in the subject as he is in recording the subject's history. It is important to look the subject in the eye. . . . " Counseling, one might say, is looking another person in the eye and leveling with her. Being honest (with each other and with ourselves) is the basis of and for counseling.

Technical Devices

Kinsey directs attention to a number of what he called "technical devices" which can be used by interviewers to establish rapport with interviewees.

It was important, Kinsey said, "to put the subject at ease." He did this, apparently, without calculation: "One does the sort of things a thoughtful host would do to make his guests comfortable." It was also important to assure privacy and to avoid interruptions. He recoiled with old fashioned moral condemnation from the dehumanizing interview he had once seen between a prisoner and a psychiatrist— "in a small room in which half a dozen persons were continually moving about and listening."

Kinsey looked carefully at the smallest details of how he asked questions. Several aspects of this art seem useful for legal interviewers, especially when you consider that lawyers are inveterate question-askers, spurred by the image of TV lawyers bullying people on the witness stand, and are trained in classrooms where students are subjected to a pseudo-Socratic technique. Kinsey emphasized that the question, if used at all, should be adapted to the interviewee:

Standardized questions do not bring standardized answers, for the same question means different things to different people. In order to have questions mean the same thing to different people, they must be modified to fit the vocabulary, the educational background, and the comprehension of each subject. It is especially important to use a vocabulary with which the subject will feel at home, and which he will understand. The college-bred interviewer needs to go to considerable pains to limit his vocabulary to the relatively few words that are employed by persons in lower educational levels. Everyday terms ... are involved: an individual [may, in his words] never [be] ill or injured, though he may be sick or hurt. He does not wish to do a thing, though he wants to do it. He does not perceive, though he sees. He is not acquainted with a person, though he may know him.

Kinsey found, in a telling instance of this, that using the sexual vernacular when he interviewed pimps and prostitutes led to information and that failure to do so left the interviewer with almost nothing. This point involves an understanding of cultural context and vocabulary at a fairly earthy level:

It is particularly important that the interviewer understand ... the sexual viewpoint of the culture to which each of his subjects belongs. For instance, it is impossible to get any number of histories from prostitutes, female or male, unless they realize that the interviewer understands both the sexual situations involved in prostitution, and the social organization of a prostitute's life. A single phrase from an understanding interviewer is often sufficient to make the subject understand this, and such an interviewer wins a record where none would have been disclosed to the uneducated investigator.

With trust in the present reader's ability to translate Kinsey's vivid experience, here is a telling example:

One starts by asking the [prostitute] how old she was when she turned her first trick (but one does not ask how old she was when she was first paid as a prostitute). She is then asked how many of the tricks return after their first contacts with her. Considerably later in the interview there is a question concerning the frequency with which she rolls her tricks (robs her customers). The [prostitute] who reports that few of the men ever return, and who subsequently says that she never robs any of the men, needs to be ... assured that you know that it doesn't work that way. If she doesn't roll any of the men, why don't they return to her? This question is likely to bring a smile ... and an admission that since you appear to know how these things work, she will tell you the whole story, which means that she robs every time there is any possibility of successfully doing so.

Part of this is a demeanor that does not telegraph the answer one expects to get. Kinsey found—and several studies of legal interviewing have found— that open-ended interview questions produce the fullest answers; precise, non-leading questions produce less information; and "cross-examination" produces still less.

Kinsey warns against being evasive on tender topics. (And who should know better about tender topics?)

Euphemisms should not be used as substitutes for franker terms. In some of the previous studies, many sexual terms are avoided: masturbation becomes "touching yourself" ... and sexual intercourse becomes "relations with other persons," or "sex delinquency".... With such questions the subject cannot help but sense the fact that the interviewer is not sure that sex is an honorable thing, and a thing that can be frankly talked about. Evasive terms invite dishonest answers.

Lawyers commonly notice the same evasion in interviews involving other taboo topics, such as death or suicide. Many "estate-planning" interviewers say, "What do you want to do if something should happen?" instead of, "What do you want to happen when you die?" Kinsey found it imperative to frame questions so as not to invite evasion. His style also implies a willingness to accept the answer he is given. He would not ask, "Have you ever ... ?" He would ask, "When did you first ... ?" He avoided multiple questions for the same reasons.

Lies

An occasional obstacle to the trust that runs from lawyer to client (and an obstacle to getting the facts) is the lawyer's suspicion that clients lie to lawyers. When it does occur, it is often the product of distrust. The usual lawyer devices for dealing with it (bluster, threat, cross-examination) make it worse. These devices reduce the diminishing sense of trust and increase dishonesty.

Even the best efforts of the attorney to establish rapport with the client, based on trust and understanding, will not necessarily prevent client distortions and untruths. Legal techniques, such as cross-examination, may work in court to catch liars, but they do this at the price of reducing the flow of information. For that reason they rarely work in the interview setting. How then should the attorney handle a client's misrepresentations? The most direct approach is open confrontation: "I feel that you are not telling the truth, and it is going to make things more difficult for both of us." (We are not, of course, suggesting that every untruth be confronted.)

It is important to notice that false information is not always a lie. Andrew Watson found that factual distortions were more frequently due to unconscious factors than intentional deceit on the client's part. The problem is attributable to the tendency of the lawyer "to presume ... that his client is a rational being, capable of good recall of past events and capable of communicating objectively with little self-serving omission or interpretation of the facts." If Watson's thesis is correct, the attorney hoping to be an effective interviewer in, say, a divorce case must look beyond purely factual information. The attorney must expect the client to distort events and omit pertinent facts. These evasions, omissions, or distortions then become facts in their own right. It is this kind of fact that helps explain who the client is and what he wants and needs.

It may be better to be the sort of lawyer who is occasionally taken in by liars and con-artists than to be the sort of lawyer who finds it hard to trust her clients. That would be part of a "lesson on lies" that Kinsey might direct to lawyers. The other and probably more important part of a "lesson on lies" is that distrust is best brought into the open and openly resolved, because clients will sense its presence and may perceive it as worse than it is. Their sense that they are distrusted will result in their withholding facts. In any case, as diCavour said, "The man who trusts other men will make fewer mistakes than he who distrusts them."

Morals

Kinsey did not, of course, prevent falsehood and fraud in his interviewees. He does seem to have held both to a minimum. His techniques for detecting and dealing with dishonesty may be useful, but they require a comment on morals. First, the Kinsey technique:

If it becomes apparent that the subject's first answer is not correct or sufficient, one should ask for additional information, and re-phrase the original question in a way that will make him prove his answer or expose the falsity of his reply. In a rapid fire of additional questions, it is difficult for a dishonest subject to be consistent. With unedu-

cated persons, and particularly with feeble-minded individuals, it is sometimes effective to pretend
that one has misunderstood the negative replies
and ask additional questions, just as though the
original answers were affirmatives; whereupon
the subject may then expose the truth by answering as though he had never given a negative
reply. "Yes, I know you have never done that, but
how old were you the first time that you did it?"
is a question which, amazingly enough, may
break down the cover-up of a feeble-minded individual. With such a technique, on the other hand,
it is especially important to make sure that the
subject's final admissions are not fictions which
the interviewer has suggested to him.

Our reactions to Kinsey's apparatus for trapping
falsehood are mixed. It is repulsive to say to any-
body—"You say you've never done that; now, how
often have you done it?" and it is not surprising
that it only worked with people for whom Kinsey
(and his generation) used the phrase "feeble-minded." But that is no way to treat people. Part of our
moral objection turns on the fact that the other is
being treated as an object and manipulated for a
purpose which seems extraneous to him. Purpose is
not the essence of the revulsion, though. It wouldn't
improve the situation very much to be able to say
that the manipulation is benign—"for his own
good"—or for some higher purpose such as the
discovery of truth. Every evil, from the most trivial
to our era's recurrent campaigns of genocide, is
explained by relating evil to high purpose.

But there is something admirable in the interchanges Kinsey describes, something that seems to us morally opposite to manipulation. Kinsey tried, some of the time, to deal with falsehood by openly confronting it. He did that when he set aside his notes and said, "Okay, now tell me the truth." In that moment he trusted his own instinct for recognizing truth, and he trusted his interviewee enough to confront him with the truth of the interpersonal moment. The truth of the interpersonal moment was: "I don't believe you and you seem to know it." It would have been less sticky, less scary, to have stood up, said, "Thank you very much," and gone home and torn up the notes. Lawyers sometimes do that with clients and witnesses. It is easy and it is safe. But what does that behavior say? It says: "I don't trust you enough to suppose that you could ever tell me the truth. I don't trust you enough to risk having my heart in my mouth and sweat on my palms. I don't trust you enough to level with you about how I feel." The client has another of those experiences of rejection that say to him "you are a bad person." Not "you are in this instance wrong or mistaken," but "you are bad." The evasive behavior needs to be confronted; the counseling issue is how to confront it. Consider this: If you loved the interviewee (and love means at least that you do for him rather than do to him), what course would you follow? "Love does not rejoice in what is wrong," St. Paul says, "but love rejoices in the truth." Apply that to Kinsey's interview with the "feeble-minded" liar. If Kinsey loved that man, the best course would have been an open, trusting, loving, but clear, confrontation: "I feel that you are not telling the truth, and I want to tell you that it is going to affect our relationship." That is, in our opinion, a response that might bring an interviewee around to reconsidering an untruthful answer.

MECHANICS

Notes. Should I take notes? Many pundits say not, but Kinsey found a way to do it (he thought) without its becoming a distraction:

> In the literature on interviewing, it is customary to advise that records should not be made in the presence of a subject, but that they should be made after the subject has left at the close of an interview. This is the commonest procedure among many psychiatrists, clinical psychologists, and among social workers. It is supposed that a subject is embarrassed at seeing his statements put on paper, and that he will talk more freely if he feels that he can say some things that are not recorded. It has been said that there is a loss of rapport when the interviewer records during the interview.... After the first few months of this study, we began to record all of the data directly in the presence of the subject, and there has been no indication that this has been responsible for any loss of rapport or interference with the subject's free exposure of confidences. We have become convinced that any loss of rapport which comes when data are recorded directly has been

consequent upon the longhand method of writing out answers while the subject sits in silence waiting for the next question. This is the thing that is destructive to rapport. By using a code for recording, it has been possible in the present study to record as rapidly as one can carry on a conversation, without loss of rapport or blockage on the subject's part.

Many modern interviewers (but surprisingly few lawyers) use a tape recorder, which, most of them say, can be explained to the client and, if explained candidly, does not become an interference. The tape serves the same function as notes; it also records inflection and mood, which notes do not. Taping also affords the interviewer a way to assess his own performance. This last point is a significant one, especially for novices in law-office practice. One student in a legal-counseling class said:

I get more out of listening to myself on the tape several times than from the comments of others.... I realize now, after several interviews, that a person can begin to develop style as to questioning, summing up, giving the solution or "advice." I feel that one's style is just as much a tool of the trade as one's verbal skills. The important thing to be kept in mind is that the "style" and verbal skills should be a means of establishing a personal contact between the lawyer and his client—as two people in a counseling context, and not simply to play out a scene where one person puts on a lawyer mask and cuts himself off, as a person, from the client.

Forms. It was inevitable that lawyers would decide to save time by asking their clients to respond to questions on a form rather than through interviews. And there is something to be said for obtaining information outside an interview to avoid the kind of tiresome and unnecessary inquiry we see represented in the following interview:

L: Okay, now, on that furniture: It makes a difference, in terms of the amount of taxes you'll be paying—later. We don't want to lump in, with the real estate, the value of the personal property. In other words, we'll show it as a total price of sixty three five, but we ought to put a value on personal property. This way you're not being taxed on personal property under the guise of real property, and also you might be avoiding some capital gain. Okay. So—what personal property's going with it?

C: Uh. The refrigerator—

L: Okay. (Writing).

C: And the living room furniture. There is a davenport and rocking chair and a matching chair. And—

L: Okay. (Writing).

C: A dining set—uh—table, two leaves, and four chairs—

L: Wait, now. You're getting ahead of me here. Davenport, rocker—(Writing).

C: And a matching chair.

L: Matching chair. Okay. (Pause, writing). And—

C: Dining table, with two leaves and four chairs.

L: Four chairs. (Pause). Okay.

C: And I told you the refrigerator. (Pause). And stove.

L: And stove. Right.

C: That goes with it.

L: Yeah. Okay.

C: The stove's built in and that's part of the house.

L: Okay. Well, roughly, what value do you think we should attach to this ... ?

The most important points about using forms to obtain facts from a client are: (1) that the device be confined to facts that are easier to write down than to speak; (2) that the forms demonstrate an openness and acceptance of the client even before they are filled in, and (3) that forms be introduced only after a working relationship with the client has been established. If a client receives a form to fill out even before he meets his lawyer, he draws conclusions about the lawyer, and about the law, from the form. The first conclusion he draws is that he is being treated impersonally, treatment of the kind he expects from the IRS or the welfare office. That conclusion can be avoided if the forms are withheld until a working relationship is established.

* * *

Some forms ask for information that can perfectly well be put on a form, but asked for it in an inhumane way. Here is a form prepared for wills clients, and sent to them with instructions to write out the answers before they come to the law office for an initial interview:

Your name: Birth Date:
Spouse: Birth Date:
Former Marriages: Who:
Any Obligations?

Forms such as these condition people to expect the worst; they bring back feelings we had about the stubby pencils and "All right, last name, first name, middle initial," in our first days of military service. They are like filling out the hundreds of forms we complete in everyday life. A profession ought to be able, always and everywhere, to do better than that.

CHAPTER SIX

THEORIES AND MODELS FOR HELPING RELATIONSHIPS

BASIC THEORIES OF COUNSELING

Lawyers can learn from psychological counselors. We study *theories* of counseling because psychologists (the ones we read and admire) are concerned about the process level of interaction between a "professional helper" and one who seeks help and is willing to pay for it. There are things about ourselves and our clients we do not understand, and over which we seem, at least on first appearance, to have little control. The more we understand the psychology of human interaction, and the counseling done in law offices, the more we find to learn from "professional counselors." Legal counselors need to know what a psychological counselor does and the knowledge they have about their work might be of use to a lawyer who wants to better understand his clients (and himself).

We have argued that counseling is a function of how we listen to and talk with clients. Counseling, for better or worse, involves a simple choice: Can the client be seen as something other than a problem? Psychological theories of counseling can be analyzed according to the way they attempt to

153

respond to this question. There is at least one theory of counseling, developed by Joseph Simons and Jeanne Reidy, that refers to the ideal counselor as a friend. Other counselors who adopt this approach to counseling prefer "companion" to "friend." They argue that people have special and idiosyncratic definitions of "friendship." Lawrence C. Porter, a counseling psychologist, defended the preference, in a personal letter to Shaffer: "For me, being a friend and being friendly are different kinds of things. My energies allow me to be friendly to a great number of people (on buses, in ticket lines, in various chance encounters), but a friend to only a very small number, because being a friend is such a complex and significant enterprise. I guess that's why *companion* seems so much easier a word for me to deal with. If I have any kind of case load as a lawyer, it will be impossible for me to deal with very many of those clients truly as friends." The choice for the counselor is significant, as it is for the lawyer.

When counselors sort themselves out according to training and theory they tend to cluster around one of four prominent theories of counseling—the companionship theory, the non-directive theory, the interpretive theory, and the directive theory:

Companionship

The companionship idea is that counselor and client seek to exploit the bonds of mutual interest in a relationship—one who needs help working with one who has been trained to provide help. It begins by inquiring into the initial attraction which brought the client to the counselor. It seeks to build that initial attraction into the basis for a productive, working relationship. It resists client dependence and works toward mutuality and collaboration in solving problems. It insists upon openness and candor in the counselor.

The initial obstacle to a companionship theory of counseling is the idea that in working with the client to solve a problem, a professional must be objective and detached, that a professional relationship is characterized by minimal involvement with clients. We imagine our clients *as* clients, not as friends or companions. We do something *for* a client, not *with* him. Lawyers are taught detachment as a professional ideal, an ideal that depends on emotional distance. When our relationships follow the ideal of detachment, they are, in Martin Buber's terms, I–It rather than I–Thou; the client is an It, not a person. Clients then become nuisances; we serve our clients because we are paid to do so.

The images of the lawyer as a companion, and of legal counseling as the practice of companionship, are integral to our thinking about the talking and listening that lawyers do. It explains how our talking and listening as lawyers can be more consciously viewed as counseling. The companionship theory of counseling is a moral ideal as well as a behavioral theory for a professional relationship. In practice, companionship is an amalgam of ideas and sentiments about the way professionals relate to their clients (and about the way we want to feel at the end of a day working with clients). Companionship is a style of interaction that is so natural for some counselors and some lawyers that they do not associate it with either theory or ideal. (Standard reference works on psychological counseling do not discuss the companionship theory as a separate school of counseling.)

Non–Directive

The idea of non-directive counseling is that clients contain within themselves all of the resources necessary for making choices they need to make and need only be freed from the judgmental paternalism (including that of professionals) to make needed choices. The best way to help clients toward competence and freedom is to demonstrate that they are better at doing what we assume they have persistently failed to do—make informed choices to better their lives. This approach to counseling, given prominence by Carl Rogers, turns on "active listening" in which the counselor aims to show that she hears (and accepts) the client by restating the feelings and fears expressed by the client and by attempting to show the client that she understands how the client feels, that she has empathy for the client. (See the Reflective Exercise at the end of Chapter Three.) Rogerian counselors seek to avoid client dependence and try to promote the client's growth by focusing on that part of the client's life and personality that is healthy and intact. The counselor rigorously avoids judgment. She concentrates on the climate of the relationship, by: (a) attempting to accept client feelings, whatever they are; (b) manifesting empathy (not merely sympathy, which is intellectual, but an attempt to feel the situation as the client feels it); and (c) demonstrating congruence between her own feelings, especially those toward the client, and her actions in the counseling relationship.

The principal criticisms of non-directive counseling are that it does not avoid, but rather encourages, client dependence, because it fosters and comes to depend on a strong empathic relationship between counselor and client; and that it is inefficient because it does not quickly enough produce choices, decisions, and plans of action.

Directive Styles

The feature that characterizes directive schools of counseling is that the counselor is active, relatively combative, often giving orders. Albert Ellis, for instance, gave his psychological clients homework. The "Gestalt" counselors (Frederick Perls, for example) believe in confronting clients with how their behavior appears to the counselor, a confrontation that goes beyond interpretation. Practitioners of "transactional analysis" (Eric Berne) relate client behavior to communications between parties in what is called a "transaction." Communications are related to parent, adult, and child "ego states" that set the tone for the relationship and are the basis for failures in communications. Eric Berne, the father of TA (transactional analysis), helped us see how feelings are embedded in the frames of reference (orientation, perspective) (Berne called them ego states) that channel and structure all of the talking and listening we do with another person. In the directive school of counseling the counselor uses specific, often dramatic, techniques to intervene and provoke change in a relationship. These techniques and interventions bring the underlying process level of relationships to the surface, where it can be observed and related to the client's behavior.

Interpretive Theories

The key in an interpretive approach to counseling is to find the underlying basis for the problem. The idea is that the client will seek to resolve his problem once he understands it. The means to this resolution is a perceptive person who will listen and help the client see how the problem works, how it got to be a problem. In order for the expert's presence to be taken seriously, though, this person must be seen as significant and reliable. Interpretive counseling may encourage dependence (transference) and tends to identify resistance (to the therapy and to the therapist's interpretations) as significant.

There is a long-standing debate about the value of classical, Freudian-style psychotherapy, where counseling relationships tend to be complex and extend over long periods of time. There would be wide agreement, though, that this style of counseling is best accomplished in the practice of depth psychology by trained therapists, those who have themselves experienced a long period of psychoanalysis. Since it involves psychological acumen it is a difficult orientation to teach and master in other professions. (See Chapter Four for a discussion of transference and countertransference.)

* * *

We borrow, in theory and in practice, from each of the four main theories that we have presented. We have drawn deeply, as we think all counselors must, on the seminal work of Sigmund Freud and C.G. Jung, the founders of psychoanalysis and analytic psychology. We realize that both Freud and Jung are controversial figures in the psychological community, but we acknowledge our dependence on their work and their commitment to understanding the unconscious and how it makes its way into everyday life, especially into professional relationships. We think it important for lawyers to be aware of the fact that basic theories of counseling can be used to understand our work with clients in law offices. (It is also important to note that different counseling theories share important assumptions, every bit as important as it is see the distinctions among the theories.)

The schools of counseling we describe are not mutually exclusive. An experienced counselor tends, amidst a proliferation of theories, to think of herself as eclectic. From the various psychological perspectives described in this chapter and in Chapter Five, we find the following points of interest to lawyers:

— The counselor is willing to ask her client for help. Alfred C. Kinsey, the researcher who first delved into the subject of contemporary Americans' sex lives, succeeded because he said to his subjects: "Would you be willing to help me?" This is often the most functional way to gather information from clients, and may be the best way to approach an understanding of their problem.

— The counselor recognizes that the client has resources, talents, and insights that bear on what her client sees as a problem and on how the relationship can best proceed—that is, on the client's resolution of the problem.

— The counselor recognizes that, as a professional, she exercises certain "priestly" functions, not because of superiority but because she has a license to prescribe drugs, argue in court, preside in church, or stand at a podium. These priestly functions imply knowledge and ability, but have little or no bearing on competence in counseling. We argue (Chapters Three and Eleven) that when this "priestly" function results in wearing a professional mask, counseling is significantly, and often adversely, affected.

— The counselor has a healthy respect and is attentive to needs that put distance between a lawyer and her client—needs to be in charge, to compete, not to become involved in the pain and travail of another person.

— The counselor is honest, with himself and his client, about his biases, his need to control and dominate, his tendency to hide things or to reveal them in an obscure way, and his instincts to compete. He respects particularly the fact that part of his professionalism lies in his special knowledge of a limited part of human experience (and that this "special" knowledge may delude him into assuming that he knows more about life in general than he actually does).

— The counselor regards his relationship with his client as an adventure, as a sanctioned, privileged, awesome intrusion into the infinite reality of another human life.

FOUNDATION FOR A COMPANIONSHIP MODEL

We have selected here four discrete theories—Gestalt, transactional analysis, the Johari window, and psychoanalytic theory—for more extensive description. These four theories provide a framework for our counseling and teaching; we view them as foundations for the client-centered, companionship model we present throughout this book.

Gestalt

Gestalt is a theory, a school of psychology, as well as a way of doing counseling and therapy. It is most often associated with the work of Frederick S. (Fritz) Perls, a bigger than life character, who drew on his experience (and failures) as a Freudian psychoanalyst to develop a new form of therapy (more accurately, a way of working with others, since much of Perls's work was done in groups, not in individual psychotherapy). Gestalt work, like psychoanalysis, tends to follow well-prescribed rules. The Gestalt-oriented counselor is more directive and confrontive than most other counselors.

Gestalt follows a set of "ground rules," ways of interpreting and interrupting behavior so that learning and change can take place. The ground rules aim for enhanced awareness, at separating what a person does that is real and authentic from what he does that is phony and manipulative. Awareness comes out of confrontation, encouraged by the therapist or others in the Gestalt group, confrontation of the person with his actual behavior, and with how that behavior affects others.

Jerry Greenwald, writing about the ground rules in Gestalt therapy, suggests that "much of the work in Gestalt therapy involves increased awareness of obsolete attitudes and behavior patterns which were learned in the past and continue despite their frustrating effect on the person's well-being in the present. While he adopted these as the most effective way he could find to cope with conflicts in his past life, he may begin to see that they no longer fit present reality. As he becomes aware of these archaic responses, he may begin to experiment by taking risks in letting go of them and discovering new, more effective attitudes and behavior. The energy that had been diverted into frustrating or non-nourishing activities is then freed and available for more meaningful experiences in the here-and-now."

These general comments can be amplified by a more extended description of the Gestalt "ground rules":

(i) Gestalt work is done through exercises that focus on *awareness,* and the most direct form of awareness is knowledge of one's *feelings* and an attempt to stay in the *here and now,* in contrast to explanations about feelings based on something that happened in the past, or on something that might happen in the future.

(ii) Gestalt work seeks out conflicts that are out of awareness but influencing present behavior. These conflicts are explored through role playing and dialogues with those who we think are angry at us, or want to love us, or those we fear will abandon us.

(iii) Gestalt work in a group requires that each person take responsibility for his own feelings, his relations with others in the group, and for his own learning (learning that being in the group makes possible). Individual and personal responsibility is a cardinal rule of Gestalt practice. The most direct way to enforce the rule of personal responsibility is to use the personal pronoun "I" when we talk about ourselves. We have been taught, in speech and in writing, to avoid "I." Gestalt work teaches us to say "I," to speak in the first person.

(iv) To learn what our feelings mean, how we are perceived by others, and how our interactions work, requires that we take risk. Gestaltists see risk as fundamental to change. Risk is inhibited by old patterns and by perceived fears. Gestalt work in a group makes possible risk-taking, which involves confrontation with fears, explicit and secret.

(v) Gestalt group work focuses on the here and now, on learning from what we are presently experiencing. In the Gestalt perspective "intellectualizing," "psychologizing," and giving advice (gratuitous or otherwise) are discouraged.

The Gestalt rule against advice extends to any kind of talking, lecturing, or story-telling about oneself or someone else. Participants are asked to focus on their experiences of the moment. "The emphasis," Greenwald says, "is on nonintellectual awareness as opposed to thoughts and speculations." One of the ways to avoid intellectualizing and to encourage the focus on one's own feelings is to avoid questions. "Questions," Greenwald points out, "frequently ask a person to explain, defend or justify some aspect of himself or of his existence. Questions often are attempts to manipulate other people; they can usually be restated as first person statements."

(vi) Participants in a Gestalt group address each other and follow a "no gossip" rule. Greenwald explains the rule this way: "To enhance feelings of contact and interaction, each person is asked to make statements directly to the other person. For example, instead of saying to the group leader about another participant: 'He makes me angry with his intellectualizing,' the person is asked to make the statements directly to the participant toward whom he feels angry; *i.e.,* 'I am angry at your intellectualizing.' "

(vii) The purpose of the "ground rules" is to create an atmosphere in which each participant in the group can learn from his or her experience in the group. The rules minimize old patterned ways of interaction and make it possible to take risk and learn new modes of behavior.

Psychoanalytic Theory

The lessons of Freudian psychology for the lawyer counselor were first presented to the legal community by Andrew Watson, a psychiatrist who taught at the law school at the University of Michigan. Watson found that the problem that we talk about may not be the problem at all. And even when we find the courage and the will to talk about the problem, we are prone to select a "helper" for reasons that, upon examination, turn out not to be the real reasons at all. The unconscious, it seems, plays a significant role not only in what we are able to say about our own lives (and the problems we confront and create for ourselves) but also affects the choice of those we will ask for help and the kind of help we will permit them to give us.

Psychoanalytic theory is a model of the mind, a frame of reference, a perspective, a map, a language for talking about the unconscious and internal mental processes (motivations, intentions, hopes, dreams, depression, feelings). Freudian psychology is of continuing interest to lawyers because intra-psychic forces affect the way we relate to our clients, other lawyers, judges, and ourselves; they affect our professional decisions, as well as the way we live our personal lives. Watson's scholarship explored these realities in reference to legal ethics, classroom teaching methods, and legal education, as well as counseling.

Lawyers tend to be more interested in ideas and skills that affect communication, that explain the obstacles to getting facts and the idiosyncratic ways of their clients, than in the specifics of a technical theory such as Freudian psychoanalysis. But it is in the actual use of psychoanalytic theory, in the work that Freudian therapists do with patients (who are called, in psychoanalytic literature, analysands), that we learn something of value about the human psyche that can inform our counseling in law offices and legal settings.

The psychoanalytic method requires that a subject relate experiences, feelings, emotions, and fears to the analyst, who guides the patient or client in recognizing and understanding the workings of the unconscious. In this process of "working through" the unconscious material, the client gains insight that can be put to use to reduce the effects of unconscious forces that provoke emotions that create problems in a relationship.

The psychoanalytic method also involves a specific technique for bringing forth this unconscious material. It is based on an assumption described by

Theodore Reik, an analyst: People "reveal themselves—all their emotional secrets—when they talk freely about themselves; not just when they talk about their secrets, but about everything concerning themselves. They give away what bothers them, disturbs and torments them, all that occupies their thoughts and arouses their emotions—even when they would be most unwilling to talk directly about these things."

In psychoanalytic terms, this technique of spontaneous utterance is called *free association*. The analyst asks the patient to free associate to words, feelings, and images in dreams, to say everything that comes to mind. The goal is to disengage the intellect that requires thoughts to be linear and rational. Freud found that the unconscious operates by a different set of rules, rules that violate the ideals we associate with the intellect. Karen Horney describes free association as the "endeavor on the part of the patient to express without reserve, and in the sequence in which it emerges, everything that comes into his mind, regardless of whether it is or appears trivial, off the point, incoherent, irrational, indiscreet, tactless, embarrassing, humiliating. It includes not only fleeting and diffuse thoughts but also specific ideas and memories ... memories of experiences at any period of life, thoughts about self and others ... beliefs in religion, morals, politics, art, wishes and plans for the future, fantasies past and present, and, of course, dreams." As practiced in psychoanalysis, it constitutes a process of spontaneous word and thought association that, in theory, overcomes the patterned ways we censor our thoughts.

(We are not being as precisely accurate with our terms as a psychiatrist would be. Analysis, in the strict sense, is a prolonged process of controlled self-discovery. The devices and techniques used in analysis are also used in shorter-term and more focused treatment—or counseling—that is probably more accurately referred to as psychotherapy.)

The point here is not that lawyers learn to use *free association* with (or on) their clients, but that to get at the basis of a human situation sometimes requires extraordinary measures, skills, and techniques that break through the crusty, impacted, surface areas of our lives. Freud's exploration of the unconscious produced a wealth of information, not only for doctors who deal with mental illness, but for professionals like lawyers who work with others and have a need to understand human behavior.

We are aware that Freud's theories are now controversial (Freud has always been controversial!), and in some instances discredited. We are not sure that the Oedipus complex is a universal phenomenon, as Freud and some of Freud's followers suggested. And we are confident, in the light of contemporary research, that Freud was mistaken about penis envy, and much else that he had to say about the psychology of women. But Freud is also controversial because he did so much in the area of psychology that cannot easily be ignored, creating for those in the field of psychology what Harold

Bloom, the literary critic, calls "the anxiety of influence." Freud is controversial because his system of psychoanalysis grew out of empirical findings (Freud viewed himself as a scientist) and out of the art of human healing. (Freud was a notable writer, and a creator of what James Hillman calls a "healing fiction," but most of all he was a physician.) Psychoanalysis remains today both a method of treatment, a theory of social science, and an eloquent, literary achievement that makes Freud a continued subject of discussion and study in the humanities as well as in the field of psychology.

Contemporary psychoanalysts and psychologists and other academic scholars are reworking and revising Freud's theories and are using them not only as the basis for a method of treatment but also for an understanding of human motivation and human behavior of use in the social sciences and the humanities. (See Chapter Four for a discussion of Freud's theory of transference.)

There are two other psychological models—the Johari window and Eric Berne's transactional analysis—that draw heavily on Freud's insights, recasting Freudian concepts of resistance and repression, and the unconscious itself, in a different language.

The Johari Window

Joe Luft and Harry Ingham developed what has come to be known as the Johari Window, a pictorial representation (a structure) that maps what we know (or think we know) about awareness in human behavior and human interaction.

	Known to Self	Unknown to Self
Known to Others	I OPEN	II BLIND
Unknown to Others	III HIDDEN	IV UNKNOWN

[B2909]

The four quadrants in this representation reflect the presence and absence of awareness (the knowledge that we have of who we are and what is happening in a relationship). The Johari Window applies Freud's insights in psychotherapy (resistance, repression, differentiating the ego and the unconscious, the ego's involvement in self-deception, and the difficulties of self-scrutiny) to our relations to others. The knowledge gained by physicians in treatment of neurosis is recast as knowledge for understanding personal and professional relationships that can be put to use in the law office.

Turning to the quadrants of the Johari window: Quadrant I is *Open,* that part of our interaction of which we are fully aware, that we readily share with others, and that others know as well as we. When we say what we want, or need, express our feelings, and are heard by another, who reflects back to us what we are saying and feeling, the interaction and communication are taking place in Quadrant I. In the interactions confined to Quadrant I we are known to self and known to others.

Many of the interactions of everyday life, and the conversations and work of the lawyer, take place in this quadrant. So long as the lawyer and the client follow the game plan, do what is expected of them, play their roles, say what they mean and do what they say, then the interaction remains in Quadrant I. If we were perfect human beings, it is conceivable that there would be nothing but Quadrant I interactions; all of our communications would be adult-adult, I–Thou, open, mutually reinforcing, and fully understandable. No person would be able to manipulate another by withholding information: To get the information you need, all you would have to do is ask for it. Dishonesty would be a rarity. Gossip would lose its appeal. Secrecy would be so dysfunctional that it would become obsolete.

That all our interactions might take place in Quadrant I suggest a utopian world, a world we sometimes aspire to, and wish for in times of misunderstanding. Lawyers would flourish in this utopian world, which raises doubt whether it is a world we would truly want. Without secrets there would be no awe and mystery. Without misunderstanding and misreadings (we misread others the way we misread all texts), there would be no curiosity about human motivations. We would, in a world dominated by Quadrant I communication and interaction, have created a totally bureaucratic universe, and a leveling of the human spirit.

Quadrant II is comprised of behavior, feelings, motivation that are known to others but not to self. It is a realm of interaction in which we are *Blind* to what others can see. Freud and Jung, as much as any contemporary or past figures in psychology and psychiatry, were masterful explorers of this region. The ego that helps us test (and create) a reality from our experiences, and to find a place for ourselves in the world, cuts us off from certain kinds of knowledge about ourselves (giving rise to self-deception). When the obstacles to self-understanding become absolute barriers, as in the case of self-destructive behavior and neurotic adaptions (ways of living that are so dysfunctional that they produce extreme unhappiness), we (those who live and must share the world with the person) become painfully aware of the pathology created by behavior to which the person is blind, but others see.

Quadrant II is significant in the attorney-client relationship. We argue that the client is a resource, and has information, knowledge, insights and understanding that can be directed to the resolution of problems. (See Chapter Nine). But the client is a resource in a broader sense, a resource for the lawyer—the client sees the lawyer as he cannot (will not) see himself. One value of the feedback we give one another is that it tells us about behavior and feelings more apparent to others than to ourselves.

Quadrant III, the *Hidden,* is the realm in which what we know about ourselves is unknown to others. The conscious elements of what Jung called the "shadow" are found here, as are all secrets, and knowledge of negligence, incompetence, mistakes, and errors. It is Quadrant III which gives rise to manipulation and lies; in this realm of interaction we find a fertile ground for guilt (as Quadrant II is the ground for depression). Quadrant III involves interactions that produce the moral tensions that pull at lawyers: confidentiality, conflict of interest, and the ideal of zealous representation arise in those settings in which what we know, but which is unknown to others, results in harm to others.

A poignant example of the Quadrant III moral tension can be found in a story told by David Hilfiker in his book *Healing the Wounds: A Physician Looks at His Work*. Dr. Hilfiker, at the time of the incident he describes, was practicing medicine in a rural health-care clinic in northern Minnesota, two hours by automobile from Duluth. Hilfiker had delivered Barb Daily's first baby and considered himself a friend of Barb and her husband, Russ. Barb thought she was pregnant again, and there was no reason to think that Barb Daily's second child would present complications. Hilfiker explained: "At her appointment that afternoon, Barb seems to be in good health, with all the signs and symptoms of pregnancy: slight nausea, some soreness in her breasts, a little weight gain. But when the nurse tests Barb's urine to determine if she is pregnant, the result is negative." The test is not always accurate; Hilfiker had Barb leave a urine sample so that another test could be run. When the second test came back negative, Hilfiker was puzzled and troubled: "Perhaps she isn't pregnant. Her missed menstrual period and her other symptoms could be a result of a minor hormonal imbalance. Maybe the embryo has died within the uterus.... I could find out by ordering an ultrasound examination. This procedure would give me a 'picture' of the uterus and the embryo. But Barb would have to go to Duluth for the examination. The procedure is also expensive. I know the Dailys well enough to know they have a modest income. Besides, by waiting a few weeks, I should be able to find out for sure without the ultrasound: either the urine test will be positive or Barb will have a miscarriage." This information was conveyed to the patient. A month later she returned to see Hilfiker and nothing had changed—still no menstrual period and no miscarriage. Barb was now confused and upset because she felt pregnant and both she and her husband wanted the baby. Hilfiker's concern intensified when a third urine test was negative. Possible explanations for Barb's condition included a hormonal imbalance and even tumor, explanations which Hilfiker ruled out, concluding that the most likely explanation was that Barb was carrying a dead embryo and that her body had not followed the usual course of miscarriage to get rid of the dead tissue.

Hilfiker again explained the situation to his patient: "Barb is disappointed; there are tears. She is college-educated, and she understands the scientific and technical aspects of the situation, but that doesn't alleviate the sorrow. We talk at some length

and make an appointment for two weeks later."
When the patient returned, with her husband, there
still has been no menstrual period, no miscarriage,
and there was another negative pregnancy test, the
fourth. "I explain to them what has happened. The
dead embryo should be removed or there could be
serious complications. Infection could develop, Barb
could even become sterile. The conversation is emotionally difficult for all three of us. We schedule the
dilation and curettage for later in the week.

"Dilation and curettage, or D & C, is a relatively
simple surgical procedure performed thousands of
times each day in this country," but with Barb
things did not go easily. What should take ten or
fifteen minutes stretches into a half-hour. The body
parts I remove are much larger than I expected,
considering when the embryo died. They are not
bits of decomposing tissue. These are parts of a
body that was recently alive!

"I do my best to suppress my rising panic and try
to complete the procedure. Working blindly, I am
unable to evacuate the uterus completely; I can feel
more parts inside but cannot remove them. Finally
I stop, telling myself that the uterus will expel the
rest within a few days."

Hilfiker learned from the pathologist's report,
confirming his worst fear, that he had aborted a
living fetus, of about eleven weeks. "My meeting
with Barb and Russ later in the week is one of the
hardest things I have ever been through. I described
in some detail what I did and what my rationale

had been. Nothing can obscure the hard reality: I killed their baby."

Every doctor and lawyer makes mistakes. As Hilfiker puts it, "They happen; they hurt—ourselves and others. They demonstrate our fallibility. Shown our mistakes and forgiven them, we can grow, perhaps in some small way become better people. Mistakes, understood this way, are a process, a way we connect with one another and with our deepest selves." The process and the growth that Hilfiker envisions is stunted if we hide our mistakes from others and ourselves. Hilfiker's book is a moving chronicle of pain and honesty in professional life—of transferring experience and knowledge from Quadrant III to Quadrant I. It is, finally, a powerful moral argument for growth through truthfulness. (See Chapter Ten).

Quadrant IV, the *Unknown,* is that area of human interaction that is out-of-awareness for both parties in the relationship. Joe Luft, one of the creators of the Johari Window, provides the following examples of feelings and needs that are difficult to confront and that take up residence in the quadrant of the Unknown:

— feelings of inadequacy, incompetence, and impotence;

— sensitivity to rejection, avoiding displays of affection;

— need to punish or to be punished;

— passive-dependent feelings, especially in men and women who have high achievement aspirations;

— intense feelings of loneliness and isolation;

— qualities in the person that one cannot tolerate in others;

— feelings of unworthiness and despair.

Using the Johari Window

The Johari Window suggests a model for analyzing the hidden agendas in lawyer and client relationships and a framework for understanding our interactions with clients. Imagine a lawyer (A) and his relationship with client (B). The lawyer and the client may be in any one of four postures. The lawyer (A) may be identified with the various Quadrants of the Johari Window. For example, he may be in Quadrant I in the Window represented as:

A

This is a state of open awareness (i.e., aware of himself and open to others).

The lawyer may be unknown to himself, but known to others (not aware but open; Quadrant II, the blind area, in the Window):

In this state, he is, of course, vulnerable to manipulation—because he literally does not know what he is doing. Clients manipulate lawyers, particularly when competition is in the air (see Chapter Four). Lawyers manipulate one another. The Quadrant II posture is an unfortunate position in negotiation, for example.

Our lawyer might be aware of himself but not open to others:

This situation is rare; we are not as able as we sometimes think to live with a poker face. It is extremely difficult to be accurate about one's feelings unless one is able to project them on other people; this is probably what Jung meant when he talked about individuation. But the situation is at least theoretically possible, and would correspond to Quadrant III (avoided or hidden) in the Johari Window.

Finally, the lawyer may be closed both to himself and to others; this is Quadrant IV (Unknown) in the window.

$$\boxed{A}$$

If you take the simplest sort of human interaction—two people (lawyer/A and client/B) in one-on-one legal counseling—there are twelve contexts for human interaction:

A	A	↻ A	A
B			
B			
↻ B			
B			

In some situations both parties deal with one another openly:

$$\boxed{A} \underset{\longleftarrow}{\overset{\longrightarrow}{}} \boxed{B}$$

There are situations in which one party deals with the other in vain, as if he were trying to break through:

$$A \longrightarrow \boxed{B}$$

Many law-office situations are scenes in which neither participant is aware of his own feelings, so that each participant is vainly attempting to influence the other:

$$\boxed{A} \underset{\longleftarrow}{\overset{\longrightarrow}{}} \boxed{B}$$

There are situations in which both parties deal with one another on a basis of mutual non-communication:

There are situations in which one party is manipulated:

And there are situations in which neither party is communicating with himself or with the other:

Transactional Analysis

Transactional Analysis (TA) was developed by a psychiatrist, Eric Berne, author of several widely read psychology books, including *Games People Play*. Berne's contribution was a road map for ordinary application of traditional Freudian teaching on the unconscious. The theory of TA was premised on the presence (during personal interaction) of a series of "ego states" or ways of being with other people, and on the observation that when one "ego state" meets another, the interaction is as likely to be dysfunctional as it is to be productive. The "ego states" are: Parent, Adult, and Child (corresponding, roughly, to stances of domination, awareness, and manipulation). Games occur on two levels—an apparent, or social, level and a psychological or ulterior level.

Berne's paradigm case was "If It Weren't For You." (His games typically had catchy names; they came, Berne said, from patients who used his analytical system in group therapy.) "If It Weren't For You" (IWFY) is a game between (old-fashioned) husband and wife. He says, "You stay home and take care of the house." She says, "If it weren't for you, I could be out having fun." At the social level, the dialogue is between parent ("restricting husband") and child:

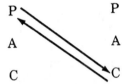

H: "Stay home."

W: "If it weren't for you.... "

At the psychological (ulterior) level, the game that is being played is a game of mutual terror: The husband is afraid that his wife will leave him; the wife afraid to go out into the world and deal with other people; both are children:

H: "You must always be here when I get home; I'm terrified of desertion."

S: "I will be if you help me avoid phobic situations."

As long as the interaction works in these ways the game can continue; thus families develop games for dealing with deviant (*e.g.,* alcoholic) members; business associates go along coping with one another in neurotic ways; and professional (*e.g.,* lawyer-client) relationships are conducted according to the model of domineering paternalism.

What stops the Bernian game and requires a realignment of positions and new behavior is what Berne identified as the crossed transaction. If, for example the wife in IWFY were to insist that she is going to go out into the business world and get a job, the social-level transaction would be crossed by an adult-to-adult communication from her, one that would stop their social game:

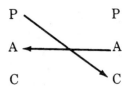

H: "Stay home."

W: "I want to get a job."

Crossed transactions can stop the ulterior game, too—sometimes in what Berne's patients identified as "blow up." A blow up is what brings people to professional helpers, including divorce lawyers, or to blows, or to both.

One of our classes in legal counseling considered a case in which the client, a young woman, was not forthcoming about her case. The student-lawyer who worked on the case managed, though, to find out that her husband cheated on her; and that he was brutal, financially irresponsible, rather dashing, and more or less indifferent. She came in asking the lawyer to do something about the husband's current affair, and saying she was not sure she wanted a divorce. She was apparently vulnerable to being influenced toward divorce, but seemed to be ambivalent about it, and she was filled with hurt and outrage and vindictiveness. The student lawyer made suggestion after suggestion, none of which, it seemed, the client was likely to follow. We found it useful to analyze that interview in terms of another of Berne's games, called "Why Don't You—Yes But" (WDYYB). It appears to be an adult conversation:

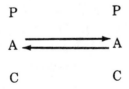

C: "Tell me what to do."

L: "This is what to do."

C: "Yes, but I can't, because.... "

The ulterior or psychological transaction here was child-to-parent; the client was saying, "See if you can help me, and I'm betting you can't." The game, then, looked like this (dotted lines being the psychological transaction):

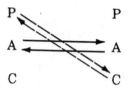

We find this sort of game played by ambivalent clients and eagerly adopted by lawyers who are determined to provide advice quickly. It can be stopped by refusing to play. When we rethink the interview, we see how it might go: (i) A lawyer might stop the game by non-evaluative listening; in that situation the client has no ball to hit because the pitcher isn't throwing. (ii) A lawyer can be more confrontive. She might suggest that the client is blaming her husband, or her husband's lover, for personal inadequacies. Either solution provides room for further discussion; the present point is that they stop the game. They prove that games can be stopped if the client is initiating them and avoided when the lawyer is attempting to initiate them.

A REFLECTIVE EXERCISE: COUNSELING THEORIES

We have identified four approaches to counseling in this chapter: companionship, non-directive, directive, interpretive. They are not meant to be all inclusive, nor anything other than handy references for use in understanding how counseling may differ according to the perspective, model, orientation, and philosophy of the counselor.

Given our cursory description of these orientations, which comes closest to the way you assume that lawyers actually work with clients? Can you identify what it is in the description of any of these models that makes you feel uncomfortable with it?

A student interested in counseling will want to find out more about different "schools" of counseling and the diverse philosophical and psychological sources of counseling theory. We have found that a "school" of counseling theory and practice turns out to be more than merely a set of principles or a prescribed way to do therapy. Professionals, lawyers included, are required by the demands of their work and their clients to change, to react to new situations, new problems, new people. The counseling theories we explore here (and others we have not presented) say something about how we learn and how we change, how we value ourselves and the situations in which we are cast as helpers and professionals.

Determine which of the basic counseling orientations you most identified with, and the one you identified with least, and see if you can find out more about them. Read something that one of the founders or followers of each of these "schools" wrote. As you learn more about the school that you find most interesting, try to learn more about the one with which you have the least affinity. (It is important that you read something that was written by the principal figures in these schools of counseling. Psychology books that describe psychological theories tend to bland description or biased dismissal.)

The temptation of lawyers and students who have not worked at understanding counseling skills is to dramatically underestimate what a "lay" counselor can do. Students sometimes argue that it is not the role of lawyers to play therapists to their clients. And we agree. Our effort is to locate and develop and improve counseling skills, not because we think lawyers should be therapists, but because counseling is what lawyers do. We aim for a personal, productive climate in the law office, one that works, one in which feelings can be treated as facts. The climate in which a professional relationship grows is important. It matters to the client because it affects the way his or her case will turn out. It matters to the lawyer because the lawyer wants to be effective and to leave the office at the end of one day looking forward to the next. It matters to the lawyer and the client because each of them wants to be treated as a person, not as a problem to be solved or a nuisance to be tolerated. Each of them wants the opportunity to grow, to lead a meaningful life.

CHAPTER SEVEN

INTERVENTIONS AND SKILLS

PHASES IN LEGAL COUNSELING

Counseling clients in a law office usually proceeds through and around four distinct stages. The first is fact gathering (Chapter Five). It is analogous to evidentiary hearings in administrative law, a legislative investigation, or the presentation of evidence at a trial. The skills involved in gathering facts from clients are interviewing skills. The second, third, and fourth stages can be identified as choice, decision, and solution. Each stage is associated with the questions a client puts to a lawyer. In the *choice* stage the question is: What do I want to do? In the *decision* stage the questions are: How am I (how are we) to do it? What legal strategies can we use? And in the *solution* stage the question is: Will my appeal to lawyers and the law get me what I want (or need)? These different aspects of counseling are presented as stages (which suggest a chronological sequence); each is often identified with a distinct (and explicit) closure that signals a movement to the next stage. It would be overly simplistic however to suggest that all counseling relationships follow this basic progression.

The first kind of result that normally issues from a process of helping the client is the tough choice: This is what I want to do. Choice as we are using it (and as non-legal counselors use it) is the direction clients determine to take as a result of counseling in the narrow sense. Counseling in the broad sense is the process of helping a client make up his mind.

The second kind of result issues from a process of working with the client toward a decision. Decisions in law offices are analogous to decisions in courts or legislatures. They are in an essential sense "legal." They are precise; they can be implemented. They are similar to legislative decisions following legislative choices: The legislature may make a choice for the state. For instance, legislatures decided in the 1960s to pursue policies of racial equality. Some of them then, more precisely, made decisions to implement their choices through fair employment practices commissions. Some legislatures chose racial equality and then came to a decision against enforcement of equal rights. They contented themselves with admonitions. Law office decisions are, in a similar way, answers to the client's second question—How am I (how are we) to do what I (we) have (already) chosen to do? Decision follows choice.

Take the distinction between choice and decision one step further: To carry out the legislative decision in favor of fair employment practices, a legislative lawyer must plan and draft a complex, comprehensive statute and resolve in it the expectations of legislators and the needs of people in minority groups. This is the third kind of result. In looking at law office practice, we are calling this operation problem-solving, and its result a solution.

Some examples:

— A client decides that she wants to terminate her marriage. She and her lawyer working together decide that the way to do that is to seek a separation rather than a divorce. And her lawyer, now taking up a technical aspect of his work, figures out a solution to the problems of how, when, and where to file; how to seek child custody; what position to take on support; and what sort of strategy to pursue with the husband's lawyer. (We don't suggest that the client is not involved in problem-solving. The difference is more narrow legal expertise, more initiation by the lawyer than is involved in arriving at choices or making decisions.)

— The lawyer and client make the decision to merge the client's twenty corporations and reincorporate them; the client decides that he wants the new corporation to be publicly owned; and the lawyer arrives at a solution to the problems of timing, tax saving, which state to incorporate in, stock restrictions, and the form and content of prospectuses and "blue sky" statements. Note that solution could come before decision here, or even before choice. (Sometimes the cart precedes the horse.) Note, too, that fact gathering and interviewing may not occur exclusively at the beginning of the process. Lawyer and client usually need to return to the facts throughout the process.

— The client decides she wants to sue the trucking company whose truck she collided with, rather than accept a token settlement. She and her lawyer decide that the way to carry this out is through litigation and the lawyer arrives at a series of solutions on forum, strategy, motions, trial time, and evidence. (Query: How should we classify her determination not to include the driver of the truck as co-defendant?)

The lawyer's function differs from one stage to another and between interviewing and the three second-tier operations that produce closure or result.

Interviewing skills are involved at the fact-gathering stage. Those were explored in Chapter Five. Counseling skills (in the narrow sense of "counseling") are involved in helping the client choose what he wants to do. These are, broadly, to provide information and a climate of freedom in which a choice can be made. Some speak of these skills as a matter of "presenting options." The counseling skills involved include such things as alert reaction, accurate reflection, congruence, acceptance, understanding, empathy, and the ability to listen.

The skills that lead to decision about how to do what the client chooses are interaction skills, skills involving cooperation, coordination, explanation, foresight, and a sense of consequence. John Dewey talked about socially-conscious judges following a "logic of consequences." Much the same quality is involved in working toward collaborative law office decisions.

The skills that result in a solution involve more lawyer initiation, more substantive knowledge, and, most of all, a high level of creativity. The analogy to courts is instructive. The great creative judges—Cardozo in the *McPherson* case, John Marshall in the cases that established the independence of the federal judiciary—set an important example for law office problem solvers.

These operations are not as discrete as the stages of a trial. It is best to think of them as functional rather than chronological: A client says he wants to disinherit his errant son. His lawyer then asks about life insurance beneficiaries and what to do about grandchildren; and then, suddenly, the client demonstrates that he has not really chosen what he said he wanted to do. The lawyer may then need to set his collaborative or creative skills aside and get back to helping the client choose what he wants to do. They may even have to return to fact gathering. The process of problem-solving (in drafting a will or planning a securities registration) may turn up key areas for collaboration, or even for tough choices, which require the lawyer to put his pencil down, close his book, and think more carefully about his relationship to this unique client with his unique concerns.

These four functions are not chronologically discrete but they are valid categories and the skills appropriate to each function can be identified. Lawyers who approach clients as problems and not people are not likely to notice the varying skills involved, but there is a difference between solving problems and facilitating choices. Lawyers who press for implementing decisions where the issue is tough choices may find neither decision nor choice but, maybe, a client who decides to go to another lawyer.

Richard Wallen proposed a diagram for organizational development consultation that we adapt here to illustrate the stages of counseling after fact gathering and after essential client choices have been made:

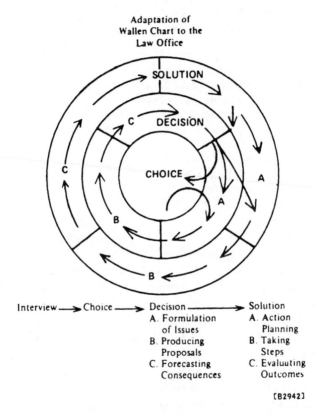

Adaptation of
Wallen Chart to the
Law Office

Interview ──→ Choice ──→ Decision ──────→ Solution
                         A. Formulation   A. Action
                            of Issues   Planning
                         B. Producing   B. Taking
                            Proposals   Steps
                         C. Forecasting   C. Evaluating
                            Consequences   Outcomes

[B2942]

The chart serves three useful purposes. First, its circles and arrows suggest that the process is dynamic and does not proceed in a linear fashion. Second, the points of choice suggested by the lines and arrows indicate that collaboration may result in further collaboration, that problem-solving may require a return to collaboration (or even a return to tough choice). Finally, Wallen breaks down collaborative decision making into further steps, so that our outline can be expanded a bit:

   I.   Interviewing (facts)
  II.   Counseling (tough choices)
 III.   Consulting (collaborative decisions)
        A.   formulation of issues
        B.   producing proposals for decision
        C.   forecasting consequences and testing proposals
  IV.   Problem-solving (creative solution)
        A.   action-planning
        B.   taking action steps
        C.   evaluating outcomes

Consider the following example: A young married couple with two pre-school children want their wills drawn. Fact gathering will involve information on assets, family relationships, and biographical data (ages, state of health, employment). The first meeting with the couple after the initial consultation involves an hour of fact gathering. Most lawyers obtain the information they need, the old-fashioned way, by personal interview (supplemented when necessary by use of forms). We have also considered fact gathering (Chapter Five), and find that even in this modern era the custom is to do this kind of work in person, with questions and answers and yellow pads.

The clients must then choose what they want to do. If the wife dies first, does the family wealth pass to the husband outright or is it necessary to establish a system of property management for him? (We assume her share of it is to pass to him, but that too may be a tough choice.) For example, if both parents die when one or more children are minors, is management necessary? Are the ordinary assumptions about succession applicable ("all to mama and if she's dead to the kids," as the country lawyers put it)? The lawyer's professional function in helping the clients decide what to do also turns up some other, more specific areas of client choice, areas that have to do with feelings about death, about property, and about loved ones. These show up, for example, when questions are asked about disposition when parents and children are all dead and distribution must be made outside the immediate family. All of these questions and concerns involve tough choices. The skills involved are counseling skills. The objective is a personal and psychological climate in which each client experiences enough freedom to make the choices clearly and with confidence.

As the choices are made, collaborative decisions become necessary. If, for example, property-management is chosen for minor children (or for the widow or widower), what form is it to take? There is an enormous difference between guardianship (conservatorship) for a child and trust management. There is a difference between a trust administered by a bank and a trust administered by a relative. This decision making process is collaborative: It involves (1) formulation of issues, (2) producing proposals for decision, and (3) forecasting consequences and testing proposals.

1.   The issue, given a decision to establish a trust for children, is whether the shares of adult children should be held in the trust until all children are of age. The lawyer usually poses this issue. ("Of age" in trust planning is a *decided-upon* age, not necessarily the age of majority dictated by statute.)

2.   Proposals for collaborative decision (coming from both the lawyer and the client) include holding all trust funds in one trust until the youngest child reaches majority; making distribution to each child as he reaches majority; and making distribution as each child either reaches majority or finishes college. Here is where it is significant that the definition of "majority" is a decision and may be a choice. The lawyer here functions as one who poses alternatives that often seem subtle to laymen but are blatant when played out in human lives. This family lawyer might, for example, suggest that the first alternative can be varied a little by giving the trustee authority to distribute principal to adult children if their educational or family needs require funds and if the minor children are adequately provided for.

3.   The proposals are tested hypothetically. If rigid share distributions are made, and one minor child has serious medical needs or proves to be a child prodigy at the violin, will trust funds be adequate? (Perhaps the trustee can function as a parent would.) The lawyer, because he has less attachment to the people and property involved in

the client's choices and decisions, is a valuable bridge to reality, a valuable barometer for the logic of consequences.

4.   Finally, as these collaborative decisions are made, the lawyer initiates the process of problem-solving. The trust for children, for example, is chosen and its main outlines decided. The clients decide that the wife's brother should be trustee. It is now necessary to solve the problems of trustee authority, beneficiary ability to assign assets, problems of accounting and bonding, and fiduciary powers over property and people. These issues are relatively technical but they involve serious consequences. They make significant differences in human lives; the drafter of a trust is important for these human lives.

A lawyer who respects his clients involves them in solving these problems, even though he will probably find that he must initiate solutions with more direction than was true when decision making was in process, and certainly with more direction than was involved when the clients were making initial choices. Using Wallen's outline:

— Action-planning points to two documents, an inter-vivos, contingent, life insurance trust and two "pour-over" wills, one for each spouse, along with appropriate changes of ownership of assets, and changes in insurance beneficiary designations.

— Action steps are taken; the documents are drafted; the wife's brother is consulted about his trusteeship; documents are drafted and the clients are asked to read them and to think about what they will mean to them and to their family.

— Outcomes are evaluated. The plan is tested against the client's needs and feelings. Clients adjust and change and re-think.

* * *

A given result may be a choice about what one wants, a decision about how to do what one wants, or a solution, depending on how the lawyer looks upon client involvement and upon his own control of the situation. Solutions involve lots of lawyer control: collaborative decisions involve less control, more partnership. Tough choices involve client control. The lawyer is, in most cases, in a position to affect, even determine, outcomes. She is also in a position to define the process by which outcomes are reached.

The primary distinction in lawyer-counselor functions that we make here is between hard choices (What do I want to do?) and collaborative decisions (How are we to do it?). Hard-choice counseling is a process in which the counselor helps the client make his own way to a choice. As "counseling" is used, in this narrow, restrictive sense, its objective is to help the client determine what she wants. The skill involved is, most of all, to provide a climate of freedom in which hard choices can be made. This skill includes the difficult ability to listen for feelings as well as to words.

When the issue is hard choice, the client does not need an expert as much as she needs a friend or companion. If the client is unsure or confused he needs companionship and safety and room to move—more than "guidance." To make good choices (choices we can live with), clients usually also need some simple information, but it should be obvious in cases like these that no amount of information, no aggregation of facts or legal rules, will substitute for the work the client must do.

A REFLECTIVE EXERCISE: HARD CHOICES AND COLLABORATIVE DECISIONS

Consider each of the following law-office cases. What kind of counseling issues do you find involved in each of these cases?

Case One

Herbert "Huck" Finley, age 18, is charged with breaking and entering a pool hall, a felony. Huck is being held for trial as an adult. The prosecutor says he will accept a plea of guilty to simple trespass, a misdemeanor, in view of the client's youth, the fact that this is a first offense, and the crowded condition of the docket. In your initial interview with Huck, he said he was nowhere near the pool hall at the time in question, and that he has never broken into and entered a building.

Comment: Huck says he did not do it, but he can avoid a prison sentence if he now says, officially, that he did. How would you respond to the counseling dilemma presented here? How does the counseling dilemma present a moral dilemma? How does the distinction between hard choices and collaborative decisions work in this situation?

Case Two

Anna Faren is distressed because she has discovered that her husband, Andrew, had an affair with another woman. She is hurt, feels betrayed, and thinks other people know about it and are talking about her. She fears for the welfare of their three children, but admits that Andrew is (or was) a good husband; she is talking to you about divorce.

Comment: Anna has to decide (choose) when enough is enough, when final is final, in the most intimate (and fateful) association a normal person has. How can you help Anna make the choice?

Case Three

Margaret Cross has nearly three million dollars (although it doesn't show), is 68 years old, loves her husband Lewis, and has two adult, well-provided-for children. She realizes that Lewis, who is ten years younger, will probably outlive her. She wants him to enjoy his widowhood, but she thinks there ought to be something left over for the children and, even if there isn't, wonders a bit about Lewis's future use of "her" money.

Comment: Margaret is making choices that will have much to do with how her husband spends his widowhood—perhaps 15 or 20 years, or more—and she is implicitly making choices about who makes the choices. What is a lawyer to do to aid Margaret Cross in getting what she wants and needs out of the choices that she is about to make?

Case Four

Charles Cross, Margaret and Lewis's son, is 31, happily married, and the father of four children, the eldest of whom is ten. He realizes, when he talks to you about a will, that he and his wife Ruth may both die before the children are adults. Lewis and Margaret could take care of the children if they were orphaned. Care by Ruth's parents would be impossible (one is dead, one an alcoholic), but Ruth's brother and his wife could take care of them. There are also friends who might take care of the children.

Comment: Charles and Ruth are making choices, in the abstract, hypothetically, that turn on factors that began to be built into their lives before they learned to sit up, and they are making choices, hypothetically, without facts, that would throw them into deep anguish if they were able to decide them on all the facts. How can a lawyer help Charles and Ruth?

THE MOVEMENT FROM CHOICE TO DECISION

Decision-making differs from counseling on hard choices in terms of the relative contribution of the parties. In choice counseling, the client asks "What am I to do?" The client must make up his mind and make a choice. The lawyer helps him make up his mind. The appropriate counselor behavior, when the issue is hard choice, is reflective and, perhaps, supportive. The counselor works best on hard choices when he thinks of himself as a companion (or friend).

In decision-making, the lawyer's role is, we think, more appropriately active. The lawyer can suggest options, provide information (about law and about other things), identify moral concerns, predict consequences, and present the interests of persons who are not in the room but who will be affected by the decision. The client is also active since the agenda involves his deepest interests and the interests of people he cares about. Most intangible information about consequences and impact are in his possession, not the lawyer's. A counselor who respects his client contributes to the decision but does not dominate it. He aims for collaboration. In this respect, decision-making is not like problem-solving. Problem-solving assumes both a client choice and a lawyer-client decision. It involves expertise in implementing decisions, and greater lawyer control of the process.

Another way to chart these distinctions is in terms of interests:

— When the client is being interviewed, the counselor's interest is a curious interest—like Joe Friday saying, "Give me the facts, Ma'am," or, better, Alfred Kinsey saying, "Would you help me?"

— When the client is making a hard choice, the interest is personal, often deeply personal. The counselor's interest is to understand, to sympathize, and to accept the client's feelings.

— When the client and lawyer are arriving at a decision, the interest is closer to the task, a mixture of psychological interest in the client and professional concern for resolving issues and predicting their impact and influence beyond the law office.

— When the issue is problem-solving, the interest is craftsmanship. It is an interest in doing a lawyer-like job of drafting, negotiation, litigation, explanation, or protection.

It is probably a useful exercise to pause once in a while when dealing with a client and ask yourself where your interest is at that moment: In the client as a person? In the task? In some agenda of your own? And where is the client's interest? These examinations of interest may help in deciding whether the lawyer-client relationship at the moment is an interviewing relationship, a counseling relationship, a decision-making relationship, or a problem-solving relationship.

SKILLS

There are discrete and practical techniques for legal counseling. We propose now to talk about three of these skills: active listening; an awareness of non-verbal communication; the effective use of questions.

Active Listening

Calvin Shrag, the existentialist philosopher, suggests that our everyday lives in coffee shops, living rooms, and at cocktail parties prepare us poorly for the business of hearing what clients say. "Talk," he says, "is a degenerate form of communication which merely expresses the accepted, average, everyday interpretations of the public. No real content is communicated, and nothing is genuinely understood. All attention is focused on the talking itself, which always uses the conventional cliches." The point is related, in Shrag's thinking, to a moral imperative he borrows from Kierkegaard: "The majority of men are subjective towards themselves and objective toward all others, terribly objective sometimes—but the real task is in fact to be objective towards oneself and subjective toward all others."

This is useful philosophy, but reducing it to a skill or a technique is not simple. As Schrag implied, to be active may be not to listen. But as Annette Garrett said, "One who frequently interrupts to say what he would have done ... is not a good listener [but] ... neither is he who sits like a bump on a log. Absence of response may easily seem ... to reflect absence of interest." She goes on to say:

Even when our primary interest in a given interview is to obtain the answers to a set of questions, we can profit much from letting the client talk rather freely at first.... [This] tends to counteract any preconceived ideas about him which the interviewer may have allowed himself to entertain. It gives the interviewer the immense advantage of being able to see the situation and the client's problem from the client's point of view.

Active listening is a way to avoid both interruption and being a bump on a log. Active listening is more than listening for facts. Fact gathering is only one aspect of listening to a client. The kind of active listening we have in mind is that of listening to the *situation.* It is a listening that involves the other senses, as in "seeing" through a surface of words, watching for clues and signs about what is really being said. Listening is not so much a matter of being quiet and passive, letting another speak, as it is an active engagement with the person as he speaks. Active listening is *imaginative* listening. An active listener is able to hear what is being said and is able to place himself in the world that he hears (and imagines) being described. An active listener is empathic; he tries to understand what the client is feeling *and* to communicate what he understands to the client.

Active listening is, then, in the deepest sense, listening to what is really being said. Each of us can remember attempting to say more than what we have managed to say in words—saying more than would have been reflected, for example, in a transcript of what we've tried to say. We usually depend on those who hear us to realize what we are saying—*all* that we are saying—and to supply what is not in the words themselves. Active listening is listening for meaning and for feeling, as well as for words. It is a skill, a technique, and an art.

One way we see the meaning in words and the feeling behind them is to listen to the story the client is telling. (See Chapter Two). Clients tell stories with words, stories that have plots. The plot in a client's story is often complex, twisted, sometimes perverse, but it is a plot. The meaning of a story is embodied in the plot, as well as in the words and the facts from which the plot appears. Listening to the story, and to the plot in the client's story, is one way to engage in active listening.

The client's story is integral to what the client is saying and essential to the fact gathering that every lawyer does in talking and listening to a client. (See Chapter Five). A story shapes and defines expectations and experiences of the client and is the best clue to "seeing" what the client wants and needs, as well as what he or she asks you to do. When a client is saying one thing and meaning another, there is some element or aspect of his story that he does not himself fully understand. (None of us is fully aware, all of the time, of the whole story we are telling.)

Another way to practice active listening is paying attention to the relationship. Finding out what the client needs (which goes deeper than asking what she wants), what she means, and something of her story is not so much a matter of psychological technique or a theory of counseling as of the lawyer's determination to establish a relationship with the client based on a set of skills that include:

— knowing that communication takes place by means other than words (listening between the lines);

— looking for metaphors and images that capture the client's sense of self and world;

— seeing the client as a story;

— assessing the emotional involvement of the client in an idea, another person, a business, an object, an injury; and your own emotional involvements which support and conflict with the client's involvements;

— being aware of unrealistic expectations and fears (in yourself as well as your client);

— realizing that some relationships are neurotic (and pathological) and that neurotic ways of relating to others and the world around us are debilitating, depressing, and anxiety provoking.

Anthony Trollope's character Lucy Morris was a good listener. Here's what Trollope said about her: "She would always be saying a word or two [not a *question* or two], just to help you—the best word that could be spoken, and then again she would be hanging on your lips. There are listeners who show by their mode of listening that they listen as a duty—not because they are interested. Lucy Morris was not a dutiful listener. She would take up your

subject, whatever it was, and make it her own."
Here are some specific suggestions for lawyers who
want to become more like Lucy Morris:

— Manner and tone are most likely to convey a
desire to help if the lawyer is aware of her own
feelings and has decided to be a companion, or a
friend. It is almost impossible to over-emphasize
the value of self-awareness as a first step in
attempting to become aware of and useful to
other people. The world would be a better place,
and so would law offices, if more lawyers spent
more time at understanding themselves. The
principal dogmas of self-awareness for the legal
counselor might be stated as follows: (a) Counseling is a people skill, not a black-letter skill. (b)
The best way to learn about people is, as Socrates
said, to know myself. (c) The second best place to
learn about people—and a good place to learn
about myself—is you.

— Discovery of something the client is not
quite aware of is most likely to be accepted if the
discovery is explained with empathy rather than
with one-upmanship. Questions ("Isn't it true
that ... ?") are almost always a poor way to
express discovery. Requests for help ("Let me see
if I understand") are almost always a good way.

— Probing for no apparent reason usually
makes the client defensive and may cause him to
avoid telling you the things you need to know;
when probing is necessary, as it often is, it should

be accompanied by explanation and assent of the client.

— Expression of the interviewer's dilemma is likely to be more successful than interrogation. If I don't understand what the client has said, I am less threatening when I focus on my reception ("I don't understand") than when I focus on his inability to be articulate ("What do you mean?"). Questions tend to focus on the client's shortcomings; they can also imply that the interviewer is superior.

— Open-ended questions work better than "cross-examination" questions; good questions go after information and not after a score ("yes" or "no" is a score); "even if questions that imply an answer do not result in false answers, they tend to give the impression that the questioner is lacking in fundamental understanding of the situation," Garrett says. Extensive research demonstrates that cross-examination, which may be a good way to catch falsehoods in court, is the worst possible way to gather information.

— Let the client set the pace; if the interview goes too slowly for the client, he will become bored, if not angry; if the pace moves too fast for the client, he is likely to experience his own confusion as a rejection by the interviewer, which it usually is.

Questions

Questions serve lots of purposes, the least of which is to learn facts. Alfred Benjamin suggests that the average interviewer uses questions too readily and without considering alternative ways to gather information. "His questions seem to keep him afloat; take them away from him and he will sink." Questions, he says, confuse and interrupt the client; they are often impossible to answer; often the questioner doesn't even want an answer, and he doesn't listen when he gets an answer. "However," Benjamin says, "my greatest objection to the use of questions . . . lies deeper":

> If we begin . . . by asking questions and getting answers, asking more questions and getting more answers, we are setting up a pattern from which neither we nor surely the [client] will be able to extricate himself. By offering him no alternative we shall be teaching him that in this situation it is up to us to ask the questions and up to him to answer them. What is worse, having already become accustomed to this pattern from previous experience, he may readily adapt himself to it. . . . [H]e will perceive himself as an object, an object who answers when asked and otherwise keeps his mouth closed—and undoubtedly his mind and heart as well. By initiating the question-answer pattern we are telling the interviewee as plainly as if we put it into words that we are the authority, the boss, and that only we know what is important and relevant for him.

> [The] unstated assumption . . . [is] that the interviewee submits to this humiliating treatment only because he expects you to come up with a solution to his problem or because he feels that

this is the only way you have of helping him. As for you, the [lawyer], you have asked your questions and gotten your answers; now show your tricks. If you do not have the solution up your sleeve, if you cannot help after the long third degree, what right had you to ask? What are you good for?

In other words, questions, in addition to all of their other shortcomings, encourage dependence.

Benjamin raises a difficult issue for lawyers—and seems to set an almost impossible standard. He recognizes, though, that we sometimes have to ask questions. Ultimately, he says, we must learn to discipline ourselves with a few protective standards: (a) We should be aware of the fact that we are asking questions. (b) We should challenge the questions we are about to ask. (c) We should examine carefully the various sorts of questions available to us and the types of questions we personally tend to use. (d) We should consider alternatives to the asking of questions. (e) We should become sensitive to the questions the client is asking, whether he is asking them outright or not.

Benjamin's pet peeve is the "why" question: The word "why," he says, "connotes disapproval, displeasure. Thus when used by the [lawyer], it communicates that the [client] has done 'wrong' or behaved 'badly.' Even when that is not the meaning intended ... that is how the word will be understood. The effect ... will probably be negative, for he will ... have grown up in an environment in which 'why' implied blame and condemnation." The result, in Garrett's opinion: "Whenever the interviewee hears the word 'why' he feels the need to defend himself, to withdraw and avoid the situation, or to attack." Benjamin gives examples of the "why" questions we have all grown up with and learned to use—"Why did you get the floor muddy?" "Why did you break the dish?" "Why did you take my bike?" "Why did you do that?" "Why don't you listen?"

Listening to What Is Not Said: Non–Verbal Communication

Miguel de Unamuno, through his character St. Immanuel the Good, says, "We should concern ourselves less with what people are trying to tell us than with what they tell us without trying." We begin to listen non-verbally when we observe the way the client presents himself. Does he act as though he were visiting a doctor? Is he treating me the way he would treat a business colleague? Does he seem wary, as if talking to someone he does not trust? Garrett emphasizes the more obvious non-verbal clues—tenseness, rigid posture, clenched hands, facial expressions, as well as the things one can observe (dress, physical condition, gait) that signal something about the client's life. We suggest that an understanding of non-verbal behavior and communication involves both broad characterization and trained observation.

The psychological research on verbal behavior suggests that accurate non-verbal communication comes across more or less in wholes, not in parts. We give meaning to the non-verbal signals of others by broad, non-verbal impressions of our own. Some examples were suggested above: What is my client's stance toward me? Does he act as if he were here to see a mortician? A principal in school? His father? His friend? The best way to take account of non-verbal communication is to become more aware of one's own non-verbal presentations and the messages they may carry. What am I saying, for instance, when I put the client on one side of the desk and myself on the other, with all of the apparatus of lawyering and mastery on my side and a bare desk on his side? What am I saying when I write notes, my eyes focused on the notepad, while the client is talking, or, worse, when I'm talking? What would I say (and what would I feel) if I moved around to the other side of the desk? Or took off my coat? Or threw the yellow pad away? What would happen if I interviewed my client at some place other than my office? (See Chapter Five, on Kinsey's interviewing practices).

THINGS TO LOOK FOR (AND DO) IN LEGAL COUNSELING

Open and Closing Sentences

First words may tell most about the client's agenda in the interview; and last words may tell most about the way he feels about his relationship with the lawyer.

Shifts in Conversation

These are probably defensive; they occur in client and lawyer statements and behaviors. That is, one wants to listen for them from the client and also to listen for them from oneself. An example is the shift that occurs when the client has touched on something he doesn't want to talk about any more (in which case, assuming the topic is relevant, it may be best to make the observation to him). Lawyers use shifts to avoid pain, even when pursuit of the topic is both germane to the discovery of facts and is something the client is willing to do. Consider the exchange between Ann Landers and one of her readers:

"My mother ... talks of nothing but sickness and death. Her favorite topic is friends who have cancer. She goes into great detail about how they are suffering. If there was surgery, she knows all about it.

"Grandma is only 52 and in good health but she takes pills for menopause as well as tranquilizers and aspirin. She invites the children to watch her take her medicine and makes a big production of it.

"I have told Mother that morbid talk is unhealthy for children. She pays no attention. It's the same story every time we go over there. What should be done about this?

Troubled."

"Dear T:

"Whenever Grandma starts to talk about illness or death, change the subject to something cheerful and happy. If she returns to the gloom-and-doom recitals, cut in and say, 'Your sad stories spoil our visit, Mother....'

"In other words, get control of the conversation and don't let go."

That is great advice for everybody but Mother; it ignores her needs and feelings. Lawyers should be more sensitive to that fact than Troubled would have been if she had followed Ann Landers' advice.

Themes, Recurrent References

A man's references to his wife, in an interview about the purchase of real estate, may tell the interviewer that the state of the client's marriage is a central concern in making the investment. "Talking in circles" may tell the interviewer that, for some reason, the client may not want to get down to the business at hand. Examples occur frequently in will interviews possibly because people don't like to talk about death, or because lawyers think they don't. Maybe it's true that the client does not want to talk about his death or his wife becoming a widow or his children becoming orphans; maybe he wants the lawyer to lead him into those subjects.

Inconsistencies and Gaps

Contradiction may indicate that the client is experiencing troublesome feelings about the subject being discussed—guilt, maybe, or confusion, or ambivalence. What is left out or expressed inconsistently is probably what is most important to the client. Garrett says: "A woman may discuss in great detail certain difficulties she has been having with the children but say nothing about her husband. The significance of such gaps or inconsistencies often becomes clearer through their cumulative force. One such occurrence may suggest a barely possible interpretation. But if ten others confirm this hypothesis, it is no longer a mere possibility."

Association of Ideas

Part of noticing how clients go from one subject to another is a matter of gathering information and part of it is a matter of avoiding interference. The interference part of idea association is a matter of the lawyer's being aware of *his own* associations. "[W]hen the client mentions ... lying, divorce, a grandmother, there may be started in the [lawyer] a stream of association which has little to do with the client's feelings about these things," Garrett says.

Concealed Meaning

A boy who says he doesn't like girls may be saying that he is suffering from a lack of girlfriends; a businessman who protests that he only "wants to do the right thing" in litigation may feel guilty because he wants to do the wrong thing.

FEEDBACK

Modern psychology borrowed from electrical engineering the term "feedback" to describe conversation that is reflective, person-centered, and, often, a bit hard to take. "Feedback" in counseling depends on honesty, even when honesty hurts. We avoid feedback because we avoid hurt. Yet, feedback and hurt are essential, or at any rate inevitable, in the stages of the lawyer-client relationship that we have called choice and decision. It sometimes comes up in interviewing (as, for example, when the client is wandering off the subject or seems seriously unrealistic or is not seeing facts that are apparent to the lawyer).

A good law office climate for tough choices needs a lawyer who will level with the client about what the client is deciding and doing, without adding to the client's feeling that he is stupid or bad or both. Carl Rogers reminded us, that, "[i]n almost every phase of our lives—at home, at school, at work—we find ourselves under the rewards and punishments of external judgments."

The counseling literature suggests these skills for effective non-judgmental feedback:

Feedback Should Describe, Not Evaluate. The client should be free to use feedback or not use it, as the client sees fit. If one pursued that idea in law practice she might decide finally that the traditional ideal of lawyer independence is overblown, or at least misapplied.

Feedback Is Specific. "John, you're trying to control the situation" may be a true observation, but it is less likely to be acted upon than "John, just now when you and I were discussing that lease, I had the feeling you were not listening to me. I had the feeling, just then, that you wanted me to agree with you, regardless of what I thought."

Feedback Is Directed Toward Behavior the Client Can Change. It won't do any client anything but injury to tell him that he is inept, stupid, or evil. What is usually involved when a "helping person" takes that tack, of course, is misdirected aggression on the part of the helper. Destructive feedback usually follows from lack of perception and unchecked assumptions. The client who is perceived as impotent because he is old or inept may simply be coming across that way. He may, out of some need of his own, be trying to appear old and inept; that may be his manipulative device ("poor little me"). If that is so, and the lawyer's perception is accurate, it may do the client a world of good to have the benefit of the perception. The challenge is to give it to him without appearing judgmental.

Feedback Is Best When Solicited. Not all law office situations imply a desire in the client for honest reaction—but many do—and the best feedback comes to him who wants it and says so. Another and more helpful way to put the point is that the most useful reaction is in terms of a question the client asks. It often takes courage to answer questions such as "Do you think I'm being selfish?" or "Does it seem to you that I'm fooling myself about the matter?" or "Do I seem to you to be vindictive?" The trick is to have the courage to deal with that sort of question honestly (we rarely do), to deal with it in a way which leaves the client free to act, and to help him without making him dependent on his counselor.

Feedback Is Well–Timed. The time to answer interpersonal questions (such as those above) is when they are asked. That's when the counselor's reaction is most honest. Delay encourages evasion or judgmental evaluation.

Feedback Is Checked. An honest reaction, based on an immediate perception, may for all its candor be wrong. One way to find out, to keep personal channels of communication intact, and to guard against evaluative feedback, is to ask if the perception seems right to the client: "Yes, I have a feeling that you are being vindictive. Does it seem that way to you, too?"

* * *

Feedback is a skill and an art. The goal of good feedback to a client is to show him the consequences of what he is doing and provoke questions about how what he is doing affects getting what he wants or needs (considering that wants and needs do not always coincide). The obstacles to tough choices may not be seen or considered by the client. The idea is to help him gear his behavior toward securing his goals and needs. The trick is to help him without judging him. And it is hard for lawyers to be non-evaluative; lawyers are moralists because the law itself is a form of moral order. Lawyer counselors know that it is our moral perceptions that bring us to law school, and law school—with its dark labyrinths of fault, malice, harm, breach of promise, good faith, and dogs who know the difference between being tripped over and being kicked—reinforces our tendencies to pass judgment. Those tendencies can do more harm than good in law office practice.

We prepare ourselves for the art of feedback when we question ourselves as we set out to enter the world of another person, when we take on (with the consent of a client) the role of helper. The questions are, inevitably, probing and personal. But then, counseling is a personal enterprise. Here are some questions posed by Carl Rogers (modified for our use here) that bear on our readiness to question ourselves:

— Can I proceed with this client in a way that will be perceived as trustworthy, dependable and helpful?

— Can I be expressive enough that who I am as a person will be perceived unambiguously?

— Can I let myself experience warmth, caring, interest, and respect for my client?

— Can I be strong enough to be separate, and am I strong enough to allow the client to be separate, to be who he is?

— Can I see things as he sees them, and accept him as he is?

— Can I be sensitive enough and accepting enough that my behavior will somehow free this client from the burden of external evaluation?

— Can we meet, in doing the work we're doing, so that neither I or the client, need to be overly bound by our roles, and our past?

INTERVENTIONS

At the everyday and most visible level, interventions consist of observations to the client, legal advice, answering questions about law, or pointing out options. Here are some illustrative types of intervention in decision-making:

Discrepancy

This intervention calls attention to a contradiction in action or in attitudes. It is useful in systems (corporations, business groups) for keeping the organization on the course it has chosen. It is a matter of reminding the client of the client's hard choices, keeping an individual client's decisions in line with his choices.

Example: Wilma Brown chose in her will to leave her property in trust for her husband. She chose to do this in such a way that her husband would have maximum access to the funds, with professional management. The present question is whether Mr. Brown is to enjoy a power to reach up to $100,000 per calendar year from the principal of the trust fund (a common provision, suggested by tax considerations). Mrs. Brown says, "No, I think not."

Example: Acme Corporation was advised by you that it had only minimum compliance duties under federal law on equal employment opportunity, but its officers, in counseling sessions with you, decided to integrate fully its manufacturing plants—to go, that is, beyond what the law requires. The issue now is whether to also integrate employee bowling teams. The plant manager says, "Do we have to do that?"

Psychological Theory

A theoretical intervention occurs when the counselor draws on theory to make a connection between an assumption and observable present behavior. In addition, theory can sometimes be useful in predicting the consequences likely to follow from embarking on a course of action.

Example: Ralph Walker insists that his lawyer in a divorce action: (a) seek custody of the children, and, (b) seek to deny to his wife visitation rights or the temporary custody of the children for vacations. But he does not appear to believe that his wife is a bad influence on his children. He appears to believe that she was and is a good mother.

Example: Mr. Knox, a rigid patriarchal figure in his family, wants his will to distribute his property among his three adult children. However, his youngest son married against his father's wishes and is in an occupation which his father disapproves. Mr. Knox wants his son's "share" of the estate placed in a tight "spendthrift" trust and parceled out to him over his entire life, with a prohibition on distribution to or for the benefit of his son's wife. The probable size of the trust is so small that half of current income each year will be taken in trustee fees.

Procedure and Consequences

The client may not understand the cause-and-effect relationship in what he proposes to do. He may benefit from an intervention that puts events in sequence and relates them logically. This is an insight at which lawyers are particularly adept.

Example: Mr. Baxter is terrified of criminal prosecution for making false statements in his federal income-tax return. These statements amount to a failure to disclose $5,000 in income on which the tax would be $1,150. He has not been contacted by the Internal Revenue Service. (Note here the difference between a procedural intervention and acceptance of Mr. Baxter's feelings, however illogical they are.)

Example: Roger and Sharon Luke have three children, ages one, five, and seven. The Lukes are in your office to make their wills and have decided on a contingent trust for the children if both parents die before all of the children are reared. They wish to have all their assets—$44,000 in physical assets and $100,000 in life insurance—held for the college education of the children.

Relationship

Relationship interventions focus the attention of clients on issues that arise among people as they work together. (We have referred to these aspects of the relationship as process.) They are needed to understand and reduce or eliminate interpersonal frictions. The lawyer here seeks to focus attention on personal feelings, especially on negative tensions that hinder mutual efforts to bring about a desired end. She acts from a belief that emotions can be examined and resolved. Everyone has been in a meeting—of directors, or business associates, or spouses—in which bickering and disagreement over apparent issues seem to obscure something else. What is being said and talked about (the agenda on the table) is not what is really at stake. Maybe there is a hidden agenda being worked out—rivalry, struggle over leadership, or resentment over events outside the room. The best evidence from behavioral science is that these struggles will prevent productive consensus, negotiation, and bargaining. The evidence also indicates that a third-party consultant's best move (and the lawyer's best move) may be to point out what she sees and senses. This is a matter of focus on the process, rather than on the content, of what is being done. This intervention does not guess at causes, or pass judgment, or attempt to read minds; it reports what the counselor sees. (See this chapter on "feedback" skills.)

Example: In a discussion of the terms of a loan agreement, among business associates in the borrowing organization, not even the most minor matters can be settled. What would happen if the lawyer said: "We seem to be bogged down here, unable to move. I can't understand the bickering—say, when Henry complained about the wording of the repossession clause and George said, sort of heatedly I thought, 'I don't split infinitives.' I don't know what's going on here, but it is keeping us from getting the job done. I think we ought to talk about it."

Example: Susan March is the president of Medical Products, Inc., a small incorporated manufacturer of cotton balls. There are 12 investors in the company; six of them are on the board of directors and three of the remaining six are executive-level employees. Susan has been approached by George Passant, an agent for an undisclosed company that wants to acquire Medical Products. Susan wants to talk to you about the possible acquisition. She has not mentioned her visit with Passant to any of her business colleagues.

Experimentation

Experimentation permits testing and comparing two or more courses of action before a final decision is taken, particularly when the way to proceed has become bound by tradition or custom. This intervention says in effect that a person or organization should be open to new ideas without assurance in advance that the ideas are safe.

Example: A number of large, prosperous law firms were built on a willingness to take labor cases in the 1930s and 1940s as the National Labor Relations Act took hold, even though those cases teemed with the unfamiliar—governmental control of employment relationships, employee elections, and "trials" before administrative agencies.

Example: Smigel says of Wall Street lawyers (quoting Beryl Harold Levy): "They helped make possible the growth of corporations 'by both counsel and by invention of new forms of credit, financing and control.' The holding company was one such device. The collapsible corporation ... another. In fact, Levy finds, 'Our contemporary, credit-industrial economy of abundance could not have been fashioned without the brilliant imagination of the daring corporation lawyers of the 19th Century who forged one device after another to lead the way, pressing far beyond existing law.' " The credit here is well placed, no doubt, but one wonders whether these devices were developed without active contribution from business people, bankers, and investors.

Example: Arthur Getliffe wants to make a will which gives his house to his wife. His house is the only asset of significance he owns, but, if transferred by will, the house becomes subject to the probate process and possibly to inheritance taxes. Does Mr. Getliffe have any options?

Dilemma

A dilemma intervention seeks to identify a point at which choices are being made unwittingly or implicitly. It often helps the client re-examine her assumptions and search for alternatives other than those under consideration.

Example: Frank Giapetto has been coming in for legal help for years. The history of his small, sole-proprietor doll shop is the history of the growth of the corporate state. He has had problems with zoning regulations, fire codes, retail licensing, sales tax, income tax, city tax assessments on sidewalks, federal and state excise taxes, electrical code requirements, adequate sewer venting, garbage collection, and weeds growing in the alley. You are able to deal with these problems as they come along—for a fee—but the price of Mr. Giapetto's dolls is already twice that of comparable, mass-produced competitors' products, and he is losing money. The issue is whether he should mortgage his shop to pay current property taxes.

Example: Sharon and Roger Luke in making their wills say that they want to talk to you about whether they should make their minor children contingent beneficiaries of Mr. Luke's life insurance or make Mrs. Luke's parents the beneficiaries, since her parents will care for the children if both Roger and Sharon die in the near future.

Example: Beth Simon's husband left town last week, without telling her. She is running out of money and the house payment is due. She says she came in to talk to you about a divorce, but in a previous session last week, when you first talked to her, she said she does not want her marriage dissolved.

Perspective

Individuals and organizations lose their sense of direction. When that happens, it is difficult to reestablish a course of action that moves the client away from momentary problem-solving toward larger issues. A perspective intervention permits present actions to be evaluated by providing a background of broader historical orientation.

Example: A common source of strain between students and teachers is that the history of one group is very short and the history of the other is generational. This is not a matter of "generation-gap" or of tradition. It is an instance of the fact that a person interprets the world from his own experience. "The past is not dead," Faulkner's lawyer, Gavin Stevens, said. "It's not even past."

Example: One of our legal counseling students said, "For me, awareness of the fact that most lawyers see themselves as dealing with problems, and not with clients or people, came this past summer while I was clerking for a plaintiffs' personal-injury firm. Initially, it came as a surprise to me that a law firm rejoiced in the gravity of their client's injuries when liability against the defendant was clear. This was especially true when pain and suffering was involved. The same sort of thing must be true of other kinds of practice. I wonder if business or corporate clients can visualize themselves as human beings being counseled on corporate matters or whether they feel like part of the cog in the corporate machine."

Structure

The structure within which clients function—familial, organizational, even personal—may need to be examined. The client's habits may prevent communication, decision-making, and the application of effort from being as effective as it might be if habits were changed. It may be necessary to confront the client and the framework (perspective) that he brings to the law-office. "Most human institutions," William James said, "by the purely technical and professional manner in which they come to be administered, end by becoming obstacles to the very purposes which their founders had in view."

Example: The managing partner in your law firm cannot understand why decisions on secretarial personnel are uniformly ill-advised. He believes lawyers who solve other people's problems should be able to solve their own. Personnel decisions in the firm are made by a committee of three lawyers; the managing partner, who is chairman, always calls these committee meetings for 5:30 p.m. on Friday, because the office is quiet at that time.

Example: An expert on job enrichment reduced tardiness, absenteeism, and other dissatisfaction among loan officers in a branch bank after the expert noticed that the entrance to the officers' area was opposite the desk of the vice-president in charge of loans. The result was that customers came first to the vice-president and then were assigned to loan officers. The expert moved the door to the other end of the officers' area and put an opaque partition between the vice president and the loan officers. After that, customers came directly to the loan officers and no one consulted the vice president except in problem cases. (See diagrams in Chapter Eight).

Culture

A cultural intervention examines traditions, precedents and established practices. Challenging culture is difficult because culture permeates actions and is salient in them. But the intervention most needed may be one that will bring culture into the area of deliberate decision-making.

Example: Miguel de Unamuno's character Antonia (in *Abel Sanchez*) "did not need to be shown anything, for she was a woman who had been born to live in the sweetness of custom."

Example: Atticus Finch, the lawyer-hero in Harper Lee's *To Kill a Mockingbird,* practices law in Maycomb, Alabama. Harper Lee tells the reader that Atticus is "Maycomb County born and bred" and we learn in the story that she tells about Atticus and his children the possibilities and pathologies in being a part of rural southern, small-town culture. When Gregory Peck came later to portray Atticus, in the movie version of the story, he said he understood Atticus because he (Peck) grew up in a small town in California.

Example: In Faulkner's *Intruder in the Dust,* a small-town, white, Mississippi lawyer successfully defends an old, rural, black man who is accused of murder. The defense is difficult and time-consuming. The lawyer, Gavin Stevens, spent weeks doing little else. At the end of the novel, the old man comes to the lawyer's office and asks, "How much do I owe you?" Stevens says, "Three dollars." The client pays him in full.

Logic

Every system and individual acts according to a logic. Some behavioral observers distinguish between a logic inherent in the activity (*e.g.,* the logic of business is profit; the logic of marriage is mutual support, or the rearing of children, or both) and an operating logic (*e.g.,* the logic of a particular business decision may be public responsibility or the preservation of tradition; the logic of a client's behavior in his marriage may be punishment or escape). An intervention that identifies the logic at work may help open up client options. This is often another instance of attending to process as much as content (see Chapter Four).

Example: Mrs. Baldwin says she has a lover and no longer cares for her husband. She asks, "Do you think I should divorce him?" You tell her what is involved in a divorce but she persists: "Do you think I should divorce him?"

Example: Mr. Van Cleve, one of several legatees under the will of his late and wealthy father, notes that his father disinherited one daughter, Mr. Van Cleve's sister, Agatha. Some members of the family feel that the fair thing to do is to pool a fund and give Agatha a share. Others feel that the right thing to do is to follow the wishes of the testator.

Solution–Seeking

Some decisions may be bogged down simply because they are being deliberated too much. It may be appropriate for the counselor to crystalize a decision which seems to him apparent but not yet expressed and to move from decision-making to problem-solving.

Example: Roger Harris represents a young man, Bennett Wilson, who has risen quickly within the ranks of one of the aggressive savings and loan associations. Harris is charged in a criminal indictment with violations of the state banking and securities laws. One of the difficult decisions in preparation for trial is whether Wilson will take the stand and testify.

Morals

Decisions may be impaired because of a moral conflict—a conflict among clients, between a client and some absent person, or between the client and her lawyer. Describing the moral issues would then be an appropriate intervention. (See Chapter Ten).

CHAPTER EIGHT

PLACE, SPACE, AND TERRITORY

PLACE

The physical setting in which interviewing and counseling take place is usually of the lawyer's choosing. Traditionally, it has been an atmosphere of tacit intimidation. She is barricaded behind an imposing desk, seated in an imposing executive chair. If the physical setting is changed, so that—for example—the lawyer and client sit as equals at a table, or in a living-room atmosphere, it is the lawyer who chooses the change. It is the lawyer who decides on the alignment of physical objects in the room; the distance between her and her client; and how vocally and visually available the two people are to one another. It is the lawyer who decides whether the lines of communication (speech and non-verbal communication) are open or closed, formal or informal, loud or soft, vulgar or elegant.

An alternative to lawyer domination of the physical situation would be to meet in the client's home or office, or in neutral territory, such as a hotel suite or a bank conference room. But even there the lawyer is usually the person who decides whether to meet on other turf. For equality in the matter, she would have to negotiate with the client whether there was to be a change of setting and if so where the new setting was to be. This sort of negotiation on physical setting is common in the literature of romantic love ("my place or yours?") and of diplomacy (seating arrangements at summit meetings and the shape of the table in peace talks); it is not common in American professional practice.

Domination is reduced and communication is usually improved when lawyer and client meet in the client's place. That law students are not trained to consider such a simple alternative is reflected in the behavior of students in a National Client Counseling Competition that had as its theme consultations with clients for business planning. The interview problems involved business people seeing a lawyer for legal help. Some of the problems were of the "should I incorporate?" genre; others involved movement into new, regulated areas of business activity; some involved buy-sell agreements and insurance funding for them. In each case the dynamics of the client's business life turned on *the presence of a place*—his office or plant, his relationship there with associates and employees, what he did there with his time, where and when he hoped and where and when he was tempted to despair. But in no case—not once—did these law-student interviewers say to the client (what seemed the most obvious, logical human thing to say): "Let's meet at your place." The time, the place, the chronology and pattern of activity, the interpersonal environment of these interviews were all the lawyers'. The place that was present was the wrong place, at the wrong time. When judges in the competition talked to practicing lawyers about this observation, the practitioners agreed that leaving the law office would have been a good idea. Many of them indicated that they did so routinely in similar situations. The image of a businessperson's lawyer leaving a book-lined office and meeting the client in the client's world, changes in a fundamental way the situation in which the lawyer and the client's work is to be done.

A REFLECTIVE EXERCISE: A SENSE OF PLACE

Plan a visit to a law office. Many law students do not see the inside of a law office until they are invited to one for an employment interview. The points we make in this chapter are best demonstrated from inside a lawyer's office. For this Exercise, schedule an interview with a lawyer, in his or her office. Tell the lawyer that you are interested in the physical arrangement of lawyers' offices and how law office ecology affects the interaction between lawyer and client. Write a report of what you learn by entering the lawyer's territory.

ASPECTS OF THE PRESENCE
OF PLACE

Formality. Tables or desks between people serve as barriers (or, in a more neutral phrase, creators of distance); they tend to produce more formal behavior.

Posture and Body Language. Studies show that strangers or casually acquainted people deal with one another less openly when they are, as the Newfoundlanders say, "side by each." That is, each presents a bodily profile to the other and turns his head when he wants to interact face to face. When people sit fully facing one another the atmosphere is more confrontive, more risky, but also probably more productive. People choose to sit facing one another because they want to confront one another, or at least because the more dominant of them wants to confront the less dominant. The confrontation can be scaled down, though, by increasing the distance between chairs or by putting a desk or table—a low coffee table—between them.

Distance. Given some minimum distance (some respect for the "critical space" of the other person), research indicates that distortion in communication varies directly with the amount of distance between the communicators. Distance also tends to indicate animosity or issues between two people, as it indicates issues of participation and membership when one of several people sits apart from the rest of a group.

Importance of Status. If status and feelings of superiority or inferiority are on the minds of the lawyer and his client, more attention is likely to be paid to increasing or decreasing tacit and physical dominance. If the lawyer is conscious of the fact that his client is of another race, for example, or of a different economic, age, or social group, he is more likely to take care that the furniture, and his posture, and other environmental aspects of the interview are consciously arranged to say what he wants to say. Arthur Train's lawyer, Mr. Tutt, obviously reserved the client chair, from which he had sawed an inch off the front legs, for particular clients.

Two-way Communication. There is always an issue in the air on whether intended or unconscious signals are received and understood by the client. What was meant to be equalization may be received as condescending or patronizing. What was meant to be a gesture of homage may be perceived as manipulation.

TIME

The temporal setting is, at one boundary, an appointment time, and, at the other, a deadline and expectation for the future. Lawyers usually—but not always—control both ends. A common modification is to leave it up to a lawyer's secretary to negotiate an appointment time. Having one's secretary set appointments can, depending on the way the secretary acts (or is told to act), say to the client either that the lawyer cares about the client's time or that the lawyer is far too busy to bother with the issue of the client's time.

The deadline issue is the question of when the meeting is to end. This can be announced or negotiated in advance, in which case the intimidation at work will be largely a function of the openness with which the lawyer considers the client's convenience. It can also be kept hidden, so that the lawyer establishes his dominance by being the one who can say, at any moment, "Time's up." Variants include noticeable glances at one's wrist watch and prearranged announcements that it is time for the next client, or for lunch, or for an appearance in court. All of these devices may have a legitimate purpose in terms of the lawyer's busy life. That is their content. They also serve as opportunities to demonstrate to the client that he, as a person, is important. That is their process message.

Deadlines, even where agreed upon, have a number of effects on the meeting. If the deadline is perceived as distant, for instance, the research indicates that the lawyer and client will be likely to relax and may even neglect the business at hand. If it is perceived as a threat, the deadline will increase anxiety, which may in turn cause the client (and, less often, the lawyer) to make hasty concessions, give simplified information, or agree to interpretations that are not accurate. A somewhat more subtle aspect of the temporal issue is its effect on the future relationship. The impact of temporal control will be different depending on: (1) whether the client's business with the lawyer is a single transaction; (2) whether the client is an established client; (3) whether she is someone the lawyer would like to work for again; (4) whether the meeting is part of a series of meetings. People act differently when they know they must depend on one another in the future. Research indicates that one-time relationships encourage the parties to exploit one another and are more likely to foster a fear of exploitation. These facts show up in institutional habits in law firms: Law firms will often let clients who are regarded as having slight significance, or who are coming to the office only once, wait for long periods of time; but let a junior associate ignore important, established business clients in the waiting room (or on the telephone) and "the Firm" will take notice, in one way or another.

DEPENDENCE

The "presence of place" may engender dependence and powerlessness in the client. There are advantages and disadvantages in dealing with powerless clients. One disadvantage is that powerless people tend to become lethargic, participate less, and their resources for the solution of problems and for creative decision-making tend to be devalued. Consider these physical factors in terms of ecology, purpose, arrangement of people, and territoriality:

Ecology

One of Ann Landers' correspondents said she was afraid that her concern for order would make her children neurotic. "I was raised in a house where the rule was, 'a place for everything and everything in its place.' Mother taught us that when your surroundings are cluttered your mind is cluttered. I know this is true because I am at my calmest and happiest when my home, closets, and shelves are in perfect order. In other words, my emotional condition is directly connected to the condition of my home."

This mother was concerned about the effect of order on others, a sensitivity not always manifest in discussions of law-office design. Some ecological factors are obvious and affect everyone in the same way. The pollution by noise—clamor, racket from machines—and clutter are obvious examples. So are ventilation, light, temperature, and humidity. Our environment contributes to fatigue, boredom, dissatisfaction, and illness. The client will have adverse reactions to an unpleasant place. She may quit and leave, or she may quit and stay, which is worse. Ecology has effects on behavior which may not be conscious. Here is the way a welfare client experienced the welfare office:

> You have to sit there for hours waiting, waiting, while the welfare "workers" drink coffee and talk and laugh together—and pointedly ignore you. The waiting room there was very warm in the winter, but I noticed that the people who came in never took off their coats. Some of them were young men who had always supported themselves but now just couldn't find work. They were so humiliated by necessity that they sat there

clutching their coats to them, as if they were protection against the cold, unfeeling system. Anyway, the experience ... made us a lot more radical than we had ever dreamed we could be.

An example we discussed in Chapter Seven involved work by an organizational development consultant for a bank. The consultant was called in because the turnover and absentee rate among junior loan officers disturbed the bank's management. He made only one change in the bank's system for treating juniors, an entirely physical (non-verbal) change that solved the bank's problem. When he came to the bank, the four juniors and the senior officer in charge of them were arranged this way:

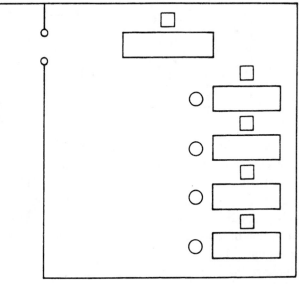

[B2827]

When he left the bank, a partition had been erected and the gate in the barrier between the open area in the bank and the interview area had been changed, like this:

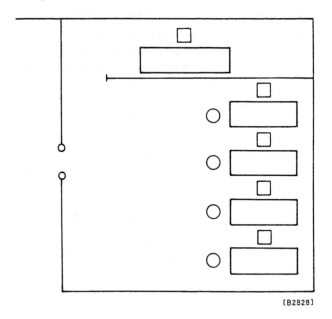

[B2828]

Before the change, no one had established a rule that customers report first to the senior officer, for assignment to junior officers. But that is what customers did. After the change, no one announced a different rule, but the customers then went directly to junior officers, as junior officers were evidently available. The physical change—without a word—changed the political structure in the bank from a supervised system to a system in which officer and client contacted one another without supervisory direction. It resulted in less absenteeism and less turnover.

Purpose

Steele notes that the presence or sense of physical environment (what we have called place) serves four purposes in the lives of those who work (and live) in a particular place. The first of these is instrumental: certain directions are, he says, "received from the physical environment." The branch-bank case illustrates that point, as does the fact that some places are more relaxing than others because they are quiet, or cordial (well lighted, say, or arranged so that the tools needed for work are easily available). Instrumental purposes may also be political: "Nothing can tell more quickly about the impersonality of an organization than seeing an area where there is very little individual influence on the space (decorations, markings, personal items, or private sense of personal space)." He mentions a new office building that featured glass interior walls and movable curtains, so that people in the office could have "a large degree of choice ... about whether they wanted an open view or a closed, private sense of personal space, and that this could be changed as they felt appropriate." But, he says, there developed a norm in the organization. The new norm said, "Anyone with nothing to hide will leave his drapes open." That norm destroyed the flexibility and the democracy of the architect's idea. The organization was stern and hierarchical, so determined to be impersonal that the architect's subtle effort to make office space more inhabitable did not take root there.

A second purpose of place is symbolic. Because of a fraternal tradition, lawyers are more subtle about rank within firms than business people are. Each lawyer's place symbolizes status. In most firms, senior lawyers have the offices at the corners of the building. These are the larger offices, and they have multiple windows, including windows on two sides. The least senior have offices with no windows at all, although this symbolic hierarchy is sometimes muted by making the interior offices larger than the offices on the outside of the building. This is a bit like the Bob Newhart sketch in which he finds his office chair moved to a telephone booth, and says, "They're trying to tell me something." Much of the symbolism of the place is subtle to the senses and blatant to the psyche. Distance is an example. It makes a difference in interviewing whether the client and lawyer sit across the room from one another, across the desk from one another, or so close to one another that they occasionally touch.

A third purpose of place is pleasure. Frank Lloyd Wright's architecture attempted to give people in a building the feeling that the natural environment outside the building was accessible to them. Considerations of pleasure cause lawyers to buy comfortable chairs for themselves and, maybe, for their clients. Disregard of pleasure causes an office to feel stifling or oppressive; for instance, a law-office waiting room which contains cast-off reading material that the lawyer no longer wants to retain rather than something the client would enjoy reading.

A fourth purpose of physical climate is to encourage the growth away from dependence of the people who inhabit the place (Steele):

An environment may ... be a force ... for learning about self, for stimulation to experimentation, and the like. It may also be neutral or negative, that is, stagnating rather than growth-producing. A space that demands that a person be aware of who he is and how he is using the space can be a positive force for growth. One that requires no consciousness to use it, such as a totally comfortable suburban house with all decisions made and no choices required, is likely to be a force toward non-growth, since the user is not called upon to think about why he prefers one thing over another, what this says about him as a person, or to deal with changes which open new ways of doing things.

Such considerations seem to speak more to the lawyer than to the client, because it is the lawyer who lays out her office. The lawyer's decisions indicate whether she wants to grow toward her client, to be open to her client, and the extent to which she considers her client as a person.

It is possible to imagine a law office in which the *client* is invited to think about "how he is using the space," is "called upon to think about why he prefers one thing over another" (Steele). Suppose every piece of furniture in the room had wheels and the client was invited to arrange the furniture before he sat. Suppose the working space in the room was a plain table with identical chairs around it, and the client was asked to choose his chair.

We know lawyers who use such possibilities as fact-gathering devices: One of these lawyers meets her new clients in a conference room with a rectangular table and identical chairs, one of which is placed at the "head" of the table. This lawyer comes to the room after a secretary has shown the client or clients in and invited him, or them, to choose their places. This lawyer says she learns a lot about the unaccompanied client when the client takes the chair at the head of the table. If there is more than one client, she learns a lot about their relationship(s) by the way they put themselves around the table.

Arrangement of People

One aspect of the "personal climate" of a relationship is established not by persons or their interactions, but by physical seating arrangements and the distances we maintain from the people with whom we communicate. A lawyer aware of this can broaden his knowledge with his own experience and experimentation. Here are a few pointers:

— People who know one another well feel emotionally closer when they are seated next to each other, but people who are not well acquainted feel less close in that arrangement and closer (and perhaps more anxious) when seated face to face. Research indicates that groups of five people communicate better among themselves when seated in a circle, but that this arrangement tends to discourage the recognition of a leader for the group.

— People inject emotional distance into situations if circumstances place them too close together. We ignore other people in a crowded elevator, for instance. Or, for a more apposite instance, invasion of the "critical space" around a person causes him to feel anxious and less able to communicate. A lawyer who sits too close to his client may find that the client scoots back emotionally, even when the client does not move away physically. Experiments with group conversation indicate that five and one-half feet is the preferred distance between people, whether they are talking across from one another or side by side; less than that appears to risk invasion of personal space. However, most furniture in living rooms is spaced ten or eleven feet apart.

— Reactions to physical closeness vary according to the personalities of clients. "Introverts," for example, prefer more distance than "extroverts" do and, if they don't get distance, are likely to become anxious. People who feel anxious want to increase distance; people who feel comfortable (because they have been praised or feel they are accepted) want to get closer. Two women may operate more comfortably within critical distances than two men do.

— The way people place themselves may express issues of leadership. People who want to be leaders, and people with high social status, tend to take the end places at rectangular tables. In one experiment, jurors who occupied the end place at a table in the jury room tended to talk more than people who sat at the sides of the table. Another experiment compared the effect on pairs of leaders by first putting them at the opposite ends of a table and then placing one on the side and one at an end. Breaking up the pairs in this fashion tended to diminish the leadership of each member of the pair.

— A person tends to talk more freely, in business settings, to someone who is opposite him than to someone who is beside him. However, if the person opposite exercises more control of the situation than is comfortable, the tendency is to direct conversation toward a third person at one's side.

Territoriality

Territory resembles critical distance, or personal space, but is not the same. A lawyer is likely to regard all of his own office, and, probably, all of his firm's premises, as his territory, when the person he is dealing with is a client. And his client will likely honor the claim. But the lawyer's critical distance, his personal space, is unlikely to be greater than a circle around his body about ten feet in diameter. The client, who will not claim territory in the law office, will retain—and may expand—his own claim for personal space.

Several significant issues of law-office territoriality have been discussed in this chapter. Two points deserve emphasis: (1) The obvious fact that a lawyer's office is his place, that it, and his claims on it, say things about his personality to clients and, if he listens, to himself. A client's reaction to the lawyer's place may be as significant in their relationship as the client's reaction to the lawyer's person. (2) A person tends to act differently when he is in his own place than when he is in another's place; this difference tends to become greater if the place of the other is also a status-heavy place (as a lawyer's office is to most people).

CHAPTER NINE

SHARING AUTHORITY AND COLLABORATIVE DE-CISION MAKING

AN ARGUMENT FOR COLLABORATION

Many lawyers are instinctively skillful at collaboration with clients. And many are not. The best argument for collaboration in decisions is the lawyer who lives a people-centered life. Here is one glimpse, a literary one: C.P. Snow's novel, *Time of Hope,* is about the professional preparation for the Bar of the lawyer who is central in Snow's *Strangers and Brothers* series. Young Lewis Eliot has read for the Bar, passed his examinations (and passed them well), eaten the requisite number of dinners at his Inn, and he is well into his internship with a senior barrister. The scene involves a difficult trial for libel in which young Eliot has his first big chance. He has been engaged to represent one of the parties. He is on display before the solicitors who can make or break him, because it is through solicitors that a barrister receives his cases. It is a crucial moment in a lawyer's career.

Snow's point is subtle. Eliot does a good job—wins the case—and probably makes a fair mark with the discriminating solicitors. But in one tense instant in the trial he becomes convinced that he should not be a trial lawyer. The moment of truth occurs during a witness examination, when Eliot asks a question that does not bear on the case. It is a question that might have turned out badly for him. Because of that question Eliot decides that he was, in that instant, more interested in the person before him than he was in the facts of the case. He was more interested in the human connection, the skeletal personal relationship he had with the witness.

Eliot decides he is not cut out to be a trial lawyer because he is more interested in people than he is in courtroom competition. He forsakes analysis for one perilous moment and finds that he prefers— sees himself preferring—the pursuit of curiosity involved in understanding another human being. Moments of insight, of self-awareness, such as that experienced by Lewis Eliot, are integral to counseling. They are why we find an interpersonal approach to lawyering much more hopeful, much more inspiring somehow, than the instrumental approach that many lawyers, some law students, and most lay persons associate with our ancient, proud, contentious profession.

This literary insight applies both to hard-choice counseling and to collaborative decision-making. The disagreement about what constitutes the best law-office practice, can be analyzed in terms of what a counselor—any counselor—is supposed to be able to contribute to her client. When the agenda is choice the counselor is there to help the client who may be stymied, frustrated, confused, or too un-informed to make a decision. When the client can-not act, the counselor is there to provide the client with a new perspective on his options.

When the agenda is decision-making, the collabo-rative principle is that there are human, economic, and social advantages in involving people rather than mastering them. The enlistment of the client, in a serious and purposeful way in his own cause, and in collaborative strategy, is the topic of this chapter, which will: (a) pursue the initial issue of collaborative pay-off; then (b) consider specific strategies in collaboration (interventions); and fi-nally (c) discuss the issue of conflict.

IMAGINING THE CLIENT
AS RESOURCE

The image of a lawyer most common in law school is of a person who is sharp, objective, takes charge, proposes alternatives, and wins arguments. The ideal of a counselor, as counseling psychology puts it, is of someone who is accepting, understand-ing, and congruent. The two ideals are not entire-ly compatible. Lawyers have difficulty reconciling them. Maybe, as a result, we function poorly in relationships with clients. Let's consider the clash more specifically:

| *lawyers are:* | *counselors are:* |
| Conscious of facts (keep their eyes on the ball) | Perceptive (conscious of human facts) |

Conscious of relevance (only the key facts, please)

Empathic (experience what the client feels)

Comprehensive (leave no stone unturned; fully prepared)

Careful listeners (try not to miss what's in the room)

Foresightful (aware of consequences; plan ahead)

Resilient (recover quickly, stay in the room)

Verbally sophisticated (can say what they think)

Open (willing to express feelings)

Orally aggressive (win arguments)

Reflective (understand what is said)

Thorough (get the job done)

Accepting, caring (avoid letting the problem undermine being fully present)

Clients and nonlegal counselors are often skeptical about lawyers and even about the law (which can be insensitive, rigid, and unjust). Lawyers can be manipulative and overbearing. Lawyers who have a broader perspective on their craft sense that clients may view the law far different than they do. But a lawyer may also know that a client's negative feelings about the law (and lawyers) serve as screens for both personal projections and the collective projections we engage in as a society. A client has a tendency not to see himself in anything as demanding as the law and may therefore identify with a competent and self-assured lawyer. For some clients, the lawyer's world is so overwhelming that he becomes docile in the presence of a lawyer. But his docility may be a psychological evasion. It may be a way for him not to see the unbending and aggressive parts of himself. It is easier to see unappealing qualities in other people, in systems, or in law itself.

There is, then, confusion and tension on both sides of the lawyer-client relationship (as there can be in any significant human relationship): The lawyer, who is in fact and in aspiration both lawyer and counselor—who is a counselor at law—and the client who both seeks and suspects the order and oral aggression associated with lawyers. The great masters of 20th century psychology would, we think, see this situation not only as a matter of tension but as a meeting of resources.

The analytical psychology of C.G. Jung, for example, is a helpful way to understand the idea that *clients are resources*. Jung diverts attention from our modern penchant for focusing on roles rather than on people. (The client role is to be docile and receptive, the lawyer role is to be informative, helpful, and—traditionally—authoritative.) Jung shows that the client has it within himself to be informative, helpful, and authoritative and the lawyer has it within himself to be docile and receptive. If the conduct of the actors in a law office does not transgress the boundaries of role it is because the actors choose to confine themselves to their roles. The evidence suggests that role conformity produces poor working relationships and poor results for clients and, we think, for lawyers as well.

Respect for the client as a resource has first to take account of the fact that clients may have personal resistances to parts of—aspects of—themselves, as well as to lawyers. They may discount their own knowledge. They may, particularly, resist the abilities and tendencies they see, not in themselves, but in lawyers. And lawyers may resist some of the values and ideals they have put aside during the course of their professional training and in their efforts to become effective lawyers. There is a psychological reality in these resistances: The client in me is afraid of the lawyer in me, and vice versa. The lawyer is afraid to let himself be soft; the "client" is afraid to let himself be hard and demonstrate that he knows what he wants. We conspire together to avoid the strength that comes from working together.

Jung's theory of psychic function is that each of us operates on two spectrums. The first is a vertical spectrum that consists of thinking (the function that tells us what things are) and feeling (the function that tells us how things are to be experienced). The horizontal spectrum is based on sensation (the function that receives stimuli from the outside world—sights, sounds, smells) and intuition (the function that, as Jung put it, lets us see around corners):

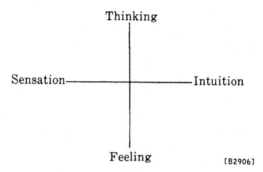

A person habitually operates more toward one end of each spectrum than the other, but she can learn to be comfortable toward the opposite (remote) function. She can learn to feel (*i.e.,* evaluate) more than is habitual for her; and she can learn to listen to her intuition as well as to immediate experience. Respect for these different functions within oneself, and for the measure of choice each of us has, on each spectrum, is a necessary first step toward respect for them in another person—a client, say.

The object, as we derive it from Jungian psychology, is to respect the client as a resource—to discover and to make use of the client's talents and abilities. But we suspect that lawyers will not seek help from clients until we are honest about our own competencies in the areas of feeling and intuition. And clients will not begin to respect the qualities a lawyer can bring to them until they begin to have respect for the rational, orderly, and manipulative side of themselves. In the absence of understanding there is a diminished respect for what the client is capable of figuring out for himself. It begins with a diminished respect for a lawyer's sense of herself that extends beyond practiced competencies.

In Jung's view of things, the client is a valuable resource because he tends to operate in psychological areas which the lawyer, out of training and habit, has learned to overlook in his own life. A person operates habitually at some point on each axis, and each person is able to operate at other points. The conventional lawyer *persona* puts a lawyer (by habit and choice) at the thinking end. A client with a troubling problem tends to operate at the feeling end. A whole person empowered with an awareness of and respect for his complete psyche can move or shift in recognition of these possibilities. When we see our own strengths, especially those strengths we do not habitually use, we are able to respect and to gain from somebody else whose habitual function is elsewhere on the scale. The heart of the idea is that there is a lawyer and a client in each of us.

SHARING AUTHORITY

Much of counseling is description and exploration of alternatives. The counseled person is often, in some sense, "hung up," unable to decide what to do or to get others to do what they should be doing. The lawyer is seen as the person who can help resolve the hang-up by some combination of information, associative thinking, and action. The client who seeks to move from hang-up to choice needs a counselor who can provide information and re-sources for that movement. Counseling skill is a proper balance of inquiry, information, and assurance that desired resolutions are possible. Lawyers may shy away from counseling and feel more comfortable with taking over (doing something, being in charge, solving problems). Taking over is not counseling; it may leave us feeling like we are real lawyers but it leaves us handicapped as counselors. Physicians, for example, are often criticized for providing too little information; lawyers are criticized for providing too much undigested information, but almost certainly for involving the client too little in the work to be done. We are less likely to leave the client in a state of ignorance than to lecture the client and leave him no room to make a choice that is his own.

One helpful distinction here is the distinction between tough personal choices and collaborative decisions. A client sometimes needs to decide what he wants. Sometimes he knows what he wants but needs to decide what to do. The difference is that a choice about *what one wants* calls for freedom (acceptance, concern, support), and a decision about *what to do* calls more for information, and for an active and collaborative counselor. The counselor has more openings for providing information, and even for giving his own opinions, when the issue is what to do. He has more openings for providing understanding, acceptance, and care, when the issue is what the client wants.

"Freedom" means leaving the client room to move. Many legal advisors smother their clients with advice, information, legal knowledge, and personal theories about how the world works. All counseling requires freedom; counseling when the client cannot decide what he wants requires a great deal of freedom. One way to look at freedom is in terms of counselor behavior, on a spectrum from telling people what they want to developing options for them (which involves organization of information), to the provision of a nonjudgmental, accepting climate (which often involves no information at all).

Client freedom is an attractive aspiration (who can be opposed to freedom?) but it is a troublesome principle. It is troublesome, first of all, because counselors argue about it a lot. There are good lawyers—that is, persons of both character and skill—who say, "A good lawyer takes charge and is in control. I would not have a client who didn't do what I told him to do," and there are physicians who take that view of their patients. Client freedom is troublesome, secondly, because the serious practice of freedom, of client self-determination, is in fact rare, regardless of the preferences we have expressed throughout this book.

Counselors Often Dominate Clients. The most common source of formal grievances against lawyers comes from the client's feeling that he doesn't know what his lawyer is doing, which is at least partly a failure to provide information. This failure seems to proceed from a conventional view of the lawyer as having knowledge and skill that makes

her an "authority." We suspect that a sense of
being an authority is easily translated into an interpersonal sense of *having* authority. The lawyer
adopts what looks to an outsider like a parental
attitude. Anthony Trollope writes of two such lawyers in *The Eustace Diamonds:* "The outside world
was a world of pretty, laughing, ignorant children;
and lawyers were the parents, guardians, pastors,
and masters by whom the children should be pro-
tected from the evils incident to their childishness."
A climate of acceptance and congruence in counseling relationships is rare. Douglas Rosenthal found
that clients of lawyers are not allowed to participate
in decisions on their automobile accident cases,
even though clients who do participate receive better financial results. A Missouri Bar Survey found
that lawyers believe their clients want domineering
parental relationships but that clients prefer friendly, open rapport with their lawyers.

Professional Disciplines Encourage Dependence.
Every professional has something to sell. Surgeons
are likely to want clients to decide on surgery.
Trial lawyers are likely to advise clients, "Sue the
bastards." Genetic counselors are inclined to advise
amniocentesis. Lawyers who know a lot about taxes believe that saving taxes is of central importance. One is inclined, always, to lead with her
strength, and, in these cases, part of the strength
is knowledge and a set of habits that the client
does not possess. Part of this—the habitual part—
is a set of official professional positions on what
clients should do. Witness the ebb and flow in

pediatrics on whether children should keep their tonsils; or the fact that it became much easier for real estate brokers to lend their skill to the racial desegregation of housing when their professional organizations (and the law) gave official disapproval to segregation. In the professions, there is a tension created when the professional tries to respond to a client as a person rather than a problem.

Professionals tend to stack the deck against client self-determination. In fact, they do it unconsciously. Clients come to professionals; professionals do not come to clients. The time and place of consultation is set by the professional, and he keeps the time clock. The space is his and is arranged to suit his tastes. Notice, for example, professional offices: The professional's chair is not only larger and behind a desk, with space on his side of the desk for legs, but it also swivels and tips back and has more padding. The professional sets the norm for proper dress, appropriate posture, access to refreshments, and level of seclusion. He decides as well how conversation is to be conducted (narrative, question-answer, cross-examination, or awkward silence).

The Tendency to Moralize. Lawyers tend to be moralistic, which makes it hard not to direct. There are even respectable professional voices which say we should be the consciences of our clients, that we should pronounce moral judgment on what they want and on how they seek what they want. The main argument against this pervasive moral evaluation of the client is that it denies the client's responsibility and forecloses the possibility that both client and lawyer may be able to learn from each other and grow together in a new adventure. As Carl Rogers says:

The major barrier to mutual interpersonal communication is our very natural tendency to judge, to evaluate, to approve or disapprove the statement of the other person. . . .

The stronger our feelings the more likely it is that there will be no mutual element in the communication. There will be just two ideas, two feelings, two judgments, missing each other in psychological space. I'm sure you recognize this from your own experience. When you have not been emotionally involved yourself, and have listened to a heated discussion, you often go away thinking, "Well, they actually weren't talking about the same thing." And they were not. Each was making a judgment, an evaluation, from his own frame of reference. There was really nothing which could be called communication in any genuine sense. This tendency to react to any emotionally meaningful statement by forming an evaluation of it from our own point of view, is, I repeat, the major barrier to interpersonal communication. . . .

Real communication occurs, and this evaluative tendency is avoided, when we listen with understanding. What does this mean? It means to see the expressed idea and attitude from the other person's point of view, to sense how it feels to him, to achieve his frame of reference in regard to the thing he is talking about.

Good counseling evolves from our respect for client self-determination. Freedom is a necessary condition for the decisions and choices that are the result of counseling. This means, at a minimum, that the lawyer is open to the conscience of the client, and respects it, and that the lawyer claims respect for his own conscience. But there is much more to client self-determination and a lawyer's moral concern than that. Counseling requires more than respect for the client's point of view. It requires, and depends on, the client as a resource—equally as valuable as the lawyer in many situations—for the resolution of the difficulty that is brought to the lawyer.

MORAL CONCERNS

Counseling, generally and in all of its vocational manifestations, involves both implicit and explicit morals. One traditional norm among American lawyers is that the client's interests come first. Another, less obvious, is that choices and decisions are for the client to make—at least in the final analysis. This client-decision norm was expressly stated in the Code of Professional Responsibility and is now found in the Model Rules of Professional Conduct for lawyers. It is implicit in the ethics of physicians, salespersons, and, usually, school counselors and pastors. It is essential (definitional) in counseling.

The ideal and the legal profession's guidelines for professional conduct are stated in the Model Rules of Professional Conduct, Rule 1.2(a):

A lawyer shall abide by a client's decisions concerning the objectives of representation ... and shall consult with the client as to the means by which they are to be pursued. A lawyer shall abide by a client's decision whether to accept an offer of settlement of a matter.

The general principle is clear, but client self-determination is, obviously, a complex subject. Our codified professional norms in fact represent *conflicting* ideals. The "comment" following Rule 1.2(a) makes the conflict explicit: "Both lawyer and client have authority and responsibility in the objectives and means of representation.... A clear distinction between objectives and means sometimes cannot be drawn, and in many cases the client-lawyer relationship partakes of a joint undertaking."

Client self-determination is a *principle* and a *goal* but the principle and the goal must be realized, constructed, negotiated within the context of a lawyer's effort to supply information based on experience, learning, and observation. Ethical rules place upon lawyers a duty to initiate a conversation with the client, about the need for the client to make choices and important decisions, to insist upon it, regardless, apparently, of how docile or uncommunicative the client is. Finally, our ethical rules notice (albeit timidly) that lawyers also have consciences. They affirm a freedom to withdraw from employment if the client seems to the lawyer to be wrong (Rule 1.16(6)(3)).

COLLABORATIVE PAY–OFF

The fact persists that many lawyers (and those apparently the most vocal) see themselves as telling their clients what to do. The assumption that a lawyer has to be domineering to be wise is perhaps the source of the querulous terror with which a young lawyer contemplates her professional life with clients. The domineering image tempts her to dread one of the greatest of life's adventures, the experience of companionship with another person, of walking in his shoes, and living in his world.

There is good authority—professional and empirical—for the point that it is better to be a companion than a domineering parent in our relationships with clients. The client benefits, materially and psychologically. We might begin to lay the ground-work to support these premises by considering Douglas Rosenthal's well-organized survey of lawyers and clients involved in automobile accident litigation in Manhattan. He assembled data from records, interviews with clients and lawyers, and from judgments made by a panel of expert trial lawyers. He then asked a series of questions about lawyering. These questions considered appropriate client behavior in the relationship, the quality of professional service and methods for judging quality, processes of decision in the law office, accessibility to lay understanding of law and fact, professional ideals and practices of the lawyers who worked in the cases, and measures of professional competence.

Rosenthal derived two models based on his data. One model, he called the "traditional," assumes that the client is pushed to be docile and dependent on the lawyer. The alternative "participatory" model assumes that the relationship is collaborative and that the client is an active partner. It is the latter model we adopt. Rosenthal went beyond aspiration. He classified the cases according to the model adopted by the lawyers he studied and put the cases to a panel of trial lawyers for evaluation and compared the panel's proposed settlement with the monetary recovery (settlement) in each case. He then determined which model produced the larger amount of money in settlement. He found that the participatory model was more lucrative for the client; clients who collaborated—were invited to collaborate—got more money.

It might be useful to look at more detailed aspects of the two models. In the traditional model, clients are expected to be passive; in the participatory model, they are expected to be active. The traditional model assumes that legal problems generally have only one best solution and that lawyers are more likely to be competent in arriving at it than lay persons are. It assumes that professional competence is a difficult thing to judge and only lawyers can judge it well. It assumes that professional service by lawyers is usually competent, that it is readily available to persons of modest wealth, and that ethical standards are high and consistently enforced. Fees, according to this model, should be set by the lawyer, and second lawyer opinions are of little use to the client.

In the participatory model, the quality of professional service is expected to vary enough that second lawyer opinions are thought to be valuable. Legal problems are complex, open to differing solutions, and open as well to a layman's common sense and first-hand knowledge. The participatory model assumes that lawyers are not as able to be disinterested as they assume, that fees should be negotiated, that laymen can judge the quality of professional services, that the middle class in America is not able to get good legal service, and that ethical standards are unclear and, even when clear, not consistently observed and enforced. These details in each model were compared against what lawyer and client in each of Rosenthal's cases said to him about his or her experience. Most of the cases Rosenthal studied fell into the "traditional" column. It was those cases in which clients were least satisfied with their lawyer, and in those cases they also recovered less money.

The choice of model is usually but not necessarily the lawyer's choice. Clients even want, often, to let the lawyer lead the way. Clients may prefer a parental (filial) relationship, and may resist their lawyer's attempt to make them responsible for themselves. (There may be here a subtle question about how domineering a lawyer can be in refusing to be domineering.) A lawyer can go so far as to terminate the relationship if a client refuses to deal with him on terms he dictates. But the choice of traditional or participatory model is always, in a sense, a shared choice.

The final pay-off in collaborative decisions is both social and personal: Collaborative decisions are less likely than lawyer dominated ones to lead to litigation. The father of preventive-law jurisprudence, Louis M. Brown, said: "Legal decisions are finalized by client and lawyer. In this context, the decisional process of the law office is as significant for a particular client as would be the decision of a court for a litigant."

The decision in the law office is assented to, worked out, by at least two people; but, like "justice" writ large, it depends for its validity on a sense of "rightness." A law-office decision must satisfy the people who are to live with its consequences. A negative way to express this is that law-office decisions should avoid litigation; a positive way to express it is that law-office decisions should rest on the implicit consent of those whose lives the decisions affect.

Non-legal counseling, by contrast, can afford to pay less attention to consequences. It aims at information and at the facilitation of choice by the client, as legal counseling does. But legal counseling is different because it is always done in the shadow of external, even institutional validation. A lawyer and client who decide that the client should seek every advantage possible in the Internal Revenue Code are making a decision with accounting consequences, risk consequences, and social consequences analogous to the consequences of the same sort of decision being made in the Tax Court. One consequence of this difference is that the legal counselor has to make up his mind; non-legal counselors often do not have to make up their minds; they often don't even want to. Non-legal counseling often need not go beyond the client's hard choices.

A REFLECTIVE EXERCISE: LAWYER INFLUENCE

Consider the two following interviews of a client by different lawyers. The client purchased an office building through a real estate broker. At the closing of this transaction, the broker who had earned a commission from the sale said he would also keep an eye out for a renter for premises in the building that became vacant in the future; the buyer said she would appreciate that. Six months later, one office suite fell vacant and the broker referred a renter. The broker then asked for a broker's commission on the rent. The buyer resisted and she and the broker then agreed on a compromise figure for the commission. At that late date, the buyer consulted a lawyer—ostensibly to find out if a roughly drawn promissory note would do to pay the settlement. The two interviews are set out below.

The object of this Exercise is to find out how you would describe the counseling dilemma presented in these interviews. How do your concerns about making and breaking promises affect your view of this client, of what the client wants to do, and of what you would do to help the client? How is the *moral* aspect of the decision approached by these two lawyers? (See also Chapter Ten).

First Lawyer Interview

C: I have no written agreement. It's all oral.

L: Well, first of all this is a point of law, as I understand it. For him getting you the tenant for that length of time there would have had to have been a written agreement, and without that written agreement, under the Statute of Frauds, you wouldn't be bound. Now at times we don't want to try to stress that, because it might cause unnecessary litigation. If there really was an agreement, which it doesn't sound like there was, between you and Mr. Baer, it might be wiser just to save you and Mr. Baer time, to work it out without having to rely on the technicality of the Statute of Frauds.

C: So, how do I work it out? I tried to work it out here with a note. If you help me, I won't have to pay him.

L: I would say the first thing I would advise you to do is to see if there are any grounds—such as perhaps, in the agreement to buy the building, which might have contained a clause that Mr. Baer should be your agent in finding tenants.

C: I'm pretty sure it did not.

L: I think that if you wish to avoid litigation, your oral agreement with Mr. Baer for $5000 is substantially below six percent, and if we found out exactly what percentage commission he should have, even if it was five percent, you would still be ahead with $5000. . . . I think there are two possible courses of action right now. I think one would be to tell Mr. Baer that we're not going to pay any money, and if Mr. Baer suggests that he is going to file an action against us, on what grounds does he think he can do that. The other course of action would be that if you don't wish to get involved in the chance of litigation, to try to write a note of the type you have here.

C: In other words, you think I should negotiate more with him.

L: I think the first step you should take is to talk to him and try to negotiate. . . .

C: Would you like to talk to him too?

L: Yes.

Second Lawyer Interview

C: I had a verbal agreement with him, but I don't know if I really have to. However, I assume I do. I don't know. I don't want to get legally involved if I can help it. Do I have an obligation to pay?

L: When he first told you that he had done this, there was no obligation to pay at all.

C: And I could have told him good-bye, and leave me alone.

L: There was nothing he could do about it.

C: Well, what are you telling me then? That I should pay him or that I shouldn't?

L: Well, I'm not saying that you should pay him or not pay him, on the basis of that. But I think that's something that, in making your decision, you have to consider—not just your legal obligations, but also other compensations, which are up to you to decide how significant they are to you. You see, the point is that we don't know how difficult it would have been for you to get somebody to become a tenant in that building, and, after all, he did go out of his way to get somebody in that building, and that person is now paying for leasing. So you're getting a benefit conferred to you, right now. Now, it's true that you may not technically be liable to him, and we're not saying that that shouldn't be an important consideration to you. Obviously.

C: Well, all right. I said before I suppose I have to pay him. How about this note now?

We would say to each of these lawyers: The one thing that is not possible in this situation is not to react. Some of us may think we can say, "Okay, whatever you want," but we cannot. Each of us is bound to have feelings in such a case, and the fact that you have feelings is bound to be picked up by the client and to matter to him. Your feelings *should* matter to you as well. The client may not perceive your feelings accurately, but he will pick up something. The lawyer who is aware of her feelings is likely to feel moral disapproval, or rebellion, or panic, or a lack of control over the situation or a need to protect the client from himself. Or you may conclude that you don't have any significant feelings. The way you feel in these situations as a lawyer, and as a person, depends on the kind of relationship you have with the client and how each of you expresses feelings and moral concerns. We know that expression of moral feelings is not easy, and there is little in legal education and training that prepares you for the task. It is something you will have to practice, a skill that you will have to learn in the law office. It is an essential skill in the craft of counseling.

CHAPTER TEN

THE MORAL DIMENSION

MORAL OPENNESS IN
THE LAW OFFICE

It strains belief to assume that the lawyer always respects the moral impulses of her client. One's explicit or implicit world-view may make respect for another's conscience difficult. Even if the disposition of Trollope's lawyer, Mr. Camperdown, to treat his clients as children is avoided, it is sometimes hard to respect a client's moral judgment. Our argument (Chapter Nine) is that a my-conscience-or-yours standoff is less likely when the client's desires have been elicited and considered and the lawyer's conscience is brought into the open and considered. By considered we mean consciously articulated and puzzled over. What we propose is moral conversation in which the lawyer's and client's moral views can be expressed. Such expression is, we think, required by the principle of openness, client autonomy, and lawyers' who honor their own conscience.

When the counseling climate is not open, lawyer conscience becomes a source of subtle (or not so subtle) pressure on the client—pressure amplified by client dependence. In such circumstances, the client's freedom to act is circumscribed as much as it is when the decision is made and imposed by the lawyer, and even more than it will be if the lawyer asserts her position and then refuses to act unless the client adopts her position. The cure for *ulterior* moral influence seems partly to be the lawyer's understanding of her own moral concerns, and partly the humility required to admit to herself that her moral impulses may be educated by way of her work with and for a client. It is possible for moral impulses to be wrong, even possible to learn how an impulse is systematically wrong and to learn how to change it. Much of a lawyer's influence and advice is moral, and moral influence and advice is, as Karl Barth put it, conditional: "He who takes the risk of counseling must be prepared to be counseled in turn. . . . Such mutual counseling . . . implies that he refrain from too much and [from] becoming thereby a lawgiver."

The principal influence threatening the ideal of client self-determination in a law-office decision is the influence of the lawyer, and, most particularly, relatively inaccessible but stubborn lawyer behavior that proceeds from undisclosed moral impulses. We may want to assume that lawyers listen to and understand moral impulses and deal with them consciously (even openly), and that every lawyer respects the moral impulses he observes in his client. In fact, though, moral impulses are subtle. They are often difficult to understand, and they are, in our "pluralistic universe," a source of conflict. This is another instance—and this book teems with them—where legal counseling requires a resolute effort to increase self-awareness.

MORAL FEELING AND MORAL JUDGMENT

Moral leadership in law offices usually comes, at least at first, from lawyers. David Riesman, a lawyer who became a social scientist, related his choice of career to this moral leadership. Lawyers are testing grounds, he said, for each client's disposition to distrust government, or business, or whatever it is the client seeks protection from when he sees a lawyer. It is probably not possible for the lawyer to turn off the client's moral sensitivity, but it is possible to discount it as a source of information or comfort or guide to law-office decision-making. And one way to do this is to treat conscience as irrelevant. The result is not a choice for professionalism and effective decision-making; it is a choice that trips up both client and lawyer. It is not possible not to choose, as Sartre would say. Morals operate whether a lawyer and client in the law office invoke them or not. They are part of what people say and do, in the law office as well as everywhere else.

Holmes' bad-man theory of law is the melancholy social principle that a citizen will do anything he can get away with. Legal decision is tested against the implicit empirical judgment that people are no damned good, that more often they are worried about money than they are principle. The theory, useful when limited, has much appeal, but carries with it great peril. In litigation—or so the Holmesian might insist—there is no room for shades of feeling, or for the fragile seedlings of conscience. Good and evil exist—crude and obvious and clear. While the bad-man theory may flourish in litigation, it has pernicious effects when brought into the law office. Most legal decisions are made in law offices, not in courts; the law-office climate is intimate and interpersonal (unless, of course, the lawyer insures that it is something else), a place where we might enact a good-person theory of law.

There is, of course, the possibility that the client may choose something horrible. There is also the possibility that the client may choose horrible methods for doing what he has a legal right to do. The moral issue for the lawyer arises because the client has the freedom that makes possible immoral choices and decisions. There is a strain of reasoning in professional ethics that says the way to avoid the horrible in professional behavior is to make sure we are not corrupted by our clients, and the way to avoid being corrupted by our clients is to make sure they do only what we tell them to do. If that line of reasoning prevails the only visible moral issue is whether the lawyer has made the right choice.

Take an example of interest to students of modern American legal ethics: Our client, a wealthy, middle-aged widower, wants to disinherit his elder daughter and give all of his "estate" (as we lawyers call it) to his younger daughter. We lawyers wonder why. (Notice that our wondering why is one moral act, and that our asking why is another.) The reason the client gives us is that the elder daughter has taken up a New Age religion. The client wants our professional help in doing something we think is wrong-headed and regrettable. Some lawyers react by saying they would refuse to help this client. Others contend that the moral issue of the proposed disinheritance is none of the lawyer's business. We find that the situation needs more analysis:

Interests. We really don't know yet what the client wants, what his *interests* are. We haven't talked with him enough, for one thing, and, for another, the notion of "interests" imposes an order on the human spirit—an order that may not even begin to accurately describe who *this* client is. As Warren Lehman put it:

> Everything we want to achieve we want ultimately because of the connection we suppose it to have to a desired feeling. Therefore, what we want is not the things we say we want, but the feelings we suppose they will produce. The list a client brings to a lawyer's office is not a ranking of desired states, but only of what the client supposes may produce them. Our judgment on issues of that sort is especially likely to be bad at the crucial time we go to a lawyer. We say we want justice when we want love. We say we were treated illegally when we hurt. We insist upon our rights when we have been snubbed or cut. We want money when we feel impotent. We are likely to act most sure of ourselves when most desperately we want a simple, human response. If this is true, the lawyer presenting himself as an uncriti-

cal [instrument] is not a satisfaction but a disappointment. The lawyer is in the deeper sense not then doing what the client wants. It may well be that in a given situation a lawyer can do no more than accept a particular client's statement of his desires. But that is not because he ought to be his client's tool or because he must be.

The Law. We could use the law, and our skill in it, to deny our client any choice at all. We could say: "The ensuing conflict and litigation could well defeat your purpose. I strongly recommend you not go this route." In this or somewhat more subtle ways we could coerce or manipulate our client into doing the *right thing*. ("Why don't you give this some thought and we'll schedule an appointment next month to decide what to do.") "About half the practice of a decent lawyer," Elihu Root said, "consists in telling would-be clients that they are damned fools and should stop." The troublesome principle of client self-determination would say that our client should be free to make the choice, and that he is not free to be right unless he is free to be wrong. A deeper moral notion would say that the client's being good (instead of right) is what is important, and for that—for becoming a better person—he needs something or someone other than a lawyer.

The Client's Morals. We could immediately make a moral objection to the client's desire to disinherit his daughter. (That is another way to read Elihu Root's observation.) We could refuse to lend our assistance to him. Or we could immediately take an instrumental view of our craft and say we will draft a will to do whatever he wants (so long as it is legal). These positions, as radically different as they first appear, both amount to saying that the client's morals are dispositive of the matter, and the lawyer can take the case or leave it. In both instances—take it or leave it—the client's morals are taken as an end statement or conclusion rather than a matter of conversation. Warren Lehman makes the more subtle observation that until we come to understand the client's morals rather than simply accepting them we won't *know* or he won't know what he wants. This means that our client could have a moral influence on *us*. Such a possibility is a risk and also an opportunity. We might even end up agreeing with the client that the right thing to do is to disinherit the elder daughter.

Moral Conversation. These two positions—that the client has to be free to be wrong, and that we are interested in hearing from him on the moral question, and even in being persuaded by it—mean that what we now have to talk about is a conversation: a conversation between lawyer and client in which the moral feelings, arguments, and principles *of both of us* are sought, learned about, listened to, and accepted as resources. It is still possible, of course, that the direction the client takes after this conversation will be one we will not take (or vice versa).

Consider, from the bad-man point of view, the client who "wants" to disinherit one of his daughters. The dynamic is to find the boundary beyond which the bad man may not pass, and then to work from the boundary into the territory of "legitimate" decision—*i.e.,* a decision that will be implemented by the courts, and that is not likely to get the client into trouble, or to fail at what the client wants. The bad-man, in this example, seeks to disinherit a daughter. It is one of hundreds of moments in the practice of law when the issue is not simply whether the law will allow it, but whether a good lawyer and a good person should do it. This is as much an issue for the client as for the lawyer, and therefore it is an issue for them together.

The essential law-office bad-man lesson here is that a will-making client can, with routine assistance from his lawyer, disinherit a member of his family. The temptation—and, often, the reality—for a law teacher is to use a hypothetical planning problem that will invite students to speculate on the legal engineering necessary, and then to scoff at the timid voice of those who suggest that the case invokes something more than lawyer craftsmanship.

* * *

Our adversary tradition—which is, to begin with, less a part of the law office than most students and some lawyers would imagine—has encouraged lawyers to suppose that the crucial moral decision is the client's and the client's alone. It is not a fit subject for conversation in the law office. In other words, lawyers have tended to work on the unstated assumption that advocacy (and, by extension, everything a lawyer does) is immune from conscience. The lawyer who acts professionally, for someone else, ceases in this view to act as a person; he is not morally responsible for what he does as a lawyer, and (maybe worse) he does not care about the conscience of his client.

A teacher encounters this view when he raises a moral consideration and is told by astonished students that lawyers should do whatever the client wants and the law permits. But newspaper reports, common sense, and even lawyer ethical codes suggest that conscience submerged in partisanship and zealous pursuit of limited goals is conscience denied. It is no more admirable in the law office than in the White House, no more defensible among lawyers than in business or medicine. Our Rules of Professional Conduct provide limited guidance on these law-office moral issues, but even these modest rules say that "a lawyer is not required to pursue objectives or employ means simply because a client may wish that the lawyer do so" (Comment, Rule 1.2, Rules of Professional Conduct). The Preamble to the Rules begins with the admonition that lawyers are "public citizen[s] having special responsibility for the quality of justice." While the Rules are less than clear or explicit about how our concerns about justice are to be reconciled with zealous client advocacy, we are left with the reminder that "a lawyer is ... guided by personal conscience...." An American lawyer's ethical duty is clear: to keep sound morals in the picture, to seek and to respect his client as a moral resource and, finally, to withdraw from either adversary or law-office relationships rather than to violate his conscience.

The principle is that we help choose, and are responsible for, whatever moral judgment the client makes or fails to make. It is not possible not to choose. Professional norms that assume that lawyers lack consciences of their own are bad professional norms, partly because they are untruthful and partly because they are unworkable. Professional norms that cause lawyers to define client interests narrowly (without really asking) are convenient and squarely wrong, both in ordinary moral principle and because the assumptions on which these norms are based are contemptuous of the possibility that morals matter in the law office.

A REFLECTIVE EXERCISE: CLIENT SELF–DETERMINATION AND MORAL CONCERNS

You represent the husband in an acrimonious divorce action. Your client, Dr. Martin Arrowsmith, has no desire to continue supporting his wife, Leora, in the manner to which she has grown accustomed in the ten years that they have been married. Dr. Arrowsmith says that he expects his wife to get custody of the children, that she is much closer to the children (a girl aged four and a boy aged six), because his work has resulted in his wife being primarily responsible for the children during their early years. You pause over this point and talk with Arrowsmith until you are satisfied that he really does not want custody of the children.

Arrowsmith is afraid that his wife's outrage over the fact that he is leaving her for a younger woman will result in an effort to make him suffer as much as possible financially. He seems particularly worried about his financial interest in a pharmaceutical business that a large supermarket chain is considering for purchase.

During the interview, Arrowsmith suggests the possibility of seeking custody of the children and using custody as a "bargaining chip" in the settlement negotiations. He wants to get matters settled with Leora and insure that his interest in the pharmaceutical business is not encumbered in any way. Leora knows of Martin's interest in the business but does not know about a potential sale. Leora is a recovering alcoholic, and after spending three weeks in a residential alcoholic treatment facility (when the children were two and four), she has refrained from drinking. Arrowsmith tells you that he knows his wife wants to avoid a custody fight at all cost, but does not elaborate.

* * *

This is the sort of law school problem that you might meet in an ethics course, or a family-law course, or a business planning course, as well as here, where we are talking about counseling.

(1) How do you feel about Dr. Arrowsmith? About this "case"? About his "problem"?

(2) Would it "bother you" (would you consider it wrong, unethical, immoral) to use the threat of a

child custody battle as a "bargaining chip" in negotiations to settle financial issues in the case?

(3) What do you see as the counseling issues involved in working with Dr. Arrowsmith?

(4) In what sense are the issues in your representation of Dr. Arrowsmith to be described as moral issues?

(5) What guidance do you find in the Model Rules of Professional Conduct?

(6) Consider the following observation of Warren Lehman in "The Pursuit of a Client's Interest," 77 *Michigan Law Review* 1078, 1079, 1091 (1979):

"Doubtless many clients, thinking they know what they want—or wishing to appear to know— encourage the lawyer to believe he is consulted solely for a technical expertise, for a knowledge of how to do legal things, for his ability to interpret legal words, or for the objective way he looks at legal and practical outcomes. It is as if the lawyer were being invited to join the client in a conspiracy of silence; the point of the conspiracy is that in silence neither shall question the assumption that the means can be truly separated from the end and that the end is the client's sole problem and solely his. Such an idea of the lawyer's job seems to relieve him of the ethical responsibility that might be his were he to assume a duty to comment on the wisdom or virtue of what his client is about. I do not think the burden of commenting upon the client's purpose can be so easily avoided. The interaction of lawyer and client is a moral event, whether morals are explicitly broached in conversation or not. The question is not whether the lawyer can or ought to comment, but what message does he convey.

* * *

"The only thing the lawyer can do for his client is be free himself, which means free to be honest in saying exactly what he thinks and feels, to confront himself. It is transcendence for a lawyer to say to a client: 'I am fearful of influencing you unduly in this matter. The tax saving is there. It may be important to you to save the money. If so, by all means defer the gift. But money saving is not everything. One should hardly organize one's life around a revenue code. I will think none the less of you whether you choose to defer or not. Some people, I suspect, may be embarrassed—odd as it may sound—to ignore an apparent financial advantage, for to do so sounds irrational. Let me assure you, I would respect more highly a [person] who will do now what seems right to him now. What sounds rational is not always humanly reasonable. . . .' The important thing about any such message is not that it be calculated to neutralize the legal-rational bias, the legal influence, but that it be honest and not intended to manipulate. Sometimes a side benefit of the speaker's honesty is a shock in the listener that shakes him loose and helps him be free."

* * *

Return now, to your client, Dr. Arrowsmith, and
to the question about your feelings about Arrowsmith. Assess those feelings as they bear on your
relationship with him. After you do this alone or
with a friend (or first alone and then with a friend),
or with a small discussion group, the information
you generate may be useful in seeing the different
approaches you and your colleagues take to counseling as a moral activity.

PROBLEMS

The struggle with client self-determination extends both to cases involving legal conduct that
seems immoral and to cases involving moral conduct that seems illegal. Examples cover: (1) cases
where the lawyer's moral influence is invoked even
beyond the informational level contemplated by ethical rules; (2) where the client proposes conduct
that seems moral to the client but not to the lawyer; (3) cases where the conduct is illegal but is seen
by the client (or by the lawyer) (or by both) as
moral; and (4) cases where the conduct seems legal
but contrary to the public interest.

Lawyer's Moral Influence Invoked

The following example occurred in the early
1960s, before modern federal (or state) civil-rights
legislation had been enacted: The corporate client
operated large industrial plants in the Deep South.
The client was a fourth-tier contractor with the

federal government, which meant then that it had very little legal duty to racially integrate its work force. The client had discussed this with a senior partner in the firm, who asked the lawyer to research the client's duties under a presidential executive order on equal employment opportunity. The lawyer picks up the story:

"I drafted a memorandum outlining the client's minimal duties. My senior, with memo in hand, telephoned the secretary of the corporation; he explained my memo ('the law'). The secretary—who was himself a lawyer—said he understood this advice but still wondered what the corporation should do. My senior in the firm then said we had reviewed the situation, and that our advice was to integrate fully in all plants. This advice had all the jurisprudential clarity and economy of *Brown v. Board of Education*. This law-office decision went beyond the letter of the law, as most law-office decisions, from income taxes to the corrupt practices act, do. Lawyer-client decision-making is not, after all, a form of technical journalism. I have often wondered why my senior gave the advice he did."

a) He may have been putting his own social opinions into the decision-making process.

b) He may have believed that the law would soon reach this client with full-integration requirements; that is, he may have been predictive. (In which case he was right.)

c) He may, in addition, have assessed the economic and human costs of compliance (which were

great in this case) and have decided that early
compliance was cheapest.

d) He may, finally, have assessed the moral implications of full integration, minimal integration, and
no integration, in terms of his own and the client's
moral posture. To have done so would have required consideration of a wide array of factors—the
consciences of the executives we were advising (the
decision-makers); corporate image; the welfare of
the workers (white and black); the social posture in
the South and the nation at that time; and, most
important, his own perception of the moral openness of the people he was advising. Any of these
factors implies a recognition of the fact that the
corporation was inevitably a moral leader in the
community.

The client in this example took the lawyer's advice. All plants were fully integrated a decade before
"the law" began to require integration of them. The
lawyer's advice here seems, by the way, to be well
beyond what the law required.

There was a right decision here, but the process
seems to have been poor. The moral decision, for all
that appeared, came solely from the lawyer. The
client may have done the right thing, but its officers
were deprived of counseling and conversation—the
important human satisfaction and growth in virtue
that comes from considering alternatives and making a praiseworthy choice. The lawyer also took
upon himself moral, as well as legal, responsibility
for the client's behavior. That could have turned

out to be professionally and emotionally troubling. (An aspect of this case that calls for more detailed discussion is the corporate lawyer's role as the conscience of the corporate enterprise. There, too, the ideal and frequently the practice is a moral conversation between lawyers and corporate managers.)

Client Conduct That Seems Immoral

Frank Cihlar gives this example, which we edit slightly: "Mr. D., a lawyer, was awakened in the middle of the night by a call from one of his clients who told him that he had decided to commit suicide. Mr. D.'s response to this information was not one of hysteria or of immediate activity designed to get his caller into the protective embrace of some life-sustaining authority. He simply indicated that he hoped his caller would not choose to take his life since Mr. D. regarded him as a friend whom he liked very much and would regret not having around. Mr. D. did not urge his caller not to take his life nor did he endeavor to reach him in person. Instead, he merely expressed his concern over the potential loss but stressed the fact that he thought the decision was ultimately his caller's. With this, Mr. D. concluded the conversation and returned to sleep." Mr. D. said later that he felt his client "had sufficient command of his faculties so as to permit him to make up his own mind in the matter." He said he would regard killing himself as immoral, but that he felt it inappropriate to intervene in his client's decision.

The example is probably more dramatic than the present point requires, but it suggests a host of less dramatic cases where clients make choices that seem wrong but that a lawyer who believes in client self-determination may feel bound to respect. Many of these choices involve more overt activity by the lawyer (drafting of instruments, negotiation, and even litigation), but the suicide example is not one of passive professional conduct; Mr. D. cannot honestly claim that he was "not involved." The fact that the caller was a client—let alone a friend— means that Mr. D. was involved. In addition, Mr. D. refrained from calling "some life-sustaining authority" and refrained as well from any attempt to interfere physically with the client.

Client Conduct That Is Illegal But Seems Moral

The most obvious example might be civil disobedience. Or consider the situation of a client who seeks legal advice concerning refusal to serve in the armed forces during some national military adventure such as the Iraq War. Those of us who had such cases in the 1960s during the Vietnam War usually found ways to avoid direct confrontation with the authorities that impose professional discipline. We were able, for example, to restrict what we said about flight to avoid military service to relatively wooden advice on what the law said (*e.g.,* analysis of the provisions of the several extradition treaties between the United States and Canada, without stating the opinion that the client should go to Canada). We gave advice on whether physical destruction of draft cards would constitute a felony under the Selective Service laws, and analyzed the law of criminal trespass as it pertained to demonstrators. In moral effect, many of us admired what our clients did and even supported them as far as our consciences would allow. (Some lawyers, of course, felt that the conduct of clients in such situations was wrong.)

Client Conduct Seems Legal But Not to Serve the Public Interest

Abe Krash gives an example that clearly involved the public interest and, for many lawyers, would have involved moral judgment as well:

For many years, the outside General Counsel for the *New York Times* was an old and distinguished New York law firm. In 1971, the editors of *The Times* informed their General Counsel that they had obtained possession of secret documents involving America's involvement in Viet Nam—the Pentagon Papers—and the editors asked counsel for an opinion as to whether the materials could be published. Counsel reportedly advised *The Times* that if they published the documents before they were declassified there was a risk of criminal prosecution. The law firm [also] reportedly advised the editors not to publish on the grounds, among others, that it would be contrary to the "public interest" to do so. *The Times* editors determined to publish notwithstanding this advice. When the Department of Justice notified *The Times* that it would seek a preliminary injunction to restrain further publication, the law firm informed *The Times* that the firm would not represent the newspaper.

Mr. Krash, himself a partner in a large law firm in Washington, D.C., said he did not disapprove of the lawyers' conduct in this case, but gave the example "to demonstrate how extraordinarily difficult it is in any given situation to know where the public interest lies." Roger C. Cramton sounded a vague murmur of dissent (and other lawyers would be more vehement in dissent): "The radical critique ... does not accept the assumption that ultimate values can be determined by the conflict of private interests. The radicals have discovered truths ... that do not depend upon the votes of the political process of the advocacy and rationality of the legal process. While the value choices that are asserted are subjective, it is also true that the preferences of the rest of us for a procedural definition of ultimate values is also ultimately subjective." In other words, there is discontent with client self-determination when the issue involves public interest, and voices of discontent can be heard. The idea of "public interest" could assume the role of limiting client self-determination, as the conscience of the lawyer limits client self-determination in other matters. Lawyers do argue, as we think they should, on whether to decline to act for clients who make choices that are seen as contrary to public interest.

ANALYZING MORAL INFLUENCE

How does a lawyer go about considering moral concerns in the law office? One way is to do what some professors do in law school—to open discussion to expressions of moral views, to hear everybody out, and then to close discussion with solemn expressions of respect for all moral opinions. That is just barely better than nothing. It implies that moral processes are immune to analysis and evaluation. It is a way to deny that morals matter in any concrete and analytical way.

A second way to proceed is to do nothing about morals. The lawyer decides by doing nothing. He pretends not to choose; he tries to hide his moral responsibility in the adversary ethic. If the lawyer resists and defies, it will often be at considerable expense to himself. A much discussed example is the lawyer who refuses to go along with his client's decision not to disclose violations of the laws on disclosure statements in securities registrations. He may end up defying both the client and other lawyers in the law firm—in which case his employment is on the line. He may feel compelled or even be required—as the Securities Exchange Commission is beginning to insist—to report his client to law enforcement officials.

A third way is to assume that moral concerns are benign and subtle, too subtle for conversation and lawyer intervention. Or, a lawyer may just assume that clients will "do the right thing," even when lawyers see no necessity either for its being done or for its being right. The client may simply announce his judgment; he may not offer it for negotiation. From the standpoint of conscience, this may be an easy judgment for the lawyer to implement, especially when the client's moral instinct is better than the lawyer's, but lawyers have been known to resist, "for the client's own good."

In many law offices the lawyer influence over client's moral choices is much larger than the client influence over lawyer's moral choices; that is, we think, typical. The reason for imbalance is the professional relationship; some of it is what psychology calls transference (see Chapter Four), some of it is lawyers taking advantage of a social role that gives them power over others. A "lay person" habitually yields independence to the professionals he employs.

If it is a desirable thing to move decisions from subtle moral influence to more explicit moral discussion and analysis, the lawyer will have to employ strategies: (1) that begin with his understanding that "feelings are facts"; (2) open communication (about his own feelings); (3) accept client feelings, understanding that "feelings are facts" and that the client's feelings matter to the lawyer; (4) demonstrate that the professional (lawyer here) understands how the client feels (best described as empathy); (5) are willing to collaborate on moral choices, a conviction that moral choices are as often what we do together as what we draw out of the dark night of the soul; and (6) show a belief that moral concerns and moral decisions can be discussed and negotiated, and that both client and lawyer benefit from such conversations.

Strategies that operate toward openness about moral judgments in the law office also include skills for evaluating morals, skills lawyers mis-learn in law school, where the principal announced objective is to learn how to evaluate legal decisions. It is probably a mistake, for example, to act always as if moral feelings can be confronted with and overruled by logic. This exaltation of the rational faculty—a faculty to be appreciated—assumes that non-rational sources of behavior are inferior. It is expressed in a number of ways in a culture such as ours:

— A moral concern is irrelevant. The values that come from moral feelings are, if useful, so intensely personal that one talks about them as little as possible. It is impolite to talk about it. ("I don't know why anyone would want to solve any kind of serious problem relying upon moral concerns.")

— Morals are relative. ("You have your morals, I have mine. What good does it do to try to explore them.")

— A person's morals are intractable. Nothing can be done about them, especially, if as we assume, they are the result of a lifetime of experience. ("If you have your personal morals and I have mine, and our morals are rooted in a lifetime of experience, what good does the talking do?")

— The morals a person ends up with are rooted in the society in which she lives. This is a variant on the-way-I-was-brought-up excuse, but the variation is significant. The fault-of-society theory assumes that "they" (the government, the schools, the "power structure") are responsible for shoddy moral judgments. It also assumes that morals are a product of manipulation; morals can be changed by social engineers, and will be, once the right engineers get their hands on the television cameras and are elected to run the government. ("We're all the products of social institutions and corporations, and to focus on the morals of an individual is to obscure the real source of a person's morals.")

— Morals are a matter of conscious choice. This is the opposite of the-way-I-was-brought-up theory and the assumption that morals are grounded in society. Or, rather, it is the disgust with which a champion of logic regards these assumptions that goes on to place morals squarely in the domain of person choice. ("You choose your morals in much the same fashion as you choose a spouse; whether for good or for bad, what you end up with is what you chose.")

These perceptions about moral concerns, and others one might identify, have two things in common: They reject the moral feeling which is at issue, and they imply that a whole person (and the good professional) subject to impulses or instincts or principles, or whatever, that tell him what he should do have no part in law-office counseling. The answer to both of these implications is that moral concerns and moral doubt are part of our professional lives whether we choose them to be a conscious part or act as if they had no place.

* * *

It is possible to identify four hypothetical principles, from all of this, for dealing with the moral impulses of clients: (1) Moral feelings are facts. Denial of them and ignoring them are poor counseling. (2) Moral feelings are a significant indicator of who the client is as a person—the way he holds himself together, the way he defends himself against the shrews' disapproval he hears from within and without, and how he makes and lives with hard choices. (3) Moral feelings cannot be submerged in logic or overcome by logic but they can be examined and evaluated by reason, even though one will occasionally look at his moral choices, and at logic, and end up saying, as William James did, "so much the worse for logic." (4) All three principles are as valid for the lawyer as for the client. She cannot fail to be a poorer lawyer if she supposes that her profession requires her to deny her own conscience.

An attitude found in legal education and in some law offices, and one we urge our reader to reject, is that morals are irrelevant, in the law and to the client. As a matter of fact, law inevitably involves moral choice. And once we get beyond the bad-man view of clients (and litigants), fostered by the adversarial view of justice, law and client decision-making are rendered accessible to moral dialogue, in the law office and elsewhere.

If nothing else, the never ending revelation of shabby practices in government, the professions, and business should cause us to be skeptical of legal educators who tell their students to put moral instincts aside when they come to law school. Karl Llewellyn told his beginning law students: "The hardest job of the first year is to top off your common sense, to knock your ethics into temporary anesthesia. Your view of social policy, your sense of justice—to knock these out of you along with woozy thinking." Llewellyn seems to be recommending a bracketing of morals that would endanger a lawyer's moral judgment and make her unworthy of the place American lawyers occupy in society. We trust that Llewellyn was aiming at a more subtle lesson, one lost in the implications of the quoted directive we present here.

CHAPTER ELEVEN

UNDERSTANDING OURSELVES

A LAWYER'S DISCOVERY

The sub-plot in John D. MacDonald's *The Last One Left* concerns a lawyer who learns to be a human being. Early in the novel the lawyer's wife leaves him because of his pursuit of the ideals our profession tends most prominently to exalt: "You are a very civilized man, dear. You are polite. You are considerate. You are thoughtful. But you demand of yourself an absolute clarity, total performance, complete dedication. There is something almost inhuman about it, really. What is lacking, I think, is the tolerance to accept—the inadequacies of things.... You have this terrible impatience with carelessness and muddy thinking and laziness. You drive yourself so hard. It isn't money hunger. You just seem to want to go around neatening up the world."

"Life itself is the basic magic, the real miracle," his wife says. "You are trying to impose your sense of order and fitness on the randomness of people and the illogic of fate. You want to refute the basic textures, the crazy mixture of life." The lawyer, Sam, resists this advice. He tells himself that his wife has ignored "the essential stuff of survival. Did

300

she want softness, apathy, amiable sloth?" Then one day he notices that he is driving his car at nearly 100 miles an hour while he thinks about what his wife said.

Sam wonders aloud, among friends, where his assumptions had come from—from himself or from "the man I have been imitating all my life." And then Sam notices that his friends look shocked, and he says: "The lawyer has flipped, huh? Ever notice how uneasy people get if you try to say some of the weird things that happen inside your head? I used to hold everything back. That's part of the incantation." And then he says, "I'm going to tell people what I think. It's going to raise hell with my law practice. But it's the only way I can think of to stop being completely alone in the world."

Sam's conversion may be expressed in the way he talks and the people he talks to, which is the way Sam says he plans to express it. It is likely also to be expressed in greater self-awareness. Sam presents an issue for other lawyers, an issue on which it may be useful to consider whether lawyers differ from other people in their psychological make-up and what means are available for a more self-conscious life in the practice of law.

ROLE AND IDENTITY

Sam's problem is indicative of a significant obstacle to the model of counseling we outline here—the conflict between a lawyer's sense of *role* (what he sees when he closes his eyes and says, "I am a lawyer") and *identity* (what he sees when he closes his eyes and says, "I am a person"). Here are some examples of the conflict and its sources:

Conflict of interest, although often denied or obscured by professional aspiration, is a constant presence in professional relationships. A trial lawyer who specializes in plaintiffs' personal-injury cases and is called to zeal for his client by Rule 1.3 of the Model Rules of Professional Conduct is, as a matter of fact, pulled by his relationship with persons "on the other side." He has many cases, virtually all of which he will compromise and settle. His livelihood depends in fact and in amount on the outcome of these compromises. The persons with whom he negotiates tend to be the same from case to case. He knows them better than he knows his client.

A busy lawyer is, for another example, often torn between his life with his family, or his personal fulfillment, and his devotion to his clients. The telephone is an ubiquitous and tyrannical symbol of that conflict. Lawyers who aspire to develop their skills as counselors are brought into conflict with hourly rates, the expectations of partners, office overhead, and the other routines and traditions that give rise to the lawyering ethos and ethic.

Still another example: The image of the lawyer as counselor, companion, and friend conflicts with the financial rewards that lawyers (and we realize that there are exceptions) seek for their services. Douglas Rosenthal, in his empirical survey of personal injury lawyers, confirms the presence of a substantial conflict. Rosenthal points out that "[t]he single source of pressure upon the lawyer most likely to affect adversely the client's interest, and which can most easily be documented, is the strain of prolonged litigation and the economics of case preparation. Simply put, a quick settlement is often in the lawyer's financial interest, while waiting the insurer out is often in the client's financial interest."

Aspirations conflict with reality. Students are confronted, within days of beginning law schools (and the beginning of their professional lives), with stories of the lawyer who allows the morals of the marketplace to erode his ideals and of the senior partner who expects his associates in the practice to produce money—big money—for the firm and therefore for him. The aspirations students bring with them to the study of law may conflict with the reality of modern day law-firm practice.

The lawyer's sense of herself as a person is broader and deeper than her sense of herself as a lawyer. Students in one of our legal counseling courses included: artists, musicians, parents, spouses, a gourmet or two, skiers, Jews, Christians, atheists, and a physician. Some of these students expressed reservations about legal education and their sense of what was happening in the profession. Many of them had doubts about becoming lawyers. They were unreserved in the belief that being a lawyer and only a lawyer was not enough. They knew, first-hand, that the lawyer role posed threats to their identity. The conflict between role and identity—lawyerhood and personhood—was and is a reality.

The traditional model of the lawyer running the show (vague and disputed as it may be) exacerbates the conflict. The image of the lawyer as a dominating authority figure—someone who has to know, to do, to tell and still be cautious and responsible—exacerbates the role-identity conflict. Our ethical aspirations insist that the law is something the lawyer uses to help the client. The determination of what to do with the law is for the client. But a lawyer such as MacDonald's Sam knows, down deep, that he cannot give up his own conscience in the process.

RESPONDING TO THE ROLE–IDENTITY PROBLEM

A student avoids the role-identity conflict by shouting it down. What follows is the occupational contours of a life that hides the conflict in values the profession finds acceptable. Professionals, doctors and lawyers in particular, are susceptible to identity formations that cut them off from others, even as they enter so-called helping professions. Richard Sennett has observed that this process of cutting-off oneself is a way for those in authority, as lawyers are, to exert "a peculiar kind of strength—a power to cut themselves off from the world around them, to make themselves distant, and perhaps lonely, by defining themselves in a rigid way. This fixed self-definition gives them a strong weapon against the outside world. They prevent a pliant traffic between themselves and [people] around them and so acquire a certain immunity to the pain of conflicting and tangled events that might otherwise confuse and perhaps even overwhelm them.... [T]he threat of being overwhelmed by difficult social interaction is dealt with by fixing a self-image *in advance,* by making oneself a fixed object rather than an open person liable to be touched by a social situation.''

There is a sort of in-the-office professionalism, by no means totally undesirable, that calls for a *persona,* wearing a professional mask that allows the lawyer to be detached, unemotional, and in control of the client, herself, and the situation. The detachment isolates the lawyer from her client's feelings, but first and more insidiously it isolates her from her own. Detachment can, and often does, become a destructive process in human relationships since feelings frame how we ''read'' a situation and provide us with a working sense of who we are.

Lawyers naturally attempt to protect themselves from unsettling feelings that arise in the work with clients, their problems, their feelings, their morals. Maintaining a facade of impersonal coolness avoids a sticky confrontation between the deeper self of the lawyer (a sense of self that goes beyond work and professional life, a sense of self that can be both expressed in and denied in one's professional life) and the real self of the client (the person beyond the client and her legal problem). Hence, the lawyer relates to the client in terms of function; she reacts to her client as a problem.

Sam, the lawyer in John D. MacDonald's *The Last One Left*, found that his professional life and his legal *persona* had taken over his private self. His legal *persona* dominated his whole personality. Sam the lawyer ate, breathed, and slept law. He talked like a lawyer, thought like a lawyer, and dressed like a lawyer. The psychological identification was complete. In such a case, as John Noonan notes, the legal persona "become[s] indistinguishable at a psychological level from other disguises of the self.... [A] judge [and lawyer] may speak and even think of the law as an invisible companion telling him what he must do." The danger that we mean to identify is that of a legal mask slipping into place, and fitting so well, working so well, that we forget we have it on. Sam found that had happened, and the result was that he became rigid and inflexible and unable to listen to what people said to him. He felt this most keenly (after he came to see what he had done) in his relationship with members of his family, but it had undoubtedly happened—and probably long before—in his relationships with his clients and with people he worked with in his law office.

One way we navigate a role-identity conflict is to develop and use a *persona*. The *persona* (and the ego which it serves) makes us adaptable, constantly adjusting to the flux and flow of the world. But the *persona* pushes much aside (everything unusable, unwanted, shameful, fearful). The urge to make ourselves presentable to the world—to be liked, respected, esteemed—an urge we make real in the energy we put into maintaining and preserving the *persona,* is strongly reinforced by the demands and expectations of society, as well as the ideals and ethics of the legal profession. Genuine and sustained reflection is absent in the lives of busy, overworked lawyers, and in the lives of many professionals. The result is that a legal *persona* which is of some functional use can become a forgotten convenience put to dubious ends.

Lawyers are blind to this *persona,* and to the evasions and manipulations it covers over and helps us justify. One of the reasons we distance ourselves from clients is to silence them from questioning matters that we have learned to deny. The *persona* has a back side, a part of the self that Jung perceptively called the *shadow.* The *shadow* contains all those elements of the personality the ego condemns, those aspects of our psyche which are intellectually, emotionally, and socially unacceptable. The *shadow,* Erich Neumann tells us, is "the expression of our own imperfection and earthliness, the negative which is incompatible with the absolute values" that we attempt to live out in our lives and our professions. The *shadow* "roots the personality in the subsoil of the unconscious, and this shadowy link with the archetype of the antagonist, *i.e.,* the devil, is in the deepest sense part of the creative abyss of every living personality." Other psychologists and counselors confirm Jung's insight. Erik Erikson found that "identity formation normatively has its dark and negative side, which throughout life can remain an unruly part of the total identity. Every person and every group harbors a *negative identity* as the sum of all those identifications and identity fragments which the individual had to submerge in himself as undesirable or irreconcilable or which his group has taught him to perceive as the mark of fatal 'difference' in sex, role or race, in class or religion." (Emphasis in original).

Freud's theory of repression makes it obvious how the *persona* and the *shadow* elect to go their separate ways: Conscious energy flows toward the *persona* while the unconscious holds back those feelings rejected for conscious life. The division of labor between the conscious and unconscious realms is functional and allows us to put aside what is socially unacceptable (every society designates behavior and thought that are shameful and to be held in disdain). But the division of labor is, in Freud's words, "overdetermined"; like all adaptive behavior it tends toward overuse, employed in circumstances far beyond its functional need.

C.G. Jung made it an explicit part of his theory and therapeutic practice to engage the patient in a process of recognizing the *shadow* and bringing it into conscious life. Jung was always careful to avoid the suggestion that bringing the *shadow* to conscious life was an argument for hedonism or social irresponsibility. To the contrary, Jung saw the confrontation with the unconscious as one of the most difficult tasks in human life, a confrontation that makes those who undertake the journey more, rather than less, socially responsible. Erich Neumann, following Jung, made this insightful comment on the confrontation with the *shadow*: "The self-experience involved in the journey of depth psychology [the first stage of which is the encounter with the *shadow*] makes [a person] poorer in illusions but richer in insight and understanding; the enlargement of the personality brought about by contact with the *shadow* opens up a new channel of communication, not only with one's own inner depths but also with the dark side of the human race as a whole. The acceptance of the *shadow* involves a growth in depth into the ground of one's own being, and with the loss of the airy illusion of an ego-ideal, a new depth and rootedness and stability is born."

Ultimately, Sam's 24–hour–a–day legal *persona* became a neurosis. It became that because the lawyer role was invested with status and prestige and the mask fit all too well. Sam imagined himself as one of those self-actualizing individuals whom Abraham Maslow described as able to "assimilate their work into their identity, into the self, *i.e.,* work actually becomes part of the self, part of the individual's definition of himself." This kind of self-definition, and integration, is both desirable and dangerous. In any case, most of us don't get as far as Sam did; what we do is switch back and forth. The diverse and conflicting professional roles of the law and the conflicts and contrast of professional and private lives create a world of constant change—from lawyer to person to lawyer, from bereaved clients to aggrieved clients to pushy clients to worried and passive clients.

The Greek god Proteus could escape those who would question his prophecy by assuming the form of various animals and even of fire and water. The "shape-shifting" of Proteus is not, in the view of Robert Lifton, a Yale psychiatrist, and others, merely a story from Greek mythology but an archetypal motif in our own lives. Lifton characterizes the Protean style as "an interminable series of experiments and explorations, some shallow, some profound, each of which can readily be abandoned...." In essence, the Protean style is the wearing of different masks and a psychological strategy that allows one to live with the psychological shifts that accompany the roles, situations, and worlds in which we find ourselves. When we admit to the fragmentation in our lives, and experience and experiment with the wearing of masks to help us adapt to diverse roles, we imitate the Greek god Proteus. Lifton observes that "while he [the Protean personality] is by no means without yearning for the absolute, what he finds most acceptable are images of a more fragmentary nature than those of the ideologies of the past. And these images, limited and fleeting though they may be, can have enormous influence on his psychological life."

The paradox for the Protean person lies in the quest for a sustainable identity in the chaos of flux and change. Erik Erikson, reflecting on the ambiguity and conflict in the Protean personality, captures the paradoxical quality of this Protean energy, a god who "knew the past, the present, and the future of all things, and it was in order to avoid having to tell that truth that he assumed the pseudo-identities of animals and elements of nature. Only when caught napping and held down before he could escape into different beings was he forced to be himself and tell what he knew. So there was a real and lasting Proteus in the original Protean personality, a tragic core-identity in the multiplicity of elusive roles."

For the Protean lawyer, playing diverse roles, wearing a lawyer mask, offers relief and liberation, but also poses a danger. Erikson, questioning the Protean style, asks:

But what if role-playing becomes an aim in itself, is rewarded with success and status, and seduces the person to repress what core-identity is potential in him? Even an actor is convincing in many roles only if and when there is in him an actor's core-identity—and craftsmanship. Comparably, there may well be some character types who thrive on Protean possibilities, even as there is, by definition, a developmental period (namely, youth) when the experimentation with a range of roles and alternating states of mind, can be a way of personal growth. What is described as a Protean personality today may, in fact, be an attempt on the part of adolescent personalities—and America has always cultivated these—to adjust to overwhelming change by a stance of deliberate changeability, of maintaining the initiative by playing at change so as to stay ahead of the game . . . . Those who are gifted in this game, and, therefore, truly playful in it, may with luck make it an essential part of their identity formation and find a new sense of centrality and originality in the flux of our time.

The story of Proteus connects with our own lives, lives in which it becomes increasingly difficult to avoid wearing masks. But even if we cannot avoid the masks we can tell the truth about them and be aware that there is a self behind them.

TOWARD SELF–UNDERSTANDING

Our motivations for actions and ways of being serve purposes of which we are, in part, unaware. While we see ourselves in our own actions, thoughts, beliefs, fantasies, and dreams, the problem is that we do not see ourselves as clearly as we sometimes assume we do. We do not know how to be honest with ourselves. (More "thinking" about ourselves, as we know from Freud, seldom results in the truth about ourselves.) Yet, each of us has the capacity to reflect on the way his own life works. The path we choose shows up in the way we talk and listen to clients, and in the kind of counselors we become. While it may not be possible to rid ourselves of *all* self-deception (a fact that will persuade many not to make the effort), it is possible with curious exploration and work to be more self-aware.

To the extent that we eschew reflection and the effort to see ourselves, our ideas, theories, and dreams more clearly, we become submerged in the world. The emphasis on doing rather than being makes our *persona,* philosophy of life, and moral perspective, more and more inaccessible to awareness. A lawyer can easily practice law and engage in a course of conduct that seems—on first appearance—to involve no significant moral choices. You can live a life oblivious to moral choice, oblivious to the conduct that shapes and ultimately defines your own character. How does this happen? How do we let a *persona,* a philosophy, and even social and moral illusions, guide our lives? To what extent is the philosophy we live out with clients hidden from us—hidden as we go about being-in-the-world as lawyers? We argue that the ultimate philosophy of counseling is found in our interaction with those we serve.

How do we let a *persona,* an implicit philosophy of life, and even social and moral illusions, guide our relationships with clients? A good counselor becomes aware of illusions, those of the client and her own. It is the exhortation we find scattered throughout philosophy—to lead an examined life— that is the theme of this chapter.

The task is to lift the veil of ignorance that obscures the philosophy we live out in the talking and listening we do with clients. What we need most is possession of what is closest to us—insight into who we are as we work, the way our work shapes and distorts our character. Socrates taught that philosophical truth comes only from persistent reflection and introspection which cast light on the darkness of self (to Jung we might rephrase this as the darkness of an unexplored, unintegrated *shad-*

ow). To follow Socrates we must learn to do our own thinking, to value reflection, and to learn from our own inner world, even as we learn from our colleagues, our lovers, and our clients; in both cases we must choose to listen.

Freud and Jung insisted that the way to understand others is to understand ourselves. Freudian and Jungian analysts undergo the same therapy they later undertake with their patients. The doctor (psychiatrist, therapist, counselor) sees the possibility of healing (understanding, listening) in light of her own experience of being heard, understood, and healed.

We bring Freud and Jung into our discussion here because they provide a working theory of human motivation that makes clear the importance of being aware of how the unconscious affects our personal and professional lives. Freud and Jung are of continuing relevance to the lawyer, because lawyers have a need for self-awareness, a need all too easy to resist. Freud and Jung showed that our lack of self-knowledge, and our failure to engage in self-scrutiny, is not caused by laziness so much as by deep-seated resistance. Established beliefs and patterns of thought and interaction resist change, a point we can make without appeal to Freud and Jung. But these giants of psychology make this resistance to self-scrutiny, and to psychological development, a focal point of their theory: Resistance is a powerful force that stands between the ego and our awareness of the unconscious and "internal" world that affects our everyday decisions, our personal and professional interactions, and our relationships with clients.

Even if the lack of motivation is overcome (and how is it that one overcomes a resistance that is itself unconscious?), there are serious obstacles to self-scrutiny. The difficulty in gaining access to unconscious motivations may prove the undoing of even the most dedicated. The psychoanalytic explanation for the difficulty lies in the "repressive forces" that keep unconscious material unconscious. Psychological repression serves as a watchman who refuses to allow passage of stirrings and intuitions of the unconscious into conscious awareness.

Resistance is not limited to the obstacles thrown in the path of the analyst prying into deep recesses of the patient's mind. (Freud observed that "one hardly comes across a single patient who does not make an attempt at reserving some region or other for himself so as to prevent the treatment from having access to it.") Resistance serves as a censor to avoid conscious awareness of emotional experiences that have been lodged in the unconscious. Freud found that resistance to unconscious material seriously cripples insight and understanding and indicates that an individual's "critical faculty is not an independent function, to be respected as such; it is the tool of his emotional attitudes and is directed by his resistance."

A word more about resistance: Given the intellectual and psychological resistance in the service of repression which censors and blocks unconscious motivations from awareness, it becomes clear that the obstacles to insight through self-scrutiny are extraordinarily difficult to overcome. However, these resistant, protecting, unconscious motivations do not doom the process of self-scrutiny. In fact, it is the appearance of the resistance that signals the existence of what has been denied, the very thing (thought, feeling) that would, if it could, create a conflict. Therefore, the resistance, rather than posing an insurmountable problem, serves as an indicator that material is being repressed. This is the point where, in psychotherapy, the resistance itself is pursued.

The first point of this excursion into psychoanalytic theory on resistance is a point about our ability to keep the uses of the lawyer role under the control of the moral self: Self-scrutiny has an emotional complexity that requires more than intellectual effort. The second point is that self-scrutiny is worthwhile. All of us fear the unconscious and some of us are unwilling to experience the painful and unsettling awareness of a deeper self. Some even believe that digging around in and opening ourselves to the unconscious is dangerous. The testimony of psychologists is that the danger is overstated. Karen Horney who wrote far more about self-scrutiny than most psychologists, found such harm or danger "so rare as to be negligible. Observation in every analysis shows that patients are well able to protect themselves from insights they are not yet able to receive."

The typical reader of this book, who will be engaged in self-scrutiny and a study of the legal *persona* outside the psychoanalytic setting, does not have the advantage of "working through" unconscious conflicts and repressed drives and thoughts with an analyst. The question then is whether insight from self-scrutiny is possible outside a psychoanalytic setting where one is guided by a psychoanalyst (Freudian), an analytical psychologist (Jungian), or a psychotherapist. Horney, who has dealt at length with the obstacles to self-scrutiny and the potential of self-observation, gave a tentative yes in response to this question. We believe that self-scrutiny is possible. We have oriented this book to provide encouragement for such an exploration.

Lawyers and law students—and those who write for them—undertake the study of law and psychology in order to understand the people we deal with professionally—clients, brothers and sisters at the bar, judges, juries. We argue throughout this book, however, that one of the principal lessons for counselors is the importance of learning about ourselves. This lesson about self-awareness is of greater significance for lawyers as they realize that they have a tendency to avoid their own feelings and as they begin to discuss the psychological importance of the elements of their counseling relationships.

A REFLECTIVE EXERCISE:
PROFESSIONAL
AUTHORITY

Louis Auchincloss, a renowned novelist and Wall Street lawyer, begins one of his stories, "Equitable Awards" (which appears in a collection of work entitled *Narcissa & Other Fables*) (1983), with a scene in the law office of Miriam Storrs. What follows is the beginning of an interesting story, and an instructive one for the student of counseling:

Gwendolen Burrill sat facing her lawyer across a broad desk, the very bareness of which, except for an unspotted green blotter and a black pen stand that was obviously never used, suggested that its occupant, in the business of offering simply a brain full of ideas, operated more efficiently without encumbrance. But the stripped neatness of the desk, matched with the bleakness of the chamber, chaste except for a large, dull print of Bowling Green in the 1840s, depressed Gwen, making her feel that her own rather faded attributes—curly chestnut hair streaked with gray, skin more smooth than pink, a decayed girlishness that showed its forty-six years—were being harshly exposed, laid out, so to speak, one by one, on a long board, to be picked up appraisingly and then, presumably, put down again.

(L–1)   "Let me explain how the ... divorce law works, Mrs. Burrill. It is based on the theory that marriage is a kind of business partnership. The court will assess the value of what you as a wife have contributed to this partnership and award you accordingly. And the division will encompass not only income but principal. In your case I'd go so far as to suggest that we're justified in asking for a fifty-fifty split right across the board. Half of your husband's total wealth, and, of course, a full half of his earned income until your death or remarriage."

(C–2)   "But how," Gwen protested, "can you argue that I contributed to his success in his law firm? He's slaved away there, day and night, for the last twenty years! Just the way you all probably do here."

(L–3)   "And how could he have done that if you hadn't been doing your part? Mr. Burrill has been able to give himself totally to his profession only because you have lifted the weight of his private life off his hands. Who looked after the home, the children, the vacations, the entertainments? Who freed him of all his petty cares, even his major ones? Why, Mrs. Burrill, I'll bet you even bought his shirts!"

(C–4)   "It's true. I did."

(L–5)   "And now that you've given him half your life, now that you've lost your chance for a professional career in which you might have done at least as well as he, are we to let him cast you aside like an old shoe? Excuse the expression! I'm afraid I got carried away."

(C–6) Gwen smiled as sweetly as she was able, but it was less to spare the lawyer's feelings than to hide her own pain. Old shoe! but of course, wasn't that just how this young woman would regard her? Miriam Storrs, juris doctor, couldn't have been more than thirty, probably less, and she had none of the masculine tailored firmness that women of Gwen's mother's generation (and some of Gwen's) liked to associate with their career-oriented sisters, smugly deeming it the price they had to pay for their success in a man's world. But Miriam Storrs was blonde and even possessed of rather baby-blue eyes, and the fineness of her figure was only too apparent under that silly white dress with the flowered hem.

(C–7) "Excuse me for asking a personal question, Miss Storrs. Are you married?"

(L–8) "Oh, yes. My husband's a doctor. A pediatrician."

(C–9) "And do you have children?"

(L–10) "Not yet, but we hope to."

(C–11) Gwen sighed. What a useless, idle creature she must seem to such a couple! A life wholly dedicated to domesticity—and a domesticity that had come to this!

(C–12)   "Do you like divorce work?"

(L–13)   "A case like yours, yes."

(C–14)   "Because you consider me a victim of male chauvinism?"

(L–15)   "Not really." Miriam's demeanor of bright professional sympathy faded a bit, and Gwen had a sudden glimpse of how her counselor might look to an adversary in court. "I assume you chose your own life and chose it freely. But you gave up certain opportunities when you did so, and your husband accepted that sacrifice. He shouldn't be allowed now to renege on his part of that implied contract. He must make you whole."

(C–16)   "How can that be done?" Gwen shrugged sadly as she rose to go. "But, of course, you mean only to the extent possible. Very well, I'm in your hands. I leave it all to you."

* * *

Pause now, to note your reactions and your feelings. Can you imagine yourself as a lawyer in a similar situation? How do you see yourself responding to Gwendolen Burrill? Would you respond as Miriam Storrs did? Consider how your response would have differed from Miriam's?

What kind of psychological counseling issues do you think will emerge for Miriam Storrs, the lawyer, as she talks and listens to her new client, Gwendolen Burrill? Of what significance, psychologically, is it that Gwendolen's husband is a lawyer? And of what significance is it when you also learn in the interview that Mrs. Burrill's father selected and made the arrangements for his daughter to visit Miriam Storrs?

Consider your feelings about Gwendolen Burrill as she is presented by Auchincloss in the scene. Do you have immediate, strong impressions, or feelings? How do you account for these feelings? And if you do not have such feelings, given what you have read and now know about Mrs. Burrill (or will you call her Gwendolen?) can you imagine that your view of her and your feelings about her might change over time? Of what psychological significance to the relationship is the fact that Miriam Storrs is a woman? That she is substantially younger than her client?

And of what significance to the outcome of the case, and your, and Miriam Storrs's, representation of Gwendolen Burrill, is this business of the way Sidney Burrill has practiced law? Gwendolen says: "He's slaved away there [in the law firm], day and night, for the last twenty years! Just the way you all probably do here." Do you see this remark as an attempt at humor? An effort on the part of Gwendolen to establish rapport with her lawyer? How would you respond to a client who made such a remark?

After leaving Miriam Storr's law office and the discussion about a divorce, Gwendolen reflects on how her parents had let it be known that if she was to marry a lawyer, that it be a lawyer who would make his name and then go "into government, or diplomacy, or some sort of higher education."

"But Sidney, with that pale skin, that dark, faintly unshaven look, those staring red-lined eyes that seemed to search for a problem and a solution in the simplest things, with his way of losing himself and the world in work, could never break away, or perhaps even want to break away, from those cool, aggrandizing clients who were shrewd enough to know, without ever being big enough to tell him, how indispensable a tool he was to their daily machinations." And when you learn that Mrs. Burrill sees her husband in this way, what do you imagine as the outcome of this perception on her feelings toward Miriam Storrs, her lawyer? Toward *you*, if you were her lawyer?

SELF–UNDERSTANDING AND CREATIVE PROBLEM–SOLVING

Danzig–Nevis International developed a series of exercises on self-evaluation that center on obstacles which keep us from being creative in our work. If, as we suspect, creativity is associated with deeper levels and functions of the core self, then understanding the blocks to creativity may be suggestive for lawyers. These obstacles to creativity are important to lawyers because there is an area, beyond hard choice and collaboration, where the expertise, knowledge, and craftsmanship of the lawyer must be deployed to devise creative solutions. Solutions often depend upon creativity and the blocks to that creativity:

Custom Rules. One way to examine the extent to which custom blocks creativity is to ask where one's values come from. From tradition? From myself? From others? And to what extent are these values functional for me? One way to look at lawyers as problem-solvers is to see that lawyers in our society have a hand in social and institutional change. The issue is whether adherence to custom—to, if you prefer, unexamined values—makes it hard to accept and implement and use change in a creative way.

Need for Order. An inability to live with disorder and ambiguity often cuts a good lawyer off from problem-solving resources in himself and his client. Andrew Watson has identified in law students an unusually high need to master the environment, to line things up, organize, and impose structure. Many law students become anxious as they find that very little in the law is settled and what is settled is being challenged. But seeing one's own life and the law as a process, as undefined, is often a way to release creative energy. It is probably why so many great lawyers in the common-law system have been history buffs and have tended to explain law more in terms of its development than in terms of its logic.

Fear of the Unknown. Lawyers like to know what they're doing; this is the problem-solving side of Andrew Watson's theory that lawyers have a high need for order. The unknown knows no order. An example of this need, this habit of mind, is the old aphorism that a good trial lawyer never asks a cross-examination question unless she knows what the answer will be. If one pursues that rule in office practice she will work to avoid the world that the client brings into the law office.

Misplaced Certainty. Lawyers who are not over-certain in their lives with clients have mastered the ability to be flexible. They have less routine in their lives and are less likely to think of clients as problems with labels or in categories. As a result, their problem-solving is not a stereotyped operation; a lawyer who is not over-certain for example, might solve a civil-rights riddle with antitrust law; she might solve collection-agency oppression with the rules on unauthorized practice of law. (The growth of the common law is, for the most part, traceable to flexible advocates.) A lawyer who is blocked by over-certainty tends to persist in professional behavior which restricts how they think the job is to be done; she tends to be guided by unexamined assumptions.

Lack of Appreciation for Contradiction. Synergy is one way to express this idea. The object is to move things away from the poles of opposition—to see how contrasting points of view, for example, can contribute to a good solution; that conflict can be used rather than suppressed. If anything is clear in the substantive law it is that circumstances alter cases, that few things are perfectly clear. From a philosophical point of view, it is possible to see professional life as a dualism, a we/they, win/lose game. It is also possible to look for and find a wholeness in the world, and that perception may be what I need to relax and let myself be creative.

Fear of Failure. Someone who has dissolved or reduced this block is able to take risks, to take chances, and to seek change. Our profession is built on adventurous lawyers—Horace Binney, for example, who vindicated charitable trusts in the United States by arguing, from 16th century English court records, that the Supreme Court should reverse itself; Louis D. Brandeis, who built his career on challenges to concentrations of wealth; Thurgood Marshall, who was able to attack racism in public education by convincing the Supreme Court to overrule its own clear precedent.

Impoverished Imagination. It is possible to ignore or distrust parts of my mind, of my life, that are real and may even be pressing—my dreams and day-dreams, and images, and visions of glory. Robert Browning could have been speaking to lawyers when he said a person's reach should exceed his grasp. And much of one's reach is a matter of psychic life. And yet there is a pervasive belief that if one looks at what is deep inside himself he will see guilt and shame and ugliness, that being our true selves will unleash a "psychic Nazism." It is hard and fearful to look at a deeper sense of self that it is possible to befriend.

Reluctance to Let Go. It is possible to try too hard, to work too long, to forget how valuable and rejuvenating it is, once in a while, to just walk away. It is especially tempting to forget that the best resource in problem-solving is oneself, and that in the interests of getting the job done we still need to protect and preserve that resource. This block has other dimensions, too—the tendency to get nervous about what we do and the attendant neglect of the people we are doing it with; anxiety about getting things done so that we cannot let ideas incubate or ripen or, maybe, just go away; so much need to control the action that we sell short capacities in other people.

Failure to Appreciate Play. A lawyer who has overcome this block tends to think of her work as play, as intrinsically enjoyable. She sees humor—not grim humor, but ironic humor—in many of the things she and other lawyers do, in the solemn pretensions of the profession. She doesn't worry about seeming to be silly; she is, at times irreverent, and enjoys it. A friend, Terrence Kelly, of the Colorado Bar, was making a difficult argument to a three-judge federal court in Denver. He had exceeded his time. The presiding judge said, "Mr. Kelly, don't you think you ought to give the other side a chance?" Kelly, who has a superbly creative sense of play, looked at the bench, and at opposing counsel, and said, "Gee, your Honor, I thought by now they would be convinced." He not only defused the occasion, he captured it.

Impoverished Emotional Life. Feelings are facts. A client's feelings have to be built into the relationship and acted upon as a guide to how we are to work together. They are part of the raw material of problem-solving. The lawyer's feelings are also facts. It takes energy to hold them back; solutions that ignore feelings are incomplete, weak, unstable. Awareness of self and others is a professional asset.

Sensory Dullness. We walk on carpets, and sit in padded chairs, surrounded by artificially cooled or heated air, and listen, if we're very unlucky, to piped music that we are not supposed to notice. An environment can numb the senses. How does it feel—to walk on freshly-cut grass, to smell a pie baking, to taste the new richness of an egg from a free range chicken? To awaken to an experience like one of these is to suggest how easily we adapt to an environment.

The counseling disciplines nourish and preserve a stubborn dogma about creativity—a hope that the average among us is creative enough. Creativity in Shakespeare's and Mozart's range may be a gift of the gods, but we need not be driven mad about it, as Salieri was. We can, despite the inexplicable occasion of genius, still insist that there is enough creativity in each of us to make life better for ourselves and those who need us. The agenda, then, is to locate and remove the habits and hang-ups that keep a lawyer from working at her creative best.

A REFLECTIVE EXERCISE: PROFESSIONAL AUTHORITY

During the course of Miriam Storr's representation of Mrs. Burrill, Gwen Burrill revealed a host of perceptions and feelings about her husband and his work as a lawyer. Assume that you learned each piece of information as Auchincloss presents it in the story and in the order we present it below. How does each disclosure affect your feelings toward Mrs. Burrill and your working relationship with her?

(1) Mrs. Burrill's parents "had never thought him [Sidney] good enough for her."

(2) "She had not suspected his [Sidney's] almost compulsive habits of work before they were married. She knew that he labored hard, but then so did all the other young lawyers among her new, post-college friends. She considered that she labored fairly hard herself. She was a secretary in a publishing house and shared an apartment with her former Vassar roommate."

(3) "Sidney seemed to have inherited a brain from nowhere and to be quite willing to place it a hundred percent at the service of his employers. He never looked beyond his firm; he never questioned

its right to use every bit of Sidney Burrill for its general purposes. He was like a faithful hound that needed but a single master, and that would probably be just as content with a second if anything should happen to the first. But the very exclusiveness of this loyalty created in him an odd independence about other things. Sidney was, as Gwen boasted, a free soul—outside his firm. He had no prejudices, no boredoms, no tiresome idiosyncrasies. He was gay and easy with people at parties; he liked to drink and, as she soon discovered, to make love. She had no doubt, when he first became serious about her, that she would be to his heart what his law firm was to his mind. But it had not taken many months of marriage to teach her that if she had his love, his time belonged to others. And the years simply confirmed this.''

(4) ''She remembered thinking that things would be different when Sidney attained his ambition and became a partner in his firm. Then he would take more time off, and they would do things together. But her father had warned her against this illusion. 'Lawyers and businessmen in Sidney's league can't afford to slacken the pace,' he had told her, rather complacently, as it now struck her. 'They might make the unpleasant discovery that they had prepared themselves for nothing else in life.' ''

(5) ''When he [Sidney] wasn't working, he could be charming: affable, amiable, open-minded, funny and interested in all the little things that were going on around him. In the country he loved to identify birds and flowers and to take the boys

[Sidney, Jr., and Fred; at the time of the Miriam Storrs interview, both sons are in college] on long walks. The intensity that he brought to his law practice was also available for the mixing of a cocktail, the solution of a crossword puzzle, or the fixing of defective plumbing. The trouble with these periods of relaxation was only their briefness.''

(6) Sidney, in turn, ''was perfectly aware of the problem that his industry posed for her, and perfectly frank in the remedy that he always put forward. 'You should get a job. You've much too good a mind to waste it all day.' ''

(7) Mrs. Burrill has had discussions, some quite emotional, with her husband about the kind of clients he represents. When she relates a statement that her father had made about Sidney's clients being a ''nest of pirates,'' Sidney tells her, in no uncertain terms, ''I think your old man has one hell of a nerve to slam people who make a go of it in fields that he was too dainty to put a toe in! [Mrs. Burrill's father was a political scientist.] How the hell does he think the money was made that lets him sit on his ass and write beautiful prose about wicked governments? And it isn't even as if he had enough to make you independent of me! By the time he kicks the bucket and Uncle Sam has taken his cut, you may be thanking your lucky stars for your grubbing husband. . . .''

(8) Mrs. Burrill realizes that ''perhaps she should have been taught a little more respect for the men

who had to make the money. The trouble might have been that she had been brought up to be unworldly without being wholly unworldly, and that she had not been one of those able to work out the necessary compromise."

(9) " 'All last night, I kept thinking of what you'd said about how I'd contributed to Sidney's career. About my looking after the children and entertaining for him. But it's not true! We could have afforded a nurse, and both boys went off to boarding school when they were fourteen. And as for entertaining, I was never warm and cozy with Sidney's clients the way I was with my own friends.' "

(10) "There's something else. I had an affair. . . . " Gwen's affair was with a tennis pro that she met at the club that she and Sidney belonged to when Sidney was sent abroad to run the French office of the firm. When the tennis pro left the apartment after their second meeting in the apartment, Sidney came home from the office with an inflamed sore throat and saw the tennis pro, whom he recognized from the club, in the lobby of the apartment. Gwen confessed to the affair, before Sidney could voice any suspicions. Sidney seemed to take the news well and there was, following the incident, a brief renewal of romantic interest on the part of both Sidney and Gwen in their relationship.

(11) After Gwen and Sidney returned from France the relationship fell apart rather quickly, but without any dramatic incidents. "Sidney slept

in the boys' bedroom and rarely came home for dinner. Finally, after an extensive business trip to the West Coast, he moved to a hotel directly on his return and wrote her that he would be staying there indefinitely."

CHAPTER TWELVE

EPILOGUE: ON LEARNING ABOUT PEOPLE

If you have read this far you have come a long way. We understand that you may not yet see yourself as a skilled counselor; it may be comforting to note that even graduates of counseling programs often share this feeling of being unskilled. This feeling of not being fully qualified as a counselor is itself a valuable asset. If you take that feeling into your relationships with your clients, most will understand that you are a learner (although a few will not), and you will have a different sense of your work (in listening and talking) with clients than a lawyer does who ignores the counseling dimension in professional life. Knowing that you have something to learn is an attitude that gives rise to good listening ("active listening") and to talking with a client rather than talking at him.

The ideal next step in learning about counseling would be to learn more about people, and the person to begin with is yourself. You are your own best resource in learning about people; you might think about yourself as a "text" that can be read and studied. The Exercises we have provided in the book are nothing more than an opportunity for you to think about and to reflect on your own experience, your feelings and your fears, your own wonderment about who you are and what you are becoming.

Much learning from your own text, from yourself, can be done alone—by a process of watching and listening and putting questions to yourself. Much of psychology developed that way, particularly the introspective depth psychology of C.G. Jung. Much of Freud's theory on normalcy is based on introspection; he was his own principal subject in *The Psychopathology of Everyday Life* and *The Interpretation of Dreams.* The psychology we find in the philosophical works of Aristotle, Aquinas, Nietzsche, and William James is that of introspective thinkers who did not merely think, or even think and then write; they thought and wrote in conversation with themselves, learning from what they wrote, experienced, and dreamed, and then tried to work out in writing what they were learning. Jung's analyses of his own dreams are remarkable instances of this—as are Freud's little detective stories on why he left his umbrella at home, or how he came to use the wrong word in a conversation. To wake up with a feeling of sadness from a dream, to find that you are depressed for no reason, to realize that you are sexually attracted to one client and always angry with another, that you feel powerless and out of control with still another, are the experiences from which your own psychology of lawyering must be understood.

We find literature of use in this project of learning about people and learning about ourselves as well. Trollope's making flesh-and-blood people out of the lonely daydreams of his wretched youth is an example. "There is a gallery of them," he said, "and of all in that gallery I may say that I know the tone of voice, and the colour of the hair, every flame of the eye, the very clothes they wear." His characters were with him when he went to bed, he said, and as he woke from his dreams. They were alive because they were real. Each of them told Trollope about people, as people told him about his characters and as both told him about Trollope. And thus C.P. Snow called Trollope one of the greatest *natural psychologists.*

One of the most powerful, immediate, and provocative means of making a study of oneself is to work in a group that makes what happens in the group the subject of study, that, as the researchers say, generates its own psychological data. The object of such groups (T-groups, encounter groups, human-relations skills groups, sensitivity groups, problem-solving groups; any small group that focuses on process as well as content) is to provide information about how we interact, who we are as we try to make our way in a world of other people. The idea of a T-group (T stands for training, and the training that is envisioned is training in the skills of inter-personal relations) is that the group's task or agenda is the process of how the group works, how each member of the group interacts within the group. The idea is that the "process" of the group is assimilated and brought back into the group, so that members of the group can "see" what is happening, to themselves and to others. Those who use

T-groups claim they are the most immediate and accessible and least costly way of discovering how each member of a group relates to the people in his life outside the group. Another idea in T-group work is that being surrounded by people who share the goal to learn about themselves will free you (and them) to be candid—to be candid most of all to yourself. When the agenda of the group is process, that is, when a group does not set as its purpose some specific task, goal, or problem to be solved, then we become for each other a screen on which feelings are projected and can be examined.

T-groups were, during the late 1960s and 1970s, a significant teaching device for learning the skills of interpersonal relations and a means of personal self-development. While T-groups receive less public attention today, and were never made an integral part of undergraduate and graduate programs in psychology, such groups continue to exist and are used in the training of business leaders, managers, teachers, psychiatrists, clergy, and others who work with people and realize the need to know more about themselves and their relations with others. We know of no other educational tool that provides the kind of learning that takes place in a T-group in which people come together to learn from their own immediate experience. (We participated in various small groups, received training as group leaders, and used small groups to teach legal counseling.)

REFLECTIVE WRITING

We tell a story in our work, in the briefs we write, the cases we try in the courtroom, and in law office conversations with clients. The art of counseling turns on telling stories and listening to them being told. Many lawyers seek a life that is more truthful, more revealing, than the stories reflected in the routines of their day-to-day work. This is how one student expressed that need: "In legal writing it is possible to steer wide of anything that matters to you as a person, but the attraction for such analytical writing passes quickly. I need to face my feelings; that need becomes a craving. Until the craving is satisfied by writing—really writing—my dreams become wild, my attention to detail lags, and my restlessness insures my unhappiness."

Over the years, the authors have invited and encouraged students to engage in reflective and introspective writing. We see reflection and introspection as a necessary lawyer skill. These skills, largely ignored in legal education and by lawyers with crowded and busy lives, are now the focus of a growing body of literature that contends that we all have a need to say something imaginative (and truthful) about life, about the world in which we live.

A basic way to teach and learn reflective skills, one now commonly practiced and sometimes written about, is the use of journals. We (the authors) have worked with journals over the years, used them in our teaching, and asked our students in various law school courses to keep journals as a way to learn about themselves and to monitor the changes they undergo in law school. And we have kept journals ourselves.

Keeping a journal can be difficult. If it were easy, everyone would do it. Knowing that introspective journal writing is good for you, that you can learn about yourself by doing it, is not enough to prompt most of us to actually keep a journal. (It's not at all clear how one gets to be a journal writer.) The fact that so few lawyers and others in public life and leadership positions keep journals and do the kind of introspection that we suggest here reflects not only the difficulty of doing a journal but an attitude toward introspection more generally. Abraham Zaleznik and Manfred F.R. Kets de Vries, in their book on corporate leaders, *Power and the Corporate Mind,* argue that "Leaders, who orient themselves to power and action, are usually indifferent to the notions of psychic truth; instead, they care about practicality and feasibility." Zaleznik and de Vries could well be describing lawyers here.

The habits of journal writing and introspection are discouraged by the routines of everyday life— the meetings with clients and other lawyers, court appearances, papers to be drawn up and filed, briefs to be written—routines that keep us so busy, our lives so crowded with practical matters we have no time to think, much less write, or keep a journal that seems to serve no purpose other than peace of

mind. Busy people who long ago quit reading have
no time for making a text about themselves. The
busy lawyer tends to justify his life by telling himself, "I don't have time to do anything else." And it
is exactly this kind of experience, of being rushed,
of not having time, that is carried into our relationship with clients, that impoverishes our counseling,
that gives our lives the feel and the "texture" they
have. This experience, of lawyering and everyday
life, and the conflict it creates and the frustration
and burn-out it ultimately produces, can itself be
made the subject of journal writing. Even the ordi-
nariness of everyday life is an entry-way or opening
into a deeper understanding of who we are and
what we have become as lawyers, how we have
found a place for ourselves in the world (or how we
continue to search for that place).

* * *

When we ask our students to write journals, to
use them to learn about themselves, we do it because the felt experience in one's life as a student is
significant to the substantive knowledge that is
being taught and learned in law school and how it
will be used with clients. Many students end up
writing about their experience of writing and their
feelings about doing a journal.

One interesting aspect of reflective journal-writ-
ing is that it can, for some students, be a kind of
therapy. This is the way one student explained it:

I write to survive. Whenever I feel a lot of pain, I
write to some unknown individual, just spewing

out my rage and pain. It has a cathartic effect.
Sometimes when my feelings and thinking are at
odds with each other, I attempt to make decisions
through stream-of-consciousness writing. I make
a deliberate attempt to write everything about a
feeling or thought. After a week or so, I reread
my writing to see how the situation has changed.

Keeping a journal is thus a way to deal with pain,
disappointment, confusion, conflict, and failure.
These experiences, the ones we hate so much to
admit, the ones we dread having, the ones we hope
will just go away, are the kinds of experiences that
journal writing helps us experience more fully. In
introspective journal writing we get our hands in
the dirt of shadow material—all that stuff we just
want to go away (but that never quite does). The
journal claims experience and shadow as something
that can be admitted, owned up to, explored, even
appreciated.

A journal works as therapy, when it works (sometimes nothing seems to work), because it gives
whatever is troubling us, pulling us down, or moving things too fast or too slowly, a chance to speak
for itself. The ego crowds out the many voices of our
lives that don't fit the *persona,* or the demands that
our clients (and the world) make upon us. The
therapeutic value of journal writing that students
(and the authors) experience comes from becoming
more attentive to those voices trampled in the rush
of everyday life. One student writes:

Without regard to the purpose of this journal, the process of drafting it over the semester has been a valuable experience in itself. I have thought about things in depth, whereas without the journal, I would merely have let them pass. I have questioned and criticized, whereas without writing the journal, I would have been apathetic. But, most importantly, I have forced myself to take a step back from "all of this" [law school] and try to gain a perspective on it, whereas without writing the journal, I would not even have attempted this. In essence, the journal has been very beneficial to me, even if I have not created a "purposeful" or "good" journal.

Journals and introspective writing help us see what is truly important in our lives and to see that apprehension, anxiety, anger, and fear, as much as happiness, contentment, and achievement, are inevitable and valuable in our lives.

Journal writing is an "outlet," or as one student dramatically puts it: "This journal has given me an outlet to plug all my frustrations and problems and ideas into. It has been my psychiatrist." Another student speaks of the journal as a way of seeing and understanding her own life:

This has been an excellent outlet for me and my frustrations and tensions. I write down my problems, insecurities, feelings and then come back and read what I have written and it gives me a different and clearer perspective on the situation. Sometimes just by the actual "writing" physical tensions are released and frustrations calmed. It has been an excellent way for me to look deeper and find out new things about myself.

To counsel another person, to attend to her problems, and the concerns and fears that are related to her problems, it is necessary for the counselor to "see" and to reflect on what is happening in her own life. The work that a lawyer does, the listening and talking we do with clients, the way our encounters and interactions with clients are imagined, conceived, and executed cannot be divorced from the feelings, fears, failures, hopes, and dreams of the lawyer. Only if the lawyer were able to view herself purely as a technician, only if her professional work were purely routine, would it be possible to study and understand, to learn and perform the lawyer role without it having an effect on who she is as a person. A student writes: "This journal has made me confront myself as a person. If this writing serves no other purpose, that is enough."

A journal is a way of keeping a record, as well as an exercise in reflection. For some students, writing is a way to stay on an even keel; it keeps them on track, moving in the right direction, helps them be more clear-headed about the world they inhabit. One student says: "I am depending on the journal to keep my thought processes keen, even in the tide of overwhelming amounts of case material and demand for one-lane thought." But the ego that gets into journal writing—and it is the ego that worries about being effective and realistic, setting goals, and achieving them—also has a penchant for ignoring aspects of our lives that don't get expressed by being on track, by the linear movement from goal A to goal B to goal C. There are needs and purposes that bring one to a professional life that are sacrificed in the making of goals and achieving them, in doing what teachers and clients demand of us. Goal-oriented achievement poses no small danger, even as it gets us to where we have chosen to go (and many of us do less choosing than we want to admit). One student writing on this point recognizes that law school is a great adventure and one that calls for sacrifice: "This journey is probably the greatest adventure I have ever embarked upon. This [journal] is a record of my development, a living account of the adjustments and sacrifices that I have made to accomplish a goal that was set so long ago." The journal is a way of seeing what our purpose is and where we have been—if not where we are going:

> I want to see myself in my journal. I have saved my writings for over ten years. By re-reading these writings, I can see many facets of my personality. I can read about how I express anger, love, worry, hopes, dreams, and pain. I can compare how I feel now with how I felt ten years ago. I can evaluate the changes. My collection of writings keeps me aware of what I have been through, and helps me focus on my goals.

Another student comments:

> My journal is still full of questions for me to resolve. Hopefully, every time I am in doubt my journal will be a barometer to show me how far I

have veered from my course, or how well I have obtained my objectives.

Journal writing is a way to explore, to discover, to see how the goals we make for ourselves in turn bring with them restrictions and limitations:

My law school writing is, for the most part, different than my personal or imaginative writing. I am expected to accurately record and analyze divergent facts. While analysis can be creative, it is nonetheless no real part of myself. As a law student I am only reacting to factual situations or to theories already formulated by others. At most I am creating theories from separate, smaller groups of ideas already formulated. Legal writing strives for succinctness. While necessary for clarity, brevity removes one's spirit from the work. When clarity is the only emphasis, writing has no soul.

Legal writing can, however, be seductive at times. When I am tired or would rather not face up to the world or my feelings, I find it easier to analyze than to create.

Another student comments:

Writing for an assignment has always been difficult for me. I've been afraid to sound like myself—for fear that what I'm saying isn't worth listening to. I must sound authoritative and often I find myself using words that I would never use in conversation. I'm still not sure if writing is supposed to sound like me or not. I've concluded that if the assignment involves research on a particular subject, I should never sound like me.

I remember handing in a writing exercise in high school that was returned to me with every "I" and "me" circled in red ink, along with a comment that these words were used far too often in the essay. It had a profound effect on me. I'm still somewhat paranoid about personal pronouns in my writing.

In Law School all I've written are memos and a brief for the Legal Writing course. It's something you do by writing, but it isn't writing. The memos were the easiest—research and write—"it could be this, it could be that"—no feeling, no emotion permitted. The brief permitted the expression of some emotion through the need to be persuasive. This was "me" talking and it involved somewhat of an investment. I wrote alone in the apartment all weekend. I found it a painful process—almost like labor. It felt as if I had delivered this baby, and now a baby expert was going to look at it and he might tell me it was ugly—or, worse, that it was dead!

And another:

School causes us to write for our teachers, others, instead of for ourselves. We learn that we cannot write, that we are not worthy of writing for ourselves. This process continues in law school.

When I have a writing assignment, I panic. Will it be as good as the professor wants it to be? It's so hard to write for oneself when grades and jobs depend on pleasing the professor. Why are we all so caught up in pleasing others with our writing?

I associate methodical, sterile, "correct" writing with becoming a lawyer. When I write for law school, my writing is not original, it is a conglomeration of other people's thoughts and writings on yet other people's thoughts. Everything I write down has to be footnoted! Law school has made me more confident in terms of writing correctly, but not creatively.

As a woman, I write more about love, pain, coping, and relationships. It is hard to imagine a woman writing a book about fishing.

When I recently began to keep a journal, I sat down with nothing particular in mind and simply began to write. No typographical errors to correct, no misspellings, no delay in putting ideas into words. It felt good.

In journal writing there is often a sense of discovery, the surprise that there is more going on in our lives than we have been willing to admit. We think we know who we are. Journal writing questions this knowing and the imagined self and its prescribed roles. We can discover ourselves in writing, as Joan Didion, the novelist, puts it, "Writing is the act of saying I." The self we find is often one that has been in hiding.

One of the consistent themes in counseling, and one of the things that bring a lawyer to imagine himself as a counselor, is a curiosity about the lives of his clients. When we try to understand another person from his perspective, we realize that the only way that can be possible is to know something of our own perspective. One student, expressing something of Didion's notion of "writing to say I," observes:

Writing is important to me now to help understand exactly what my thoughts are. Sometimes I don't even know what I'm thinking or feeling. When I write I begin without a goal or idea in mind. I simply start out with a blank page and begin with a few general comments. Then come the thoughts, and before I know it my most closely guarded secrets are there on the page. It is as if I cannot help myself—my innermost thoughts slip so easily from my mind to my pen that I am hardly aware of it. Afterwards I feel refreshed, whole. I know that if I tried to explain my thoughts to others rather than write about them, my words would be tempered by my perception of their reactions, or their needs. Only in writing am I completely free, completely open.

Another student contends that:

My writing has enabled me, for the first time, to begin to look at myself honestly. Sometimes this is very hard to do, since I still struggle with who I am and what I want from life.

I have begun a journey, through writing, wherein I discover diverse sides of myself. So much territory remains undiscovered. I am beginning to risk expression that I never would have dreamed possible. I feel that I am growing and developing as a person in many new ways. I am no longer afraid of my writing. Rather, I look forward to being able to express myself, not only for release, but as a tool for reflection on who I am. My writing has taken on a whole new meaning. I am writing for me and it feels good.

A third student says:

Doing the journal has come at a good time for me [the first semester of law school]. It has helped me through a stressful and lonely period, a time in which the only key to survival was a dependence on the development of a source of inner strength.

Writing concretizes dreams, hopes, fears, frustrations, anger, confusion, and love. The writer takes that which is amorphous and ephemeral and makes it real. Validation of the personal voice can open avenues of expression and potential for change which stimulates the emergence of a whole inner self into an external world previously off limits.

Learning law as a student, practicing it as a lawyer, teaching it as a teacher, depends more than we have previously recognized on what we think and imagine of ourselves as persons. The continual exposure to law and legal thinking affects our inner world, the subjective world that is both source and reservoir of our images, emotions, feelings, and fantasies. Law and legal thinking, the talking and listening we do as lawyers, shape our view of the world, and become a world view. (See Chapters

Three and Eleven). In exposing ourselves and our inner world to the psychological truth exposed in reflective writing, we may discover ("see") the shape of this person we are becoming, the person present in all our professional work. When education (learning law) and the work of ordinary Wednesday afternoons in the practice of law focus exclusively on skills and knowledge—the problem to be solved, the next client to be seen—we lose sight of the human dimension of our craft. One way to retain and recover the values that are pushed aside in the rush of a busy day is to write about our "felt experience." Law is not something merely to learn, use, and do; it is something to experience. It is the experience of working with our minds in the company of clients, and of other lawyers who both contribute to and challenge our skills and knowledge, that makes our work both wearisome and pleasurable, alienated and meaningful. In writing about what matters to us, what we have succeeded in doing and what we have failed to do, things we understand and things that remain a mystery, about the lives we see our clients living and how we become a part of their lives when we serve them as lawyers (often enough, unintentionally), our lives take on a new depth and authenticity. It is this "inner experience" that Robert Redmount suggests is "the core of ... inquiry into professional conduct."

Journals are a means by which we connect our knowledge and our work with our subjectivity, our outer world with an inner sense of self. A journal honors subjective experience, brings it into view, makes it valuable. Subjectivity surrounds our learning, our knowing, our doing. Journals bring the subjectivity that is always, already there, back into conscious awareness. The journal is a way to relate knowing to being, and to confront the story we live when we become lawyers.

Postscript: A Note about the 4th Edition

We tried, in previous editions of *Legal Interviewing and Counseling*, to provide a workable "introductory" text, even as we took the liberty to follow our own interests (as every lawyer must, in some way, try to do). We wanted to present an introduction to counseling, and to the various theories and models that have most engaged us as lawyers and teachers. In following this approach we realize that there are developments in the counseling literature which we would not try to incorporate.

Since the first edition of *Legal Interviewing and Counseling* appeared in 1976, there have been significant developments in legal scholarship which deserve attention. Feminist jurisprudence is now a recognized "school" of contemporary jurisprudence, a school of jurisprudence from which one might outline a feminist approach to counseling. If the law itself has the markings of its masculine construction, then we might expect the law's masculine virtues to find their way into the law office and into the lawyer-client relationship. Given the work of feminist legal scholars, we suspect that some of the ideas and theories presented in *Legal Interviewing and Counseling* look different when viewed from a feminist perspective. Just how different we cannot say. We would hope that the differences would be more personal than ideological, more a matter of style than of substance. We have followed, with interest, the scholarly writing in feminist jurisprudence and assume that our client-centered, self-reflective approach to counseling is not alien to feminists. There has not, to our knowledge, been developed in the legal counseling literature anything resembling a full-scale feminist critique of the eclectic, psychological, humanistic, client-centered perspective presented in *Legal Interviewing and Counseling*. We have not focused on gender differences (noting as we do that these "differences" are contested and disputed) and have decided not to add a "gender differences" chapter to the 4th edition.

Another significant development, if less well-established, is the emerging "cultural studies" approach to law. We have attempted, if indirectly, to present legal counseling as an art and a skill practiced in a "legal culture" by a culture of lawyers. Lawyers in their interactions with clients are obviously, significantly, and pervasively influenced by the law office, law firm, and legal culture. If there is a single identifying mark of this legal culture it is the adversarial nature of our system of justice. The adversarial nature of the system, and our work with it, is at once cultural, definitional, and troubling. It is definitional in the sense that it shapes and frames and limits not only the way we solve problems brought to us by our clients, but also in the way adversarialism seeps into our consciousness and our character. It is the adversarial quality and nature of our work and the tension that follows from it, that underlie the moral fault lines in legal work and the common pathologies we associate with lawyers and their work. A culture—an adversarial culture—is the central feature (if not the map of the terrain) on which our work with clients, and our effort to counsel them, takes place.

We might well use a "cultural studies" approach to legal counseling to push our thinking about counseling in two different (and perhaps contradictory) directions: ideological and anthropological. We find persuasive the argument that in the adversarial system, lawyers are deeply affected by legal culture as an ideology. This means that lawyers in their work with clients represent (and resist) the ideological features of the legal culture (positive and negative). In one sense *all* lawyers represent law's ideology as they "do" the culture's work; they represent law as a living symbol and are participants in its continued enactment. In still another sense, a lawyer may, by the organization of a law office, and in her efforts as a counselor, work with a client to understand the ideological features of the LAW and swim against the force of the ideological tide. There is, of course, an on-going examination of this cultural perspective of law, and a critique of law as ideology, which serves as the substance of the various schools of contemporary jurisprudence. We could have used *Legal Interviewing and Counseling* to present the cultural/ideological features of lawyering in a more focused and penetrating way than what we have to date attempted.

A cultural studies approach to law might, in contrast to a theory-driven study of ideology, adopt an anthropological perspective. What is it, exactly and precisely, that happens in the law office when clients bring a problem to a lawyer and a lawyer must figure out what to do in response? How does the client talk to the lawyer? And how does the lawyer talk to the client? An anthropological imagination would have us curious about the nature of the language lawyers use and the language that clients use. How do lawyers and clients define a legal problem (and the context, the world, in which that problem has arisen)? And how will the client and the lawyer perceive the character of the work that the lawyer claims must be done to resolve the problem? And how does the use of this language (by lawyer)(by client) affect the character of each of them as the work is undertaken? There are obstacles (ethical, cultural, personal) in getting access to the language-in-use that takes place in the law office, the conversations in which counseling takes place. Nonetheless, there has been notable scholarship of just the kind of anthropological work we describe here, and we have found this work valuable and important. We welcome it and encourage law students and lawyers to pursue it (and make use of it) in their education. Every lawyer (and student of law) needs to be more aware of the cultural effects of law on our interactions with clients.

Religion too, just lately—and perhaps for the first time since World War II—is beginning to be a serious and acceptable focus in scholarly explorations of the moral lives of American lawyers. This new acceptance of religion as a focus of serious, scholarly, jurisprudential interest may also be of interest in thinking about ourselves as counselors. Until the 1990s, it was considered bad form, even in church-related law schools, to relate legal ethics and counseling issues to religious ethics and pastoral counseling. A vague commitment to the separation of law (as a discipline) from theology (as a discipline) has now given way to some theologizing among a small sub-group of American law professors. Some university law reviews (notably the *Fordham Law Review*) have devoted symposia to such topics as "faith and the law," and it is not uncommon to find essays on theological subjects even in elite law reviews. If this new development, in particular the scholarly exploration of religion and legal practice, turns out to have any influence, it may prompt lawyers to be more willing, as they think and talk to one another and to their neighbors, to bring conscience out of the closet—at least a little bit—and in doing so, to subject conscience (and the entanglements of conscience and legal thinking) to the disciplines of philosophical and theological ethics. We may find, in the turn to theology, an opportunity to confirm, buttress, and re-configure our thinking about the lawyer as counselor.

There are still other areas of legal scholarship that might provide the basis for an expanded (if not altered or revised) view of legal counseling. We note—with no pleasure, and a sense of growing alarm—a growing body of "unhappy lawyers" scholarship. The disaffection of growing numbers of lawyers with their professional lives is now so pronounced that it has become commonplace. Polls and empirical studies report that a substantial and significant number of young lawyers tell researchers they would prefer to be in a different profession. We will not attempt here to survey the various reasons being advanced for this situation, and we do not claim that a focus on the lawyer as counselor will provide immunity against professional malaise. We do believe, and believe strongly, that a better understanding of the psychology of law, lawyers, and lawyering, and a sustained effort at self-scrutiny, can offer insight into the lawyer disaffection phenomena, if not relief from professional malaise. There are, of course, social, political, and culture features of lawyering that an individual lawyer— even one well equipped psychologically—cannot amend or change. Obviously, we do not mean to imply that the best use of psychology is to better adapt ourselves to law work and a law culture which leaves so many lawyers on edge, depressed, stressed-out, leading unbalanced and unsustainable lives. So, it is not adaptation, or for pursuit of happiness (read in the limited sense of that term), that we prescribe psychology and attention to the lawyer-as-counselor in response to the "unhappy lawyer" phenomenon. But what psychology and counseling do, in both the best and worst of times and cultures, is to help us deal with the "who I am" vs. "who the world would have me be" problem.

This self-world problem (a manifestation of the role-identity conflict which so many lawyers experience) is always with us. As a constant feature of modern day existence, the conflict requires each of us to locate ourselves in, between, and beyond the alienation-conformity axis of our existence. We find psychology generally, and self-scrutiny in particular (especially as it draws on the discipline and theories of psychology, literature, and journal writing), to be essential as a first response to professional malaise. We think psychology (configured as serious self-study) can—if it cannot cure unhappiness, which is unlikely—prevent a slide toward a more serious condition, a form of neurosis we associate with the "working wounded," a pathology which may require sustained therapy and professional counseling.

We have made frequent references to lawyers in literature, and we could have made many more. Fictional lawyers tell us a great deal—more than one might suspect—about lawyers and legal culture. What we learn about the lawyers we find in novels and short stories provides exemplars of good lawyering and good counseling and an array of characters who present the full array of negative examples, or what Jung would call the "shadow" side of lawyering. The pathologies of lawyers are found in abundant examples all around us (and in our own lives), but they are nowhere better studied than in literature and popular literary fiction. If psychology is the single most important discipline outside law to which we turn for guidance on counseling, literature turns out to be an equally important resource for sharpening those ill-defined features of the good lawyer—creativity, imagination, risk-taking, and an understanding of human motivation and character (neurosis and pathology). We have focused on self-learning and psychology as a way of learning about other people, especially the people we meet and work with as clients, but we also think of literature (and legal fiction) as a rich source of learning about others and about ourselves. We use stories in our teaching (and draw upon literature) because of the intrinsic pleasure we experience in exploring stories, and because we know that what we learn about lawyers from fiction can be put to use. We're pleased that our own turn to literature and the value we place on stories is now widely recognized in the impressive (still growing) scholarly literature on "legal storytelling," "narrative jurisprudence," and the "law and literature" movement.

APPENDIX A

THE COUNSELING PROFESSIONS

There are occasions in the practice of law (as in the work of virtually every professional who deals directly with people) when you will need help in dealing with the problems confronting your client, help with a problematic client, or perhaps, help with problems you have created for yourself and your client. One of the realities of contemporary society is the division of labor in the helping professions. Few lawyers will be willing to help their clients resolve all the problems (especially protracted psychological ones) they bring with them to the law office.

In this Appendix we describe various mental health professionals for the purpose of giving you some idea about who clients can be referred to for further help.

Psychiatrists are medical or osteopathic doctors who have specialized in psychiatry; they operate the way other medical specialists operate (on referrals from other medical or osteopathic doctors) and tend to practice on the medical model. (This last is a very broad generalization; there is growing diversity in psychiatry, in both assumptions and methods.) Almost all psychiatrists have the M.D. or D.O. degree; some have specialist certification in the field of psychiatry and some do not.

Psychoanalysts are usually psychiatrists who use psychoanalytic methods—that is, the methods of depth analysis devised by Freud and his followers. There are a few "lay" analysts who do not have the medical degree. "Psychoanalysis" is sometimes used to describe Jungian psychotherapy, although Jung and his followers preferred the term "analytical psychology" to describe his method. Some Jungian analysts are medically trained but many are not. The Jungian method of counseling, like psychoanalysis, is time-consuming, intense, and expensive. One distinctive feature of both Freudian and Jungian psychotherapy is that the analyst has himself been "analyzed," has received the treatment that he now provides his client.

Psychologists, except where the term is used in its most general sense to mean anyone who works with others using psychological and counseling theories, are specialists with academic degrees and field training but they are not medically trained (and generally have not been clients for the kind of help they now seek to provide as professionals). Clinical psychologists are licensed in most states and engage in a broad range of counseling, therapy, and testing. They are trained at the Ph.D. level in universities and, typically, have undergone periods of internship in mental institutions or as counselors. Some psychologists limit their practices to the administration of psychological and personal development tests.

Many clinical psychologists now provide psychological services on a private-patient (or "client") basis, on a model similar to that followed by medically trained psychiatrists. Psychologists do not prescribe medication but sometimes have consulting relationships with physicians who prescribe medication on the psychologist's recommendation.

Psychotherapy is a generic term which usually means intensive therapy. There is a wide array of methods of psychotherapy, ranging from the non-directive methods of Carl Rogers to the technique-oriented Gestalt work (pioneered by the legendary Frederick Perls) and the TA (transactional analysis) theories of Eric Berne and Thomas Harris. Most psychotherapeutic methods have in common a setting in which professional and client talk about the client's problems.

Psychotherapy is sometimes practiced by persons with degrees in education, nursing, and religion and who have not received training at the doctoral level. Typically these practitioners have credentials at the master's degree level in psychology or social work. Many community mental health clinics provide counseling and therapy through psychiatric social workers and psychologists trained at the master's degree level.

Marriage counselors are trained at the doctoral or master's degree level, in non-medical schools of counseling, and practice in institutions, in agencies, and in private offices. Many of them are also trained (and certified) as clinical psychologists. The American Association of Marriage and Family Counselors says, about one of its members, that she "has met rigid education and examination requirements, and is licensed by the state in which she practices where regulated by law; is knowledgeable in areas of human growth and development, behavior, family dynamics and interaction; is skilled in counseling techniques and processes; is committed to a stringent code of ethics; is experienced—she has served at least two years in supervised clinical internship; is an active member of a professional association serving marriage and family counselors; and welcomes your inquiries about her methodology, background, and experience."

The clergy are also counselors. The traditional member of the clergy relied on experience and the grace of God for human-relations skills, and was often ill-served from both sources. (But, then, much the same could be said of the traditional lawyer.) Seminary and divinity-school training may now include human-relations skills training and many religious congregations now include among congregational clergy professionals who are certified in psychology or marriage counseling and ordained to the ministry or rabbinate. A useful conduit to such persons, and to clergy who are not formally trained but are regarded as competent in counseling, may be a local agency that acts in social matters for the religious congregations, such as the Catholic social service organizations, Council of Churches, the Ministerial Alliance, or Jewish community organizations.

CHAPTER REFERENCES

[For chapter references we have provided original publication dates from which we have (generally) drawn our citations, and the most recent publication of the work.]

Chapter Two

Alasdair MacIntyre, *After Virtue: A Study in Moral Theory* (1984)(1981); Louis Auchincloss, *The Great World and Timothy Colt* (1987)(1956); Clifford Geertz, *Local Knowledge: Further Essays in Interpretive Anthropology* (1983); Gerald P. López & Alison Grey Anderson, unpublished ms.; James Boyd White, *The Legal Imagination: Studies in the Nature of Legal Thought and Expression* (1973).

Chapter Three

Richard Bandler & John Grinder, *The Structure of Magic: A Book About Language and Therapy* (1975)(vol.1); Fred Rodell, *Woe Unto You, Lawyers!* (1939); James Boyd White, *The Legal Imagination: Studies in the Nature of Legal Thought and Expression* (1973); David B. Saxe & Seymour F. Kuvin, "Notes on the Attorney–Client Relationship," 2 J.Psychiatry & L. 209 (1974); Stuart A. Scheingold, *The Politics of Rights: Lawyers, Public Policy, and Political Change* (2004)(1974); Judith N. Shklar, *Legalism: Law, Morals and Political Trials*

(1986)(1964); Murray Stein, "Power, Shamanism, and Maieutics in the Countertransference," Chiron: A Review of Jungian Analysis 67 (1984); Howard F. Stein, *The Psychodynamics of Medical Practice: Unconscious Factors in Patient Care* (1985).

Chapter Four

Victor H. Appel & Ralph E. Van Atta, "The Attorney–Client Dyad: An Outsider's View," 22 Okla.L.Rev. 243 (1969); Eric Berne, *Transactional Analysis in Psychotherapy: A Systematic Individual and Social Psychiatry* (1978)(1961); Eric Berne, *Games People Play: The Psychology of Human Relationships* (1996)(1964); Virginia Church, "Counselor–at–Law: A Game of Chess?" Trial, Sept.–Oct. 1972, p. 271; Virginia Church, "People Come to Lawyers Wanting a Good Parent, Magical Bodyguard, and Political Ally with Muscle," Student Lawyer, Dec. 1973, p. 10; Sigmund Freud, *Dora: Analysis of a Case of Hysteria* (1997)(Collier Books, 1963); Frieda Fromm–Reichmann, *Principles of Intensive Psychotherapy* (1974)(1950); Erving Goffman, "The Nature of Deference and Demeanor," 58 Am.Anthropologist 453 (1956); Raymond S. Hunt, "Problems and Processes in the Legal Interview,"50 Ill.B.J. 726 (1962); C.G. Jung, "The Psychology of the Transference in the Practice of Psychotherapy," in C.G. Jung, *Collected Works* (Bollingen, 2nd ed. 1966)(vol. 16); Carl Jung, *Analytical Psychology: It's Theory and Practice–The Tavistock Lectures* (Pantheon Books, 1968); Carl R. Rogers, *Client-*

Centered Therapy: It's Current Practice, Implications, and Theory (1965)(1951); Carl R. Rogers, *On Becoming a Person: A Therapist's View of Psychotherapy* (1995)(1961); Claude Steiner, *Scripts People Live: Transactional Analysis of Life Scripts* (1990)(1974).

Chapter Five

Louis Brown & Thomas Shaffer, "Toward a Jurisprudence for the Law Office," 17 Am.J.Juris. 125 (1972); Alfred C. Kinsey, *Sexual Behavior in the Human Male* (1998)(1948).

Chapter Six

Eric Berne, *Transactional Analysis in Psychotherapy* (1978)(1961); Eric Berne, *What Do You Say After You Say Hello?* (1985)(1972); Martin Buber, *I and Thou* (Kaufmann trans. 1996)(1958); Sigmund Freud, *Dora: Analysis of a Case of Hysteria* (Collier ed. 1963); Greenwald, "The Ground Rules in Gestalt Therapy," in Chris Hatcher & Philip Himelstein (eds.), *The Handbook of Gestalt Therapy*, 1976); Thomas A. Harris, *I'm OK, You're OK: A Practical Guide to Transactional Analysis* (2004)(1969); David Hilfiker, *Healing the Wounds: A Physician Looks at His Work* (1998)(1985); Karen Horney, *Self–analysis* (1999)(1942); Muriel James & Dorothy Jongeward, *Born to Win: Transactional Analysis with Gestalt Experiments* (1996)(1971); C.G. Jung, *The Psychology of the Transference in the Practice of Psychotherapy*, in C.G. Jung, *Collected Works* (Bollingen, 2nd ed. 1966)(vol.16); Carl

Jung, *Analytical Psychology: It's Theory and Practice–The Tavistock Lectures* (Pantheon Books, 1968); Alfred C. Kinsey, *Sexual Behavior in the Human Male* (1998)(1948)(ch. 4); Joseph Luft, *Of Human Interaction* (1969); Frederick S. Perls, *Gestalt Therapy Verbatim* (1992)(1969)(John O. Stevens ed.); Ellis Hull Porter, *An Introduction to Therapeutic Counseling* (1950); Theodor Reik, *Listening with the Third Ear: The Inner Experience of a Psychoanalyst* (1983)(1948); Carl R. Rogers, *Client-Centered Therapy: It's Current Practice, Implications, and Theory* (2003)(1951); Carl R. Rogers, *On Becoming a Person: A Therapist's View of Psychotherapy* (1995)(1961); Carl R. Rodgers, *A Way of Being* (1995)(1980); Everett L. Shostrom, *Man the Manipulator: The Inner Journey from Manipulation to Actualization* (1968)(1967); Joseph Simons & Jeanne Reidy, *The Human Art of Counseling* (1971); Andrew S. Watson, "The Quest for Professional Competence: Psychological Aspects of Legal Education," 37 U.Cin.L.Rev. 93 (1968); Andrew S. Watson, *Psychiatry for Lawyers* (1968).

Chapter Seven

Alfred Benjamin, *The Helping Interview* (2001)(1969); John Dewey, "Logical Method and Law," 10 Cornell L.Quart. 17 (1924); Annette Marie Garrett, *Interviewing: Its Principals and Methods* (1982)(1942); Carl R. Rogers, *Client-Centered Therapy: It's Current Practice, Implications, and Theory* (2003)(1951); Edgar H. Schein, *Process Consultation: Its Role in Organizational Development*

(1987)(1969) (includes Wallen article); Thomas L. Shaffer, *Death, Property, and Lawyers* (1970); Erwin O. Smigel, *The Wall Street Lawyer: Professional Organization Man?* (1969)(1964); Herbert Wexler, "Practicing Law for Poor People," 79 Yale L.J. 1049 (1970).

Chapter Eight

Carl R. Rogers, *Client-Centered Therapy: It's Current Practice, Implications, and Theory* (2003)(1951); Steele, "Physical Settings and Organizational Development," in Harvey A. Hornstein *et. al.* (eds.), *Social Intervention: A Behavioral Science Approach* (1971).

Chapter Nine

Louis M. Brown, *Preventive Law* (1970)(1950); Louis M. Brown, *Lawyering Through Life: The Origin of Preventive Law* (1986); Louis M. Brown & Edward Dauer, *Planning by Lawyers: Materials on a Nonadversarial Process* (1997)(1978); John Dewey, "Logical Method and Law," 10 Cornell L.Quart. 17 (1924); Thomas A. Harris, *I'm OK, You're OK: A Practical Guide to Transactional Analysis* (2004)(1969); Carl Jung, *Analytical Psychology: It's Theory and Practice–The Tavistock Lectures* (Pantheon Books, 1968); C.G. Jung, "Psychological Types," in C.G. Jung, *Collected Works* (Bollingen, 1971)(vol.6); Carl R. Rogers, *Client-Centered Therapy: It's Current Practice, Implications, and Theory* (2003)(1951); Douglas E. Rosenthal, *Lawyers and*

Client: Who's in Charge? (1977)(1974); C.P. Snow, *Trollope, His Life and Art* (1975).

Chapter Ten

Karl Barth, *The Epistle to the Romans* (trans. from the 6th ed., Edwyn C. Hoskyns, 1980)(1933); Eric Berne, *Games People Play: The Psychology of Human Relationships* (1996)(1964); Louis M. Brown & Thomas L. Shaffer, "Toward a Jurisprudence for the Law Office," 17 Am.J.Juris. 125 (1972); Frank Philip Cihlar, "Client Self–Determination: Intervention or Interference," 14 St.Louis U.L.J. 604 (1970); Abe Krash, "Professional Responsibility to Clients and the Public Interest: Is There a Conflict," 55 Chi.B.Rec. (1973)(Special Centennial Issue); Roger Cramton, "Comment," 55 Chi. B.Rec. (1973); Warren Lehman, "The Pursuit of a Client's Interest," 77 Mich.L.Rev. 1078 (1979); Karl N. Llewellyn, *The Bramble Bush: On Our Law and Its Study* (1991)(The *Bramble Bush: Some Lectures On Law and Its Study* (1930)); David Riesman, "Some Observations on Law and Psychology," 19 U.Chi.L.Rev. 30 (1951).

Chapter Eleven

Charles Chauncey Binney, *The Life of Horace Binney, with Selections from His Letters* (1903); Carl Jung, *Analytical Psychology* (1968); John Noonan, *Persons and Masks of the Law: Cardozo, Holmes, Jefferson, and Wythe as Makers of the Masks* (2002)(1976); Erich Neumann, *Depth Psychology and a New Ethic* (1990)(1969); Erich Neumann, *The Origins and History of Consciousness* (1999)(1954); Sigmund Freud, *The Complete Introductory Lectures on Psychoanalysis* (1966); Richard Sennett, *The Uses of Disorder: Personal Identity & City Life* (1996)(1970); Erik H. Erikson, *Life History and the Historical Moment* (1975); Robert Lifton, *Boundaries: Psychological Man in Revolution* (1970)(1969); Douglas Rosenthal, *Lawyer and Client: Who's in Charge?* (1974); David B. Saxe & Seymour F. Kuvin, "Notes on the Attorney–Client Relationship," 2 J.Psychiatry & L. 209 (1974).

Chapter Twelve

Abraham Zaleznik & Manfred F.R. Kets de Vries, *Power and the Corporate Mind* (1985)(1975); Carl Jung, *Analytical Psychology: It's Theory and Practice–The Tavistock Lectures* (Pantheon Books, 1968); Robert Redmount, "Attorney Personalities and Some Psychological Aspects of Legal Consultation," 109 U.Penn.L.Rev. 972 (1961); Carl R. Rogers, *Client-Centered Therapy: It's Current Practice, Implications, and Theory* (2003)(1951).

COUNSELING BIBLIOGRAPHY

Books

Bastress, Robert M. & Joseph D. Harbaugh. INTER-
VIEWING, COUNSELING, AND NEGOTIATING: SKILLS FOR
EFFECTIVE REPRESENTATION. Boston: Little, Brown
and Company, 1990.

Binder, David A., Paul Bergman & Susan C. Price.
LAWYERS AS COUNSELORS: A CLIENT-CENTERED AP-
PROACH. St. Paul, MN: Thomson/West, 2nd ed.,
2004.

Cochran, Robert F., John M.A. DiPippa & Martha
M. Peters. THE COUNSELOR-AT-LAW: A COLLABORATIVE
APPROACH TO CLIENT INTERVIEWING AND COUNSELING.
New York: Lexis Publishing, 1999.

Freeman, Harrop A. LEGAL INTERVIEWING AND COUN-
SELING: CASES WITH COMMENTS. St. Paul, MN: West
Publishing Co., 1964.

Freeman, Harrop A. & Henry Weihofen. CLINICAL
LAW TRAINING: INTERVIEWING AND COUNSELING. St.
Paul, MN: West Publishing Co., 1972.

Jandt, Fred E. EFFECTIVE INTERVIEWING AND A PROFIT-
ABLE PRACTICE. Cincinnati: Anderson Publishing
Co., 1990.

Krieger, Stefan H. ESSENTIAL LAWYERING SKILLS: IN-
TERVIEWING, COUNSELING, NEGOTIATION, AND PERSUA-

SIVE FACT ANALYSIS. New York: Aspen Publishers, 2nd ed., 2003.

Lisnek, Paul Michael. EFFECTIVE CLIENT COMMUNICATION: A LAWYER'S HANDBOOK FOR INTERVIEWING AND COUNSELING. St. Paul, MN: West Publishing Co., 1992.

Rosenthal, Douglas E. LAWYER AND CLIENT: WHO'S IN CHARGE?. New Brunswick, NJ: Transaction Books, 1977.

Schoenfield, Mark K. & Barbara Pearlman Schoenfield. INTERVIEWING AND COUNSELING. Philadelphia: American Law Institute–American Bar Association Committee on Continuing Professional Education, 1981.

Shaffer, Thomas. DEATH, PROPERTY AND LAWYERS: A BEHAVIORAL APPROACH. New York: Dunnellen, 1970.

Shaffer, Thomas L. & Robert F. Cochran. LAWYERS, CLIENTS AND MORAL RESPONSIBILITY. St. Paul, MN: West Publishing, 1994.

Shaffer, Thomas L., Carol Ann Mooney & Amy Jo Boettcher. THE PLANNING AND DRAFTING OF WILLS AND TRUSTS. New York: Foundation Press, 4th ed., 2001.

Shaffer, Thomas & Robert S. Redmount. LEGAL INTERVIEWING AND COUNSELING. New York: Matthew Bender, 1980.

Watson, Andrew. PSYCHIATRY FOR LAWYERS. New York: International Universities Press, rev. ed., 1978.

_____. THE LAWYER IN THE INTERVIEWING AND COUNSELING PROCESS. Charlottesville, VA: The Michie Company, 1976.

Zwier, Paul J. & Anthony J. Bocchino. FACT INVESTIGATION: A PRACTICAL GUIDE TO INTERVIEWING, COUNSELING, AND CASE THEORY DEVELOPMENT. Notre Dame, IN: National Institute for Trial Advocacy, 2000.

Articles

Appel, Victor H. & Ralph E. Van Atta. *The Attorney–Client Dyad: An Outsider's View*, 22 Okla. L.Rev. 243 (1969).

Baggett, Earlene. *Cross-Cultural Legal Counseling*, 18 Creighton L.Rev. 1475 (1984).

Bastress, Robert M. *Client–Centered Counseling and Moral Accountability for Lawyers*, 10 J.Legal Prof. 97 (1985).

Barkai, John L. *A New Model for Legal Communications: Sensory Experience and Representational Systems*, 29 Clev.–St.L.Rev. 575 (1980).

Barkai, John L. & Virginia O. Fine. *Empathy Training for Lawyers and Law Students*, 13 Sw. U.L.Rev. 505 (1983).

Binder, David, Paul Bergman & Susan Price. *Lawyers as Counselors: A Client–Centered Approach*, 35 N.Y.L.Sch.L.Rev. 29 (1990).

Bloch, Frank S. *Framing the Clinical Experience: Lessons on Turning Points and the Dynamics of Lawyering*, 64 Tenn. L.Rev. 989 (1997).

Bogoch, Bryna. *Gendered Lawyering: Difference and Dominance in Lawyer–Client Interaction*, 31 Law & Soc'y Rev. 677 (1997).

Brown, Louis & Thomas L. Shaffer. *Toward a Jurisprudence of the Law Office*, 17 Am.J.Juris. 125 (1972).

Bryan, Penelope E. *Reclaiming Professionalism: The Lawyer's Role in Divorce Mediation*, 28 Fam. L.Q. 177 (1994).

Cahn, Naomi R. *Styles of Lawyering*, 43 Hastings L.J. 1039 (1992).

Caplow, Stacy. *What If There Is No Client?: Prosecutors as "Counselors" of Crime Victims*, 5 Clin. L.Rev. 1 (1998).

Cihlar, Frank Phillip. *Client Self–Determination: Intervention or Interference?,*14 St. Louis U.L.J. 604 (1970).

Cochran, Robert F. *Legal Representation and the Next Steps Toward Client Control: Attorney Malpractice and the Failure to Allow the Client to Control Negotiation and Pursue Alternatives to Litigation*, 47 Wash. & Lee L.Rev. 819 (1990).

Condlin, Robert J. *"What's Love Got To Do With It?"–"It's Not Like They're Your Friends for Christ's Sake": The Complicated Relationship Between Lawyer and Client*, 82 Neb. L.Rev. 211 (2003).

Dauer, Edward & Arthur Leff. *Correspondence: The Lawyer as Friend*, 86 Yale L.J. 573 (1977).

Dinerstein, Robert D. *A Mediation on the Theoretics of Practice*, 43 Hastings L.J. 971 (1992).

____. *Clinical Texts and Contexts* (Review Essay), 39 UCLA L.Rev. 697 (1992).

____. *Client–Centered Counseling: Reappraisal and Refinement*, 32 Ariz.L.Rev. 501 (1990).

DiPippa, John M.A. *How Prospect Theory Can Improve Legal Counseling*, 24 U. Ark. Little Rock L.Rev. 81 (2001).

Elkins, James R. *The Legal Persona: An Essay on the Professional Mask*, 64 Vir.L.Rev. 735 (1978).

____. *A Counseling Model for Lawyering in Divorce Cases*, 53 Notre Dame Law. 229 (1977).

Ellman, Stephen. *Lawyers and Clients*, 34 UCLA L.Rev. 717 (1987).

____. *Empathy and Approval*, 43 Hastings L.J. 991 (1992).

Federle, Katherine Hunt. *The Ethics of Empowerment: Rethinking the Role of Lawyers in Interviewing and Counseling the Child Client*, 64 Fordham L.Rev. 1655 (1996).

Felstiner, William L.F. & Austin Sarat. *Law and Strategy in the Divorce Lawyer's Office*, 20 Law & Soc'y Rev. 93 (1986).

____. *Enactments of Power: Negotiating Reality and Responsibility in Lawyer–Client Interactions*, 77 Cornell L.Rev. 1447 (1992).

Fey, Steven G. & Steven Goldberg. *Legal Interviewing From a Psychological Perspective: An Attorney's Handbook*, 14 Willmette L. J. 217 (1978).

Furey, Nancy M. *Legal Interviewing and Counseling Bibliography*, 18 Creighton L.Rev. 1503 (1985).

Gantt, Larry O., II. *Ethical Guideposts for the Christian Attorney: Integration as Integrity: Postmodernism, Psychology, and Religion on the Role of Moral Counseling in the Attorney-Client Relationship*, 16 Regent U.L.Rev. 233 (2003/2004).

Gellhorn, Gay. *Law and Language: An Empirically–Based Model for the Opening Moments of Client Interviews*, 4 Clin.L.Rev. 321 (1998).

Gellhorn, Gary, Lynn Robins & Pat Roth. *Law and Language: An Interdisciplinary Study of Client Interviews*, 1 Clin.L.Rev. 245 (1994).

Gelt, Howard. *Psychological Considerations in Representing the Aged Client*, 17 Ariz.L.Rev. 293 (1975).

Gifford, Donald G. *The Synthesis of Legal Counseling and Negotiation Models: Preserving Client–Centered Advocacy in the Negotiation Context*, 34 UCLA L.Rev. 811 (1987).

Gilkerson, Christopher P. *Poverty Law Narratives: The Critical Practice and Theory of Receiving and Translating Client Stories*, 43 Hastings L.J. 861 (1992).

Glennon, Theresa. *Lawyers and Caring: Building an Ethic of Care Into Professional Responsibility*, 43 Hastings L.J. 1175 (1992).

Goodpaster, Gary. *The Human Arts of Lawyering: Interviewing and Counseling*, 27 J.Legal Educ. 4 (1975).

Hazard, Geoffrey C., Jr. *Lawyer as Wise Counselor*, 49 Loy. L.Rev. 215 (2003).

Heller, Jamie G. *Legal Counseling in the Administrative State: How To Let the Client Decide*, 103 Yale L.J. 2503 (1994).

Hosticka, Carl J. *We Don't Care What Happened, We Only Care About What is Going to Happen: Lawyer–Client Negotiations of Reality*, 26 Soc. Probs. 599 (1979).

Hurder, Alex J. *Negotiating the Lawyer–Client Relationship: A Search for Equality and Collaboration*, 44 Buff.L.Rev. 71 (1996).

Jacobs, Michelle S. *People from the Footnotes: The Missing Element in Client-centered Counseling*, 27 Golden Gate U.L.Rev. 345 (1997).

Kelso, Charles D. & C. Kevin Kelso. *Conflict, Emotion, and Legal Ethics*, 10 Pac.L.J. 69 (1978).

Kessler, Joan B. *The Lawyer's Intercultural Communication Problems with Clients from Diverse Cultures*, 9 Nw.J.Int'l L. & Bus. 64 (1988).

Kritzer, Herbert M. *The Dimensions of Lawyer–Client Relations: Notes Toward a Theory and a Field Study*, 1984 Am.B.Found.Res.J. 409.

Lehman, Warren. *The Pursuit of a Client's Interest*, 77 Mich.L.Rev. 1078 (1979).

Levinson, Sanford. *The Lawyer as Moral Counselor: How Much Should the Client Be Expected to Pay*, 77 Notre Dame L.Rev. 831 (2002).

Loder, Reed Elizabeth. *Out From Uncertainty: A Model of the Lawyer–Client Relationship*, 2 S.Calif.Interdis.L.J. 89 (1993).

Luban, David. *Partisanship, Betrayal and Autonomy in the Lawyer–Client Relationship: A Reply to Stephen Ellmann*, 90 Colum.L.Rev. 1004 (1990).

Margulies, Peter. *"Who Are You to Tell Me That?": Attorney–Client Deliberation Regarding Nonlegal Issues and the Interests of Nonclients*, 68 No.Car. L.Rev. 213 (1990).

Martyn, Susan R. *Informed Consent in the Practice of Law*, 48 Geo.Wash.L.Rev. 307 (1985).

Mather, Lynn. *Fundamental: What Do Clients Want? What Do Lawyers Do?*, 52 Emory L.J. 1065 2003.

Maute, Judith L. *Allocation of Decisionmaking Authority Under the Model Rules of Professional Conduct*, 17 U.C.Davis L.Rev. 1049 (1984).

Menkel–Meadow, Carrie. *Portia in a Different Voice: Speculations on a Women's Lawyering Process*, 1 Berkeley Women's L.J. 39 (1985).

Miller, Binny. *Give Them Back Their Lives: Recognizing Client Narratives in Case Theory*, 93 Mich. L.Rev. 485 (1995).

Mitchell–Cichon, Marla Lyn. *What Mom Would Have Wanted: Lessons Learned from an Elder*

Law Clinic About Achieving Clients' Estate–Planning Goals, 10 Elder L.J. 289 (2002).

Mitchell, John B. *Narrative and Client-centered Representation: What Is a True Believer to Do When His Two Favorite Theories Collide?*, 6 Clin. L.Rev. 85 (1999).

Morgan, Thomas D. *Thinking About Lawyers as Counselors*, 42 Fla.L.Rev. 439 (1990).

Murdoch, Lynda L. *Psychological Consequences of Adopting a Therapeutic Lawyering Approach: Pitfalls and Protective Strategies*, 24 Seattle Univ.L. R. 483 (2000).

Nelson, Robert L. & Stewart Macaulay. *Ideology, Practice, and Professional Autonomy: Social Values and Client Relations in the Large Law Firm*, 37 Stan.L.Rev. 503 (1985).

Neustadter, Gary. *When Lawyer and Client Meet: Observations of Interviewing and Counseling Behavior in the Consumer Bankruptcy Law Office*, 35 Buff.L.Rev. 177 (1986).

Nolan–Haley, Jacqueline M. *Propter Honoris Respectum: Lawyers, Clients, and Mediation*, 73 Notre Dame L.Rev. 1369 (1998).

Peters, Don. *You Can't Always Get What You Want: Organizing Matrimonial Interviews to Get What You Need*, 26 Cal.W.Res.Rev. 257 (1989–90).

Peters, Don & Martha M. Peters. *Maybe That's Why I Do That: Psychological Type Theory, the Myers–Briggs Type Indicator, and Learning Legal Interviewing*, 35 N.Y.L.Sch.L.Rev. 169 (1990).

Postema, Gerald J. *Moral Responsibility in Professional Ethics*, 55 N.Y.U.L.Rev. 63 (1980).

Redmount, Robert. *Humanistic Law Through Legal Counseling*, 2 Conn.L.Rev. 98 (1969).

———. *Attorney Personalities and Some Psychological Aspects of Legal Consultation*, 109 U.Pa.L.Rev. 972 (1961).

———. *Perception and Strategy in Divorce Counseling,* 35 Conn.B.J. 2149 (1960).

Rosenberg, Joshua D. *Interpersonal Dynamics: Helping Lawyers Learn the Skills, and the Importance of Human Relationships in the Practice of Law*, 58 U. Miami L.Rev. 1225 (2004).

Rubinson, Robert. *Constructions of Client Competence and Theories of Practice*, 31 Ariz. St. L.J. 121 (1999).

Sammons, Jack. *Rank Strangers to Me: Shaffer and Cochran's Friendship Model of Moral Counseling in the Law Office*, 18 U.Ark.Little Rock L.J. 1 (1995).

Sarat, Austin & William L.F. Felstiner. *Enactments of Power: Negotiating Reality and Responsibility in Lawyer-client Interactions*, 77 Cornell L.Rev. 1447 (1992).

———. *Lawyers and Legal Consciousness: Law Talk in the Divorce Lawyer's Office*, 98 Yale L.J. 1663 (1989).

———. *Law & Social Relations: Vocabularies of Motive in Lawyer/Client Interaction*, 22 Law & Soc'y Rev. 739 (1988).

Saxe, David B. & Seymour F. Kuvin. *The Attorney–Client Relationship: A Psychoanalytic Overview*, 9 N.Eng.L.Rev. 395 (1974).

Schoenfield, Mark K. & Barbara Pearlman Schoenfield. *Interviewing and Counseling Clients in a Legal Setting*, 11 Akron L.Rev. 313 (1977).

———. *How to Handle a Client In a State of Crisis*, 27(4) Prac.Lawyer 53 (1981).

Shaffer, Thomas L. *On Thinking Theologically About Lawyers as Counselors*, 42 Fla.L.Rev. 467 (1990).

———. *The Practice of Law as Moral Discourse*, 55 Notre Dame Law. 231 (1979).

———. *A Lesson From Trollope for Counselors at Law*, 35 Wash. & Lee L.Rev. 727 (1978).

———. *Undue Influence, Confidential Relationships, and the Psychology of Transference*, 45 Notre Dame Law. 197 (1970).

———. *The "Estate Planning" Counselor and Values Destroyed by Death*, 55 Iowa L.Rev. 376 (1969).

———. *Will Interviews, Young Clients and the Psychology of Testation*, 44 Notre Dame Law. 345 (1969).

Shaffer, Thomas L. & Robert F. Cochran, Jr. *Lawyers as Strangers and Friends: A Reply to Professor Sammons*, 18 U.Ark.Little Rock L.J. 69 (1995).

Silver, Marjorie A. *Emotional Competence, Multicultural Lawyering and Race*, 3 Fl. Coastal L.J. 219 (2002).

_____. *Love, Hate, and Other Emotional Interference in the Lawyer/client Relationship*, 6 Clin.L.Rev. 259 (1999).

Smith, Linda F. *Medical Paradigms for Counseling: Giving Clients Bad News*, 4 Clin.L.Rev. 391 (1998).

_____. *Interviewing Clients: A Linguistic Comparison of the "Traditional" Interview and the "Client–Centered" Interview*, 1 Clin.L.Rev. 54 (1995).

Spiegel, Mark. *The Case of Mrs. Jones Revisited: Paternalism and Autonomy in Lawyer–Client Counseling*, 1997 B.Y.U.L.Rev. 307.

_____. *The New Model Rules of Professional Conduct: Lawyer–Client Decision Making and the Role of Rules in Structuring the Lawyer–Client Dialogue*, 1980 Am.B.Found.Res.J. 1003.

_____. *Lawyering and Client Decisionmaking: Informed Consent and the Legal Profession*, 128 U.Pa.L.Rev. 41 (1979).

Strauss, Marcy. *Toward a Revised Model of Attorney–Client Relationship: The Argument for Autonomy*, 65 No.Car.L.Rev. 315 (1987).

Tremblay, Paul R. *Interviewing and Counseling Across Cultures: Heuristics and Biases*, 9 Clin. L.Rev. 373 (2002).

Wasserstrom, Richard. *Lawyers as Professionals: Some Moral Issues*, 5 Human Rights L.Rev. 1 (1975).

Watson, Andrew. *Lawyers and Professionalism: A Further Psychiatric Perspective on Legal Education*, 8 U.Mich.J.L.Reform. 248 (1975).

_____. *Know Thyself and Thy Client*, 1 Learning & the Law 23 (1974).

_____. *Professionalizing the Lawyer's Role as Counselor: Risk–Taking for Rewards*, 1969 Ariz.St.L.J. 17 (1969).

_____. *The Lawyer as Counselor*, 5 J.Fam.Law. 7 (1965).

Wiseman, Frederick. *Lawyer–Client Interviews: Some Lessons from Psychiatry*, 39 Bos.U.L.Rev. 181 (1959).

Zacharias, Fred C. *Reconciling Professionalism and Client Interests*, 36 Wm. & Mary L.Rev. 1303 (1995).

Zeidman, Steven. *To Plead or Not to Plead: Effective Assistance and Client–Centered Counseling*, 39 B.C. L. Rev 841 (1998).

Zwier Paul J. & Ann B. Hamric. *The Ethics of Care and Reimagining the Lawyer/Client Relationship*, 22 J.Contemp.L. 383 (1996).

RESOURCE READINGS: A SELECTED BIBLIOGRAPHY

[References are to the latest published U.S. or London edition of the book]

Books

Abrams, Jeremiah (ed.). THE SHADOW IN AMERICA: RECLAIMING THE SOUL OF A NATION. Novato, CA: Nataraj Pub., 1994.

Argyris, Chris & Donald A. Schön. THEORY IN PRACTICE: INCREASING PROFESSIONAL EFFECTIVENESS. San Francisco: Jossey–Bass Publishers, 1992.

Baumeister, Roy F. ESCAPING THE SELF: ALCOHOLISM, SPIRITUALITY, MASOCHISM, AND OTHER FLIGHTS FROM THE BURDEN OF SELFHOOD. New York: BasicBooks/Harper Collins, 1991.

Baur, Susan. CONFIDING: A PSYCHOTHERAPIST AND HER PATIENTS SEARCH FOR STORIES TO LIVE BY. New York: HarperPerennial, 1995.

Becker, Ernest. THE BIRTH AND DEATH OF MEANING: AN INTERDISCIPLINARY PERSPECTIVE ON THE PROBLEM OF MAN. New York: Free Press, 2nd ed., 1971.

Belenky, Mary Field *et al*. WOMEN'S WAYS OF KNOWING: THE DEVELOPMENT OF SELF, VOICE, AND MIND. New York: BasicBooks, 1997.

Berne, Eric. WHAT DO YOU SAY AFTER YOU SAY HELLO?: THE PSYCHOLOGY OF HUMAN DESTINY. New York: Bantam Books, 1985.

_____. GAMES PEOPLE PLAY: THE PSYCHOLOGY OF HUMAN RELATIONSHIPS. New York: Ballantine Books, 1996.

Bruner, Jerome. ACTS OF MEANING. Cambridge: Harvard University Press, 1998.

_____. ACTUAL MINDS, POSSIBLE WORLDS. Cambridge: Harvard University Press, 1986.

Carse, James. FINITE AND INFINITE GAMES: A VISION OF LIFE AS PLAY AND POSSIBILITY. New York: Ballantine Books, 1997.

Carson, Richard D. TAMING YOUR GREMLIN: A GUIDE TO ENJOYING YOURSELF. New York: Quill, 2003.

Cassell, Eric J. THE HEALER'S ART: A NEW APPROACH TO THE DOCTOR-PATIENT RELATIONSHIP. Cambridge: MIT Press, 1985.

Chernin, Kim. A DIFFERENT KIND OF LISTENING: MY PSYCHOANALYSIS AND ITS SHADOW. New York: HarperPerennial, 1996.

Cohen, David B. OUT OF THE BLUE: DEPRESSION AND HUMAN NATURE. New York: W.W. Norton, 1995.

De Beauport, Elaine. THE THREE FACES OF MIND: DEVELOPING YOUR MENTAL, EMOTIONAL, AND BEHAVIORAL INTELLIGENCES. Wheaton, IL: Quest Books/Theosophical Publishing House, 2002.

Downing, Christine. THE GODDESS: MYTHOLOGICAL IMAGES OF THE FEMININE. New York: Continuum, 2000.

Edinger, Edward F. EGO AND ARCHETYPE: INDIVIDUA-TION AND THE RELIGIOUS FUNCTION OF THE PSYCHE. Boston: Shambhala, 1992.

Egan, Gerard. THE SKILLED HELPER: A PROBLEM-MAN-AGEMENT AND OPPORTUNITY-DEVELOPMENT APPROACH TO HELPING. Pacific Grove, CA: Brooks/Cole Pub. Co., 7th ed., 2002.

_____. ENCOUNTER: GROUP PROCESSES FOR INTERPERSONAL GROWTH. Belmont, CA: Brooks/Cole/Wadsworth Publishing, 1970.

Ferrucci, Piero. WHAT WE MAY BE: TECHNIQUES FOR PSYCHOLOGICAL AND SPIRITUAL GROWTH THROUGH PSY-CHOSYNTHESIS. New York: Jeremy P. Tarcher/Put-nam Book, 1982.

Freedman, Jill & Gene Combs. NARRATIVE THERAPY: THE SOCIAL CONSTRUCTION OF PREFERRED REALITIES. New York: W.W. Norton, 1996.

Fromm, Erich. MAN FOR HIMSELF: AN INQUIRY INTO THE PSYCHOLOGY OF ETHICS. London: Routledge, 2003.

Gaylin, Willard. THE RAGE WITHIN: ANGER IN MODERN LIFE. New York: Penguin Books, 1989.

_____. FEELINGS: OUR VITAL SIGNS. New York: Harper & Row, 1988.

Gerzon, Mark. LISTENING TO MIDLIFE: TURNING YOUR CRISIS INTO A QUEST. Boston: Shambhala, 1996.

Gilligan, Carol. IN A DIFFERENT VOICE: PSYCHOLOGICAL THEORY AND WOMEN'S DEVELOPMENT. Cambridge: Harvard University Press, 1993.

Goleman, Daniel. WORKING WITH EMOTIONAL INTELLIGENCE. New York: Bantam Books, 2000.

———. EMOTIONAL INTELLIGENCE. New York: Bantam Books, 1997.

———. VITAL LIES, SIMPLE TRUTHS: THE PSYCHOLOGY OF SELF-DECEPTION. London: Bloomsbury, 1997.

Hampden–Turner, Charles. MAPS OF THE MIND. New York: Collier Books, 1982.

———. RADICAL MAN: THE PROCESS OF PSYCHO–SOCIAL DEVELOPMENT. Garden City, NY: Anchor Books, 1971.

Harris, Thomas. I'M OK, YOU'RE OK: A PRACTICAL GUIDE TO PSYCHOANALYSIS. New York: Quill, 2004.

Hilfiker, David. HEALING THE WOUNDS: A PHYSICIAN LOOKS AT HIS WORK. Omaha, NE: Creighton University Press, 1998.

Hillman, James. A BLUE FIRE: SELECTED WRITINGS. Thomas Moore, editor. New York: HarperPerennial, 1991.

———. THE FORCE OF CHARACTER: AND THE LASTING LIFE. New York: Ballantine Books, 2000.

———. HEALING FICTION. Dallas: Spring Publications, 1994.

———. THE MYTH OF ANALYSIS: THREE ESSAYS IN ARCHETYPAL PSYCHOLOGY. Evanston, IL: Northwestern University Press, 1999.

———. RE-VISIONING PSYCHOLOGY. New York: HarperCollins, 1992.

_____. THE SOUL'S CODE: IN SEARCH OF CHARACTER AND CALLING. New York: Warner Books, 1997.

Hobson, Robert E. FORMS OF FEELING: THE HEART OF PSYCHOTHERAPY. London: Routledge, 1997

Hopcke, Robert H. PERSONA: WHERE SACRED MEETS PROFANE. Boston: Shambhala, 1995.

_____. A GUIDED TOUR OF THE COLLECTED WORKS OF C.G. JUNG. New York: Shambhala, 1999.

Horney, Karen. NEUROSIS AND HUMAN GROWTH: THE STRUGGLE TOWARD SELF-REALIZATION. London: Routledge, 1999.

_____. SELF-ANALYSIS. London: Routledge, 1999.

Jack, Rand & Dana Crowley Jack. MORAL VISION AND PROFESSIONAL DECISIONS: THE CHANGING VALUES OF WOMEN AND MEN LAWYERS. New York: Cambridge University Press, 1989.

Jacobi, Jolande. MASKS OF THE SOUL. Grand Rapids, Michigan: William B. Eerdmans, 1976.

Johnson, David W. REACHING OUT: INTERPERSONAL EFFECTIVENESS AND SELF-ACTUALIZATION. Boston: Allyn and Bacon, 8th ed., 2003.

Johnson, Robert A. INNER WORK: USING DREAMS & ACTIVE IMAGINATION FOR PERSONAL GROWTH. San Francisco: Harper & Row, 1989.

Jung, C.G. MEMORIES, DREAMS, REFLECTIONS. New York: Vintage Books, 1989.

Kirschenbaum, Howard & Valerie Land Kirschenbaum (eds.). THE CARL ROGERS READER. Boston: Houghton Mifflin, 1989.

Kottler, Jeffrey A. GROWING A THERAPIST. San Francisco: Jossey–Bass, 1995.

———. ON BEING A THERAPIST. San Francisco: Jossey–Bass, 3rd ed., 2003.

———. THE COMPLEAT THERAPIST. San Francisco: Jossey–Bass, 1991.

Kovel, Joel. THE AGE OF DESIRE: CASE HISTORIES OF A RADICAL PSYCHOANALYST. New York: Pantheon Books, 1981.

Kronman, Anthony T. THE LOST LAWYER: FAILING IDEALS OF THE LEGAL PROFESSION. Cambridge: Harvard Belnap Press, 1995.

LaBier, Douglas. MODERN MADNESS: THE HIDDEN LINK BETWEEN WORK AND EMOTIONAL CONFLICT. New York: Touchstone Book/Simon & Schuster, 1989.

Langer, Ellen J. THE POWER OF MINDFUL LEARNING. Reading, MA: Perseus Books, 1998.

———. MINDFULNESS. Reading, MA: Addison–Wesley Pub. Co., 1990.

Lasswell, Harold D. PSYCHOPATHOLOGY AND POLITICS. Chicago: University of Chicago Press, 1986.

Lesnick, Howard. BEING A LAWYER: INDIVIDUAL CHOICE AND RESPONSIBILITY IN THE PRACTICE OF LAW. St. Paul, MN: West Publishing, 1992.

Lifton, Robert Jay. THE PROTEAN SELF: HUMAN RESILIENCE IN AN AGE OF FRAGMENTATION. Chicago: University of Chicago Press, 1999.

Luban, David. LAWYERS AND JUSTICE: AN ETHICAL STUDY. Princeton, NJ: Princeton University Press, 1988.

Luft, Joseph. GROUP PROCESSES: AN INTRODUCTION TO GROUP DYNAMICS. Palo Alto, CA: Mayfield Pub. Co., 1984.

_____. OF HUMAN INTERACTION. Palo Alto, CA: Mayfield Publishing, 1969.

Maccoby, Michael. THE GAMESMAN: THE NEW CORPORATE LEADERS. New York: Bantam Books, 1978.

Maslach, Christina. BURNOUT: THE COST OF CARING. Cambridge, MA: Malor Books, 2003.

Maslach, Christina & Michael P. Leiter. THE TRUTH ABOUT BURNOUT: HOW ORGANIZATIONS CAUSE PERSONAL STRESS AND WHAT TO DO ABOUT IT. San Francisco, CA: Jossey–Bass, 1997.

Maslow, Abraham. THE FARTHER REACHES OF HUMAN NATURE. New York: Penguin Compass, 1993.

May, Rollo. LOVE AND WILL. New York: Dell, 1989.

_____. MAN'S SEARCH FOR HIMSELF. New York: Dell, 1973.

_____. THE DISCOVERY OF BEING: WRITINGS IN EXISTENTIAL PSYCHOLOGY. New York: W.W. Norton, 1994.

McCall, George J. & J.L. Simmons. IDENTITIES AND INTERACTIONS: AN EXAMINATION OF HUMAN ASSOCIATIONS IN EVERYDAY LIFE. New York: Free Press, 1978.

Monk, Gerald, John Winslade, Kathie Crocket & David Epston (eds.). NARRATIVE THERAPY IN PRACTICE: THE ARCHAEOLOGY OF HOPE. San Francisco: Jossey–Bass, 1997.

Nelson, John E. & Andrea Nelson (eds.). SACRED SORROWS: EMBRACING AND TRANSFORMING DEPRESSION. New York: Jeremy P. Tarcher/Putnam Book, 1996.

Oldham, John M. & Lois B. Morris. NEW PERSONALITY SELF–PORTRAIT: WHY YOU THINK, WORK, LOVE, AND ACT THE WAY YOU DO. New York: Bantam Books, 1995.

Pedersen, Loren E. DARK HEARTS: THE UNCONSCIOUS FORCES THAT SHAPE MEN'S LIVES. Boston: Shambhala, 1991.

Perlman, Helen Harris. RELATIONSHIP: THE HEART OF HELPING PEOPLE. Chicago: University of Chicago Press, 1983.

Pirsig, Robert. ZEN AND THE ART OF MOTORCYCLE MAINTENANCE: AN INQUIRY INTO VALUES. New York: Perennial Classics, 2000.

Progoff, Ira. JUNG'S PSYCHOLOGY AND ITS SOCIAL MEANING. London: Routledge, 1999.

Rogers, Carl R. A WAY OF BEING. Boston: Houghton Mifflin Co., 1995.

Sardello, Robert. FACING THE WORLD WITH SOUL: THE REIMAGINATION OF MODERN LIFE. New York: HarperPerennial, 1994.

Shaffer, Thomas L. MORAL MEMORANDUM FROM JOHN HOWARD YODER: CONVERSATIONS ON LAW, ETHICS, AND

THE CHURCH BETWEEN A MENNONITE THEOLOGIAN AND A HOOSIER LAWYER. Eugene, OR: 2002.

———. FAITH AND THE PROFESSIONS. Provo, UT: Brigham Young University Press, 1987.

———. ON BEING A CHRISTIAN AND A LAWYER: LAW FOR THE INNOCENT. Provo, UT: Brigham Young University Press, 1981.

Shaffer, Thomas L. & Mary M. Shaffer. AMERICAN LAWYERS AND THEIR COMMUNITIES: ETHICS IN THE LEGAL PROFESSION. Notre Dame, IN: University of Notre Dame Press, 1991.

Schank, Roger C. TELL ME A STORY: NARRATIVE AND INTELLIGENCE. Evanston, IL: Northwestern University Press, 1995.

Schön, Donald A. EDUCATING THE REFLECTIVE PRACTITIONER: TOWARD A NEW DESIGN FOR TEACHING AND LEARNING IN THE PROFESSIONS. San Francisco: Jossey–Bass, 1990.

Sells, Benjamin. THE SOUL OF THE LAW. London: Vega, 2002.

Singer, June. BOUNDARIES OF THE SOUL: THE PRACTICE OF JUNG'S PSYCHOLOGY. New York: Anchor Books/Doubleday, rev. ed., 1994.

Stein, Murray. TRANSFORMATION: EMERGENCE OF THE SELF. College Station, TX: Texas A & M University Press, 1998.

———. IN MIDLIFE: A JUNGIAN PERSPECTIVE. Dallas, TX: Spring Publications, 1983.

Steiner, Claude. SCRIPTS PEOPLE LIVE BY: TRANSACTIONAL ANALYSIS OF LIFE SCRIPTS. New York: Grove Weidenfeld, 1st Evergreen ed., 1990.

Sullivan, Harry Stack. THE PSYCHIATRIC INTERVIEW. New York: W.W. Norton, 1970.

Taylor, Shelley E. POSITIVE ILLUSIONS: CREATIVE SELF-DECEPTION AND THE HEALTHY MIND. New York: Basic Books, 1989.

Vaillant, George E. THE WISDOM OF THE EGO. Cambridge: Harvard University Press, 1995.

Weinberg, George. THE HEART OF PSYCHOTHERAPY: A JOURNEY INTO THE MIND AND OFFICE OF THE THERAPIST AT WORK. New York: St. Martin's Griffin, 1996.

Welwood, John (ed.). AWAKENING THE HEART: EAST/WEST APPROACHES TO PSYCHOTHERAPY AND THE HEALING RELATIONSHIP. Boston: New Science Library, 1985.

White, Michael & David Epston. NARRATIVE MEANS TO THERAPEUTIC ENDS. New York: W.W. Norton, 1990.

Whyte, David. THE HEART AROUSED: POETRY AND THE PRESERVATION OF THE SOUL IN CORPORATE AMERICA. New York: Currency Doubleday, 2002.

Wilkinson, Tanya. PERSEPHONE RETURNS: VICTIMS, HEROES AND THE JOURNEY FROM THE UNDERWORLD. Berkeley, CA: PageMill Press, 1996.

Articles

Alfieri, Anthony V. *The Antinomies of Poverty Law and A Theory of Poverty Law and a Theory of*

Dialogic Empowerment, 16 N.Y.U.Rev.L. & Soc. Change 659 (1988).

———. *Speaking Out of Turn: The Story of Josephine V.*, 4 Geo.J.Legal Ethics 619 (1991).

Allegretti, Joseph. *Shooting Elephants, Serving Clients: An Essay on George Orwell and the Lawyer-client Relationship*, 27 Creighton L.Rev. 1 (1993).

Araujo, Robert. *The Virtuous Lawyer: Paradigm and Possibility*, 50 SMU L.Rev. 433 (1997).

Blumberg, Arthur S. *The Practice of Law as a Confidence Game: Organizational Cooptation of a Profession*, 1 Law & Soc'y Rev. 28 (1967).

Boccaccini, Marcus T., Jennifer L. Boothby & Stanley L. Brodsky. *Client-Relations Skills in Effective Lawyering: Attitudes of Criminal Defense Attorneys and Experienced Clients*, 26 Law & Psychol.Rev. 97 (2002).

Cohen, Larry J. & Joyce H Vesper, *Forensic Stress Disorder*, 25 Law & Psychol.Rev. 1 (2001).

Cooney, Leslie Larkin. *Lawyer, Heal Thyself: Bringing Rational Expectations to the Law Firm Environment*, 22 Whittier L.Rev. 967 (2001).

Cunningham, Clark. *A Tale of Two Clients: Thinking About Law as Language*, 87 Mich.L.Rev. 2459 (1989).

Dhanaraj, Subha. *Making Lawyers Good People: Possibility or Pipedream*, 28 Fordham Urb.L.J. 2037 (2001).

Eades, Diana. *Lawyer-client Communication: "I Don't Think the Lawyers Were Communicating with Me": Misunderstanding Cultural Differences in Communicative Style,* 52 Emory L.J. 1109 (2003).

Elkins, James R. *Lawyer Ethics: A Pedagogical Mosaic,* 14 Notre Dame J.L.Ethics & Pub.Pol'y 117 (2000).

_____. *Teaching a Lawyer's Confessions,* 21 Legal Stud.F. 151 (1997).

_____. *Thinking Like a Lawyer: Second Thoughts,* 47 Mercer L.Rev. 511 (1996).

_____. *Troubled Beginnings: Reflections on Becoming a Lawyer,* 26 U.Mem.L.Rev. 1303 (1996).

_____. *Pathologizing Professional Life: Psycho–Literary Case Stories,* 18 Vt.L.Rev. 581 (1994).

_____. *Writing Our Lives: Making Introspective Writing a Part of Legal Education,* 29 Willamette L.Rev. 45 (1993).

_____. *Symptoms Exposed When Legalists Engage in Moral Discourse: Reflections on the Difficulties of Talking Ethics,* 17 Vt.L.Rev. 353 (1993).

_____. *The Moral Labyrinth of Zealous Advocacy,* 21 Cap.U.L.Rev. 735 (1992).

_____. *The Stories We Tell Ourselves in Law,* 40 J.Legal Educ. 47 (1990).

_____. *The Quest for Meaning: Narrative Accounts of Legal Education,* 38 J.Legal Educ. 577 (1988).

———. *The Examined Life: A Mind in Search of Heart*, 30 Am.J.Juris. 155 (1985).

———. *Ethics: Professionalism, Craft, and Failure*, 73 Ky.L.J. 937 (1984–85).

———. *A Humanistic Perspective in Legal Education*, 62 Neb.L.Rev. 494 (1983).

———. *Becoming a Lawyer: The Transformation of Self During Legal Education*, 66 Soundings 450 (Winter 1983).

———. *"All My Friends Are Becoming Strangers": The Psychological Perspective in Legal Education*, 84 W.Va.L.Rev. 161 (1981).

Freedman, Monroe. *Legal Ethics and the Suffering Client*, 36 Cath.U.L.Rev. 331 (1987).

———. *Personal Responsibility in a Professional System*, 27 Cath.U.L.Rev. 191 (1978).

Fried, Charles. *The Lawyer as Friend: The Moral Foundations of the Lawyer–Client Relation*, 85 Yale L.J. 1060 (1976).

Greenebaum, Edwin H. *Lawyers Relationship to Their Work: The Importance of Understanding Attorneys' Behavior*, 53 N.Y.U.L.Rev. 651 (1978).

Hetherington, H. Lee. *The Wizard and Dorothy, Patton and Rommel: Negotiation Parables in Fiction and Fact*, 28 Pepp. L.Rev. 289 (2001).

Hyman, Jonathan M. *Slip-sliding into Mediation: Can Lawyers Mediate Their Clients' Problems?*, 5 Clin.L.Rev. 47 (1998).

Kennedy, Duncan. *The Responsibility of Lawyers for the Justice of Their Causes*, 18 Tex.Tech.L.Rev. 1157 (1987).

____. *Legal Education and the Reproduction of Hierarchy*, 32 J.Legal Educ. 591 (1982).

Kronman, Anthony. *Living in the Law*, 54 U.Chi. L.Rev. 835 (1987).

Lopez, Gerald P. *Reconceiving Civil Rights Practice: Seven Weeks in the Life of a Rebellious Collaboration*, 77 Geo. L.J. 1603 (1989).

Luban, David. *The Noblesse Oblige Tradition in the Practice of Law*, 41 Vand.L.Rev. 717 (1988).

____. *Paternalism and the Legal Professional,* 1981 Wisc.L.Rev. 454.

Mansfield, Cathy Lesser. *Deconstructing Reconstructive Poverty Law: A Practice-based Critique of the Storytelling Aspects of the Theoretics of Practice Movement*, 61 Brooklyn L.Rev. 889 (1995).

Maute, Judith L. *Balanced Lives in a Stressful Profession: An Impossible Dream?*, 21 Cap. U.L.Rev. 797 (1992).

Menkel–Meadow, Carrie. *The Legacy of Clinical Education: Theories About Lawyering*, 29 Clev.–St. L.Rev. 555 (1980).

Mindes, Marvin W. & Alan C. Acock. *Trickster, Hero, Helper: A Report on the Lawyer Image*, 1982 Am.B.Found. Res. J. 177.

Nivala, John. *Zen and the Art of Becoming (and Being) a Lawyer*, 15 U.Puget Sound L.Rev. 387 (1992).

Ogilvy, J.P. *The Use of Journals in Legal Education: A Tool for Reflection*, 3 Clin.L.Rev. 55 (1996).

Pepper, Stephen L. *Counseling at the Limits of the Law: An Exercise in the Jurisprudence and Ethics of Lawyering*, 104 Yale L.J. 1545 (1995).

———. *The Lawyer's Amoral Ethical Role: A Defense, A Problem, and Some Possibilities*, 1986 Am. B.Found.Res.J. 613.

Peters, Don. *Forever Jung: Psychological Type Theory, the Myers–Briggs Type Indicator and Learning Negotiation*, 42 Drake L.Rev. 1 (1993).

Richard, Lawrence R. *Psychological Type and Job Satisfaction Among Practicing Lawyers in The United States*, 29 Cap. U.L.Rev. 979 (2002).

Riskin, Leonard L. *Mediation and Lawyers*, 43 Ohio St.L.J. 29 (1982).

Scherr, Alexander. *Lawyers and Decisions: A Model of Practical Judgment*, 47 Vill. L.Rev. 161 (2002).

Schiltz, Patrick J. *On Being a Happy, Healthy, and Ethical Member of an Unhappy, Unhealthy, and Unethical Profession*, 52 Vand. L.Rev. 871 (1999).

Seligman, Martin E.P., Paul Verkuil & Terry H. King. *Why Lawyers Are Unhappy*, 23 Cardozo L.Rev. 33 (2001).

Shaffer, Thomas L. *American Legal Ethics*, 59 Theology Today 369 (2002).

_____. *Jews, Christians, Lawyers, and Money*, 25 Vt.L.Rev. 451 (2001).

_____. *Straight Talk for Tough Times: More's Skill*, 9 Widener J.Pub.L. 295 (2000).

_____. *Towering Figures, Enigmas, and Responsive Communities in American Legal Ethics*, 51 Me. L.Rev. 229 (1999).

_____. *On Living One Way in Town and Another Way at Home*, 31 Val.U.L.Rev. 879 (1997).

_____. *The Unique, Novel, and Unsound Adversary Ethic*, 41 Vand. L.Rev. 697 (1988).

_____. *Legal Ethics and the Good Client*, 36 Cath. U.L.Rev. 319 (1987).

_____. *The Legal Ethics of Radical Individualism*, 65 Tex.L.Rev. 331 (1987).

_____. *The Ethics of Dissent and Friendship in the American Professions*, 88 W.Va.L.Rev. 623 (1986).

_____. *The Legal Ethics of the Two Kingdoms*, 17 Val.L.Rev. 3 (1983).

_____. *Christian Lawyer Stories and American Legal Ethics*, 33 Mercer L.Rev. 877 (1982).

Silver, Marjorie A. *Lawyering and Its Discontents: Reclaiming Meaning in the Practice of Law*, 19 Touro L.Rev. 773 (2004).

Simon, William. *Lawyer's Advice and Client Autonomy: Mrs. Jones's Case*, 50 Md.L.Rev. 213 (1991).

———. *Homo Psychologicus: Notes on a New Legal Formalism*, 32 Stan.L.Rev. 487 (1980).

———. *The Ideology of Advocacy: Procedural Justice and Professional Ethics*, 1978 Wis.L.Rev. 29.

Stone, Alan. *Legal Education on the Couch*, 85 Harv.L.Rev. 392 (1971).

Strong, Graham B. *The Lawyer's Left Hand: Non-analytical Thought in the Practice of Law*, 69 U. Colo. L.Rev. 759 (1998).

Stubbs, Jonathan K. *Lawyer Competence: Perceptual Prisms, Self–Scrutiny, and the Looking Glass*, 18 J.Legal Prof. 233 (1993).

Symposium: Client Counseling and Moral Responsibility, 30 Pepp. L.Rev. 591 (2003).

Vogel, Howard J. *The Terrible Bind of the Lawyer in the Modern World: The Problem of Hope, the Question of Identity, and the Recovery of Meaning in the Practice of Law*, 32 Seton Hall L.Rev. 152 (2001).

Watson, Andrew. *The Quest for Professional Competence: Psychological Aspects of Legal Education*, 37 U.Cin.L.Rev. 91 (1968)

INDEX

References are to Pages

401

References are to Pages

†